Frederick M. Shepherd has driven the literature forward in Latin American Politics by filling a gap on the influence of transnational actors. Shepherd's three levels of analysis (societal, national, and transnational) provide a nuanced 20,000-foot view of the region and the influence, or lack thereof, of transnational actors... His coverage is comprehensive yet succinct, stretching from early drug prohibitionist history to the modern drug war in Latin America and current administrations... [The book] introduces an important analytical variable of state infrastructural capacity which, when low, weakens Latin American governments' ability to address societal needs broadly.

Nathan P. Jones, Associate Professor of Security Studies,
Sam Houston State University, USA

THE POLITICS OF TRANSNATIONAL ACTORS IN LATIN AMERICA

The Politics of Transnational Actors in Latin America: Power from Afar explores the important issues of transnational actors and their influence on institutions and people in Latin America, raising profound questions of accountability, social justice, and sovereignty.

The text focuses on four particularly significant groups that transcend national boundaries: the Catholic Church, transnational corporations, transnational drug networks, and transnational human rights networks. By comparing each of their impacts on the region, Frederick M. Shepherd explores larger questions about transnational power and how it has deeply penetrated the nations of Latin America. The book's analysis delves into attempts made over the last 100 years by citizens, social movements, and governments to reassert a degree of control over these transnational actors, setting up a framework to understand how local, national, and global forces interact in a setting of transnational dominance. The volume suggests that local and national groups can use principles and power to bring about equitable and just outcomes in relation to transnational actors, and that, in some cases, transnational actors can be a part of constructive change in Latin America.

This concise volume will be of interest to students of History, Latin American and Caribbean Studies, and Political Science as well as those interested in 20th-century Latin American politics and political history.

Frederick M. Shepherd is Professor of Political Science at Samford University, USA. He is the editor of *Christianity and Human Rights: Christians and the Struggle for Global Justice* and the author of numerous publications on Latin American politics, religion, human rights, and genocide.

THE POLITICS OF TRANSNATIONAL ACTORS IN LATIN AMERICA

Power from Afar

Frederick M. Shepherd

Routledge
Taylor & Francis Group

NEW YORK AND LONDON

First published 2021
by Routledge
52 Vanderbilt Avenue, New York, NY 10017

and by Routledge
2 Park Square, Milton Park, Abingdon, Oxon, OX14 4RN

Routledge is an imprint of the Taylor & Francis Group, an informa business

Library of Congress Cataloging-in-Publication Data
Names: Shepherd, Frederick M., 1963– author.
Title: The politics of transnational actors in Latin America : power
from afar / Frederick M. Shepherd.
Description: New York, NY : Routledge, 2021. | Includes
bibliographical references and index.
Identifiers: LCCN 2020043912 (print) | LCCN 2020043913 (ebook) |
ISBN 9781138096325 (hardback) | ISBN 9781138096332 (paperback) |
ISBN 9781003017998 (ebook)
Subjects: LCSH: Non-state actors (International relations)—Latin
America. | Transnationalism. | Latin America—Politics and
government.
Classification: LCC JL960 .S53 2021 (print) |
LCC JL960 (ebook) | DDC 320.98—dc23
LC record available at https://lccn.loc.gov/2020043912
LC ebook record available at https://lccn.loc.gov/2020043913

ISBN: 978-1-138-09632-5 (hbk)
ISBN: 978-1-138-09633-2 (pbk)
ISBN: 978-1-003-01799-8 (ebk)

Typeset in Bembo
by codeMantra

CONTENTS

ILLUSTRATIONS

Figures

Tables

ACKNOWLEDGMENTS

The general idea for this book began several decades back, during work on my dissertation at Georgetown University. As a result, I'd like to thank George Crane, Eusebio Mujal-León, Arturo Valenzuela, and especially John Bailey for their practical and theoretical guidance as I made my way through my initial attempt at understanding the drama of Latin America through the lens of a three-level framework of analysis. I'd also like to thank several scholars and colleagues from my many years at Samford University, with whom I've discussed these and related matters: James Brown, Carlos Alemán, and Serena Simoni. James Waller and John Witte have provided me with great insight into issues of genocide and religion. I am especially eager to go on record posthumously thanking someone who helped me throughout the years and who always seems to appear in acknowledgments: the great Charles Tilly, whose influence is seen directly or indirectly in so many important works. I'm also particularly grateful to distinguished economist William G. Shepherd for his insights on corporate power (and his steadfast support as a parent) over the years.

More recently, I have had the chance to communicate about this book directly with a number of gracious and insightful folks: thanks to Miguel Angel Centeno; Alison Brysk; Nathan Jones; Jackie Smith; and, once again, John Bailey. Thanks as well to Cecilia Plottier at the UN Economic Commission for Latin America in Santiago, Chile, and Lauren Young at the Samford University Library for research assistance. I'd also like to thank several people for key technical support: my wife, Lorrin Etka-Shepherd, for help with the tables; Lee Walsh at the Samford Department of Political Science for countless instances of help; my colleague Scott Fisk for his help with the graphics; and my daughter Maddie Shepherd for computer assistance during crises. Many thanks also to Emily Irvine at Routledge/Taylor and Francis for her fine work in helping to get through this lengthy process.

On a more personal level, I'd like to thank my family for all their support during this project and many others. The unit we've put together, which is now growing with a new generation, is far more important than anything I put into written form. So, in this spirit, final and heartfelt thanks (again) to my wonderful wife Lorri. I'm grateful for her patience with me always, and especially as the deadline for the book neared. And there's no one I'd rather be with during a pandemic!

1

THE POLITICS OF TRANSNATIONAL ACTORS IN LATIN AMERICA

Transnational actors deeply influence the daily lives of the Latin American people, from the northern border of Mexico to the Southern Cone. Organizations based in distant lands make decisions that affect how Latin Americans work, consume, worship, and mobilize politically. They have deeply penetrated Latin American political systems, controlling national governments and directly influencing Latin American societies. Yet, even as transnational actors have thwarted states and citizens in the region, their presence has provided openings for Latin Americans to empower themselves in an increasingly globalized setting. This book focuses on four especially influential transnational actors: the Catholic Church, transnational corporations (TNCs), transnational drug networks (TDNs), and transnational human rights networks (THRNs). Their global scope allows them to transcend national boundaries and mobilize vast resources. These transnational actors have cajoled, bullied, collaborated with, and frequently superseded national governments as they have exerted their influence on the people, the political systems, the culture, the religion, and the economies of Latin America. In doing so, they have raised profound questions of sovereignty, democracy, and self-determination in Latin America.

These transnational actors symbolize the economic and political vulnerability of an entire region of the world. Eduardo Galeano presents this history with the vivid image of the "open veins of Latin America" representing transnational exploitation of the region (Galeano, 1997). Yet close scrutiny of these actors, and their interactions with the governments and people of Latin America, provides an opportunity to draw significant conclusions about globalization, government policies, and social justice in Latin America. There is no doubt that focusing on transnational actors in the region raises profound questions of accountability. How can citizens function in a setting in which powerful actors make decisions from an extreme geographical and political distance? Latin American activists have been part of a long and honorable tradition of struggle against power exerted by outside forces, and this struggle has come to define the region. Indeed, the power of transnational actors has led to complex political interactions that have occasionally empowered governments and social movements to better the lives of Latin Americans.

It is in this spirit that this book explores the impact and the actions of transnational actors in Latin America. (A more thorough discussion of the definition of the term "transnational actors" appears near the end of this chapter.) It focuses on four specific transnational actors, with one chapter devoted to each: the Catholic Church, TNCs, TDNs, and THRNs. It focuses on the **politics** of transnational actors as they interact with other institutions and forces in the region. This opening chapter sets up a three-tiered framework for analyzing the influence of transnational actors in Latin America. Analysis based on this framework points out the deep level of transnational penetration of Latin American societies, but also helps to clarify the complex relationships between transnational actors, national governments, and the societies that they ostensibly rule. It is in the complicated interactions at these three levels that seemingly marginalized states and citizens have been able to gain some degree of leverage in their relations with transnational actors.

In this regard, this book does not attempt to provide an authoritative account of each of these actors and their collective history in Latin America. Rather, it analyzes the political issues raised by overwhelming transnational influence, and the reaction among states and societies to this influence. The influence of the Catholic Church, TNCs, TDNs, and THRNs has created political distortions and tensions throughout Latin America, frustrating citizens but also, more recently, providing political openings for addressing these frustrations. This book's focus never strays far from questions of accountability in a setting of influence exerted by distant groups. But the nature of this influence and the responses to it are issues that arise repeatedly in the chapters to follow.

Using Theory to Understand the Impact of Transnational Actors

The transnational focus of this book necessitates a theoretical approach that incorporates global actors into the politics of nation-states. At the same time, this expansion of focus acknowledges the complex flow of power and influence from the most local to the most global actors and back again. In this regard, the first theoretical framework for the book is based on **three levels of analysis: the global, the national, and the local**, as depicted in Figure 1.1. Analysis at the global level focuses primarily on the four specific transnational actors, and also intermittently on other powerful global forces. Analysis at the national level focuses on the nation-state: the geographical and cultural unit of the nation; and the state—the national governing institution in all of its different

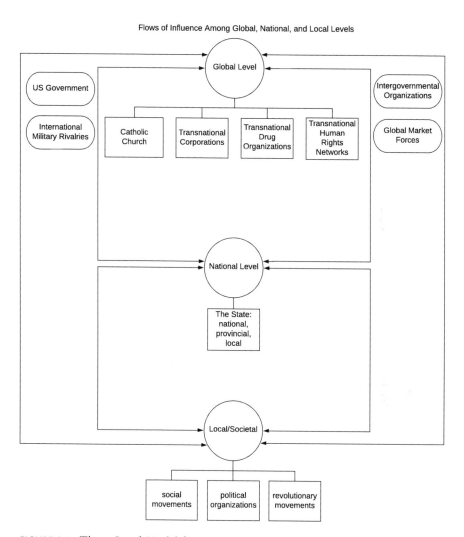

FIGURE 1.1   Three-Level Model for Transnational Influence.

forms. Analysis at the local and societal level focuses on political organizations, social movements, and revolutionary movements. (These terms, and others mentioned in this paragraph, are defined more clearly in the following pages.)

This book is organized around the influence of four transnational actors in Latin America and their actions in a globalized world. Yet it is based on an approach to globalization that acknowledges it as a multi-directional force. The idea that both bottom-up and top-down variations of globalization exist is central to this analysis (Falk, 1992; Evans, 2000, 2008). It provides the basis for assessing how influence flows among the global, national, and local/ societal levels, and serves as a starting point for explaining the visual images provided by Figure 1.1. So, from this perspective, as the multi-directional arrows in Figure 1.1 demonstrate, influence can flow up from local and societal organizations toward the state or directly toward global forces. Influence can flow downward from global actors toward the nation-state or, bypassing it, directly toward Latin American societies. As part of this top-down process (as is explained later in this chapter), additional global forces, including the US government, intergovernmental organizations, geopolitical rivalries, or global markets, can also exert their influence. However, influence can flow from the state either upward to global actors or downward to society and local actors. Groups from different levels can collaborate with or oppose one another: global groups can ally with national states against local organizations, states can ally with local organizations against global groups, and global groups can ally with local organizations against national states. And, beyond the categories presented in Figure 1.1, penetration of ostensibly "national" systems can become so extensive that distinctions among these three levels can become blurred, especially in the context of globalized societies, relatively weak nation-states, and powerful transnational actors.

These representations of the three levels of analysis provide an overview of potential power relationships that include transnational actors. A brief detour into several examples, described in greater detail in upcoming chapters, can bring these more abstract relationships to life. The first set of examples represents "unconstrained" transnational influence, in which transnational actors directly affect the lives of Latin Americans. The Catholic Church established relations with the Colombian government that, for almost 100 years, provided them with "missionary areas" in which they performed government-like functions, controlling education, levying a kind of taxation in the form of tithing, and administering justice beyond the control of government authorities. Beginning in the early 20th century, US-owned copper companies created economic enclaves and "company towns" in Chile, in which virtually all aspects of the workers' lives were controlled by TNCs. TDNs have used their vast wealth and fearsome arsenals to control entire areas of Mexico, both intimidating and gaining the loyalty of Mexicans as they buy off and supplant the Mexican state. Finally, in a more collaborative relationship, transnational "peace brigades" from North America accompanied endangered Guatemalans to protect them from a genocidal regime in the 1980s. These examples all share a basic feature: transnational actors exerting direct and disproportionate influence on the people of Latin America, penetrating national societies, and bypassing or controlling the state in the process. This unconstrained transnational influence remains an important frame of reference for understanding Latin American politics.

But much of this book is taken up with analyzing more complex relationships at the global, national, and local levels, in which transnational actors are far more constrained. Radical Catholics in Nicaragua defied the hierarchy in Managua and Rome by directly participating in the struggle to oust the Somoza dictatorship and filling positions in the Sandinista government. Bolivian social movements successfully mounted protest-based "wars" against TNCs in the oil and water sectors, leading to the election of the leftist labor leader Evo Morales in 2005 and the subsequent state takeover of key economic sectors. Colombian and Mexican governments (with massive levels of US assistance) succeeded in smashing specific TDNs even as the global drug trade has grown. And victims of human rights violations in Argentina have increasingly been able to appeal to a newly democratic government and the Inter-American Court of Human Rights. All these examples depart from the model of unconstrained transnational influence, and raise important issues of how global, national, and local actors can constrain transnational actors.

Beyond the three-level theoretical framework, this book's analysis is based on a series of theoretical concerns coming out of recent work on Latin America and the global system. The first focuses on the nature of the organizations which are the protagonists in this study, and a close analysis of transnational actors as **institutions and networks**. Their institutional makeup turns out to be crucial to how they influence Latin American states and societies. At the transnational level, the four groups which are the focus of the book vary widely in terms of how hierarchical and structured they are, on the one hand, and how decentralized and loosely organized they are, on the other hand. On one end of the spectrum is a formally integrated, tightly organized unit, acting as a single monolithic entity, with clear lines of command throughout its operations. An obvious example is a well-run military organization. Nathan Jones sees this type as marked by many "layers of management" and "organizing vast resources toward singular goals" (Jones, 2017, p. 6), even as it transcends national boundaries. At the other end of the spectrum is a far more decentralized transnational network. In their study of human rights organizations, Margaret Keck and Kathryn Sikkink note that these networks are marked by "a dense web of connections among these groups, both formal and informal," and describe these networks as "characterized by voluntary, reciprocal, and horizontal patterns of communication and exchange" (1998, pp. 8, 7). Jones, in his work on drug networks, uses similar language, pointing to "nodes" interacting with one another, "in the absence of central authority" (Jones, 2017, p. 6). When these networks take a transnational form, they are made up of multiple local, national, and global organizations, which find ways to collaborate by forming nodes of contact. In transcending national boundaries and political systems, these networks have much in common with other transnational organizations. But their formal decentralization makes them, at once, more flexible and more vulnerable than formal organizations to fragmentation in the face of opposition and violence.

The details of transnational actors, as networks or formally integrated organizations, are the subject of chapters to follow. In the most general terms, the Catholic Church and TNCs are relatively hierarchical integrated organizations; transnational drug groups and transnational human rights groups are relatively decentralized. As they extend their influence globally, each transnational actor represents a mixture of hierarchy and decentralization. But there is enough hierarchy within the Catholic Church and TNCs to refer to them as integrated, relatively hierarchical organizations. And transnational human rights groups and transnational drug groups are marked by so much decentralization and collaboration that it only makes sense to refer to them as networks. These, then, are the basic considerations for understanding the potential significance of institutions and networks in the analysis of the four transnational actors that follows.

Because of the absence of formal global governance, it may seem appropriate to view these transnational actors as acting relatively freely on a global level, constrained primarily by other global actors, specific national governments, and perhaps an occasional local social movement. But historical and recent developments make this perspective inadequate. A theoretical emphasis on **principles and norms** must be part of any attempt to understand the actions of transnational organizations and networks, and those trying to influence their behavior.

Norms come out of principles and "beliefs about right and wrong," and emerge as politically significant when they become "collective expectations about proper behavior for a given identity" (Jepperson et al., 1996, p. 54). In short, then, principles refer to ideals apart from their political setting; norms emerge when principles take on political force. Risse and Sikkink note that "[t]o endorse a norm not only expresses a belief, but also creates an impetus for behavior consistent with the belief" (1999, p. 7). Khagram et al. refer to a "life cycle" for norms as they evolve from abstract principles to meaningful norms that influence political behavior. Risse and Sikkink are even more detailed, describing a five-step "norms-spiral" (Khagram et al., 2002, p. 20). Norms can exist at the small-scale local level, at the level of the nation-state, and at the global level. One of the best examples of a norm is the societal consensus against smoking: in a complex mix of changing laws and beliefs, a completely new set of norms about the appropriateness of this addictive and harmful behavior emerged over several decades (Sikkink, 2011, p. 11). Scholars of even the most functional communities and the most democratic national political systems often point to the distance between norms and policy outcomes. Yet the study of these political units, marked by formal institutions of governance, is based on an assumption that norms can be used to pressure institutions to act based on societal norms, and that the distance between norms and outcomes can be closed by responsive governments. In certain settings, "a community able to pass judgments on appropriateness" can translate into policy outcomes based on these judgments (Risse and Sikkink, 1999, p. 7).

Scholars and policymakers are increasingly pointing to the emergence of politically significant norms at the global level. In their study of human rights, Khagram et al. describe global norms as "the shared expectations or standards of appropriate behavior accepted by states and intergovernmental organizations that can be applied to states, intergovernmental organizations, and/or nonstate actors of various kinds" (2002, p. 14). To varying degrees, norms are also relevant to the study of the Catholic Church, TNCs, and TDNs. Norms can arise from within these transnational organizations; they can also originate externally within groups attempting to influence them. In the absence of rigorously enforced laws at the global level, norms have become an increasingly important factor in assessing the behavior of transnational organizations and networks. And it is worth noting that norms have often been a central tool in marginalized groups' efforts to collaborate with or defy transnational actors.

Each of the chapters on particular transnational actors explores the political conditions and alignments that would encourage the effective use of norms, but they are placed at the center of analysis in explaining the actions and influence of the Catholic Church and THRNs in Latin America. Norms have always been central to understanding the Catholic Church in Latin America (Bettiza and Dionigi, 2015). Chapter 3 focuses on two contrasting norms: "neo-Christendom," which advocates a "close relationship with ruling elites" and "union with the public authority of the state" (Mainwaring, 1986, p. 5; Wilde, 1987, p. 4); and the "preferential option for the poor" and related norms emerging out of Vatican II in the 1960s. For THRNs, human rights norms have been at the heart of the transnational struggle for justice. Advocates and scholars have pointed to the emergence of human rights norms: articulated in a comprehensive fashion with the 1948 UN Universal Declaration but gaining political heft as transnational networks have emerged and formal legal provisions have followed. This process is central to the analysis in Chapter 6.

Principles and norms appear in a different way in Chapter 4 on TNCs and Chapter 5 on TDNs: the focus is on the extent to which norms are employed by actors outside these organizations to constrain their behavior. Two norms in particular have had a significant impact on TNCs in Latin America. First, the norm of "resource nationalism," pushed by both states and societies in Latin America, has taken on genuine political importance in certain periods and became a constant feature of Latin American political culture in the mid-20th century. Given the general weakness of nationalism in Latin America compared to other regions of the world, the emergence of this norm is particularly notable. Second, the more recent norm of "corporate social responsibility" (CSR) has influenced transnational corporate behavior in Latin America. These norms have been effectively pushed by local and transnational actors, and have also been formally endorsed by regional and global intergovernmental organizations. The main point of Chapter 5 with regard to norms is that they have been mostly ineffective in changing the behavior of TDNs, which operate largely free of moral or legal constraints.

The final major theoretical concern in this book is the ability of transnational, national, and societal actors to use resources at their disposal to both coerce and gain the loyalty of people and organizations in Latin America. The primary focus is the **capacity and power** of organizations from all three levels of analysis to influence material conditions. This approach to power and capacity will use two theoretical tools that focus on how states function in a setting of external domination: the "state in society" approach and theories of state capacity.

The "state in society" approach explores how states influence, and are in turn influenced by, societal forces. The state is viewed as a central actor, but its power is constrained by non-state forces. In this context, the state is only one of many significant actors struggling to influence society. According to Joel Migdal, "[t]he central political and social drama of recent history has been the battle pitting the state and organizations allied with it...against other social organizations dotting society's landscape" (Migdal, 1988, p. 28). He views the state as "only one organization in a mélange within the boundaries in which it seeks to rule" (ibid., p. 40). And he maintains that the central postcolonial political struggles in Asia, Africa, and Latin America "have been over whether the state will be able to displace or harness other organizations—families, clans, multinational corporations, domestic enterprises, tribes, patron-client dyads—which make rules against the wishes and goals of state leaders" (ibid., p. 31).

The state is up against a wide variety of societal challenges. An examination of Latin American history reveals that these challenges originate from both inside and outside of national boundaries, or at both the first and third levels of analysis adopted in this book. The relative weakness of Latin American states has provided the political space for local organizations to survive and defy the state; at the same time, it has allowed external actors to deeply penetrate formally sovereign nations. And these local and transnational processes have often fed off each other at the expense of Latin American states. This approach, then, assesses the extent to which a wide variety of actors can use the resources at their disposal to influence and gain the loyalties of groups and peoples within nations. This struggle can be dominated by local actors, by nation-states, by transnational actors, or by some combination of the three. One of the central goals of this study of transnational actors in Latin America is to understand not only instances in which transnational power prevails over national authorities, but also cases in which states assert themselves in relation to powerful external actors. Scholars analyzing Latin America and other regions have pointed to notable cases of "state autonomy," when national governments have exhibited surprising degrees of efficacy and political independence even as powerful external and internal forces bear down on them (Stepan, 1978; Hamilton, 1982; Rueschemeyer and Evans, 1985).

A central question in this context is the power of states and societal organizations, with power being understood in the context of classic definitions based on the ability to get people and institutions to do things or, in the words of Robert Dahl, "A has power over B to the extent that he [sic] can get B to do something that B would not otherwise do" (Dahl, 1957). Migdal's take on state power presents a variation on this idea: "the ability of state leaders to use the agencies of the state to get people in the society to do what they want them to do" (Migdal, 1988, p. xiii). Given the transnational setting for this book, it also relies on views of power coming out of theories of global politics, in which the distinction between "hard" and "soft" power has become a central point of debate and analysis (Nye, 2004). The sharp inequities that are impossible to ignore when studying transnational actors in Latin America necessitate a focus on "hard" power and the military and economic basis for it. Yet much analysis in the following chapters demonstrates that soft power, based on cooperation, culture, ideas and norms, is surprisingly relevant to understanding how transnational groups interact with states and societies in Latin America. This analysis, rather than attempting some understanding of power at the most general level, uses more specific concepts related to capacity, to more fully understand how transnational, national, and local actors influence one another.

This investigation begins with the concept of state capacity, in two different forms. The view of state capacity adopted for this book comes out of the work of Michael Mann, and it is based on a fundamental distinction between two types: infrastructural capacity and despotic capacity. Despotic capacity refers to the ability of a government to dominate all that is narrowly political in a society, to monopolize the halls of political power. Despotic power is, in Mann's words, "the range of actions which the elite is empowered to undertake without routine, institutionalized negotiations with civil society groups." Mann's literary example of this type of power is the Red Queen (from Lewis Carroll) who has the power to shout, about a political rival, "off with his head," but has little political power to do much more (Mann, 1986, p. 188). Even a cursory look at Latin American history demonstrates the tragic relevance of this type of capacity to a region marked by dictatorships and violent repression, even as it has democratized recently.

In contrast, infrastructural capacity refers to something much more profound, with far different implications for relations between a state and societal actors. Infrastructural capacity "denotes the power of the state to penetrate and centrally coordinate the activities of civil society through its own infrastructure" (Mann, 1986, p. 190). This kind of capacity includes state provision of physical infrastructure and a whole host of other functions that would transform society in material and political ways. It implies a state that could use this capacity to, at once, gain some measure of loyalty from the people and convince them, in an enduring way, to support the state and follow the rules it establishes (Mann, 2012). Scholars have attempted to measure this capacity in many ways, including levels of taxation, road building, provision of safety and policing, successful military conscription, provision of public education, and many more. Some, including Joel Migdal, measure this type of state capacity in relation to the strength of other societal non-state actors. But the larger point is that this type of state capacity is fundamentally related to the ability of the state to reach down and transform society in a way that leads to an enduring state presence in the lives of its people. On a more specific level, as this concept is applied to Latin America it becomes clear that the region is, for the mos part, marked by notable infrastructural weakness: as Miguel Angel Centeno notes, "the Latin American state has not had the required institutional capacity to perform even a limited set of tasks" (Centeno, 2002, p. 3).

These contrasting types of state capacity have significant implications for, and can be profoundly influenced by, transnational actors. The three levels of analysis adopted in this book can help clarify how state capacity can evolve in a transnationalized setting. An infrastructurally strong state would prioritize its relations with citizens, and less easily fall prey to global forces. But an infrastructurally weak state would most likely prove vulnerable to transnational actors: the inability to reach down and influence society might provide the kind of vacuum that would allow for external influence. This weakness may, in fact, be partially determined by a history of transnational domination. There are numerous historical and recent examples of powerful transnational actors moving in and, due to the vacuum created by an infrastructurally weak state, performing key functions normally performed by state institutions. In contrast, the aloofness and repressiveness that accompany despotic capacity fits well with the undemocratic experience of much of Latin America. It applies even more fully when linked to the distancing brought on by excessive external domination and by close ties between states and global actors. A state with stronger ties to transnational groups than to its own population is a state that is far more likely to be despotic in nature. And a nation ruled by an aloof, despotic state is far more likely to provide transnational actors opportunities to penetrate its national borders and influence its society. Figure 1.1 provides a visual representation of these relationships.

The analysis in upcoming chapters uses the concept of state capacity to assess the power of transnational actors in several ways. First, it analyzes the impact of close relations between states and outside actors on despotic and infrastructural capacity. Second, it explores the enduring power of transnational actors in the context of their ability to exert genuine infrastructural capacity—the kind normally associated with states. While this assessment of power and capacity scrutinizes all forms of power exerted by transnational actors in Latin America, the theoretical lens of state capacity adds rigor and clarity to the discussion.

And, as is more fully analyzed in the concluding chapter and in chapters on specific transnational actors, any full understanding of state capacity in Latin America must come to terms with its external dimensions. This global perspective is also essential to understanding the capacity of states. More specifically, a state acting with efficacy must have capacity in relation not only to its own citizens but also to powerful outside factors: whether specific actors or more impersonal political and economic forces. These interactions make up a large proportion of this book, and the concluding chapter makes a case for a revised and more globalized understanding of state capacity.

The state in society and state capacity approaches acknowledge both the constraints and the opportunities for national governments as they struggle with transnational power. There has been a shocking history of external domination in Latin America. But careful study of these events brings out a more complex reality, in which this struggle has not been completely one-sided, and states—sometimes in alliance with other global forces or internal social movements—have had some success in asserting their capacity and national prerogatives in the face of transnational power. This book explores both scenarios as it assesses the power of transnational actors in Latin America.

One final theoretical note: the three-level model of analysis represents an attempt to broaden concerns with state capacity and relations between state and society to the transnational level. In this regard it owes a great deal not only to the theorists cited above, but also to scholars who have attempted to integrate studies of states and societies with more global concerns. Charles Anderson, in his influential early work on Latin American politics, recommended that scholars incorporate what is "subnational," "national," and "supranational" into their analysis (Anderson, 1967). This was also the framework in my 1991 dissertation, which analyzed the impact of external penetration on Nicaragua and Honduras (Shepherd, 1991). Eduardo Silva and his collaborators use multilevel analysis in their work on "Bridging the Divide" between transnational and national social movements (Silva, 2013). Alison Brysk has used a similar approach in her work on human rights in Argentina and indigenous activism in Latin America, exploring the impact of social movements operating "from above and below," and analyzing how influence flows "from tribal village to global village" and back again (Brysk, 1993, 2000). Her example and informal advice have been invaluable as I have crafted the three-level approach to the study of transnational actors in Latin America.

This book is above all a study of transnational actors, distinct in their motivations from any national government inside or outside of Latin America. Nevertheless, any study of the region must come to terms with the impact of other significant factors at the global level. In this regard, the analysis also intermittently incorporates the influence of four additional global actors and forces: the US government, key intergovernmental organizations (such as the UN and the Inter-American Court of Human Rights), global economic market forces, and traditional international military rivalries (see Figure 1.1.) Depending on the circumstances, they may be central to the analysis in some cases, but may not even appear in others.

The US government appears frequently throughout the book, even as it does not occupy center stage. First, as is explained in greater detail in Chapter 2, US domination for roughly 100 years after Latin American independence helped to create the conditions for external penetration of Latin American national political systems by transnational actors. For much of this period, for example, the US government emphatically backed US-based TNCs. More recent history shows great variety in relations between the US government and transnational actors. It is not possible to systematically equate US policy with the interests of any single transnational actor—or in opposition to them. Despite all these variations, US policy has deeply affected transnational actors in Latin America (with the possible exception of the Catholic Church).

The book treats intergovernmental organizations in the same way, with a special emphasis on the UN and, more recently, the Inter-American Court of Human Rights (IACHR). The analysis points to moments when intergovernmental organizations proved crucial to transnational actors as they interacted with Latin American states and societies. Despite its shortcomings as a global governing force, the UN has been an important actor in the region since its inception, and the IACHR has, over recent decades, had an extremely important legal presence in Latin America.

Global market forces are a third significant external factor for the study of transnational actors in Latin America. These forces have always been important in a region marked by extreme levels of economic dependency. But their influence has fluctuated, and they have been particularly central to interactions among global, national, and societal actors in certain eras. Much of what TNCs and TDNs do is profoundly influenced by global markets.

Finally, traditional interstate military rivalries are treated as a potentially significant fourth global factor. A central theme of Chapter 2's historical survey is that these rivalries have been largely absent and have only rarely taken the form of conventional wars. Most accounts in following chapters point to a similar absence in more recent eras. Yet, in a few cases, these conflicts have had a significant impact. Awareness of their impact can provide genuine insight into how states and societies react to transnational influence.

Explaining Terms

It is important to clearly define the terms used for the tremendous variety of actors which appear in this study.

Societal and local actors: This refers to groups operating within nations, separate from national governments. As reflected in Figure 1.1, the first category is political groups, which often have close ties and established relationships with state structures. Political parties are the largest and most all-encompassing of these types of groups. In the Latin American setting, some parties have been a presence in national politics for long stretches of time, serving as channels for political participation in more or less democratic systems (Mainwaring, 2018). Interest groups can be more or less close to power than political parties, but they are usually formally recognized organizations that focus on one or several related issues (Thomas and Klimovich, 2014). The more mainstream versions of these groups can be clearly labeled as "political," while the more radicalized or grassroots versions can be described as belonging to social movements, the second category of local/societal organizations (noted in Figure 1.1). Labor unions can be included in either category. Social movements often eschew conventional political participation and engage in behavior such as strikes, marches, and demonstrations; the field of "subaltern" studies focuses on the most marginalized social movements (Darnovsky et al., 1995; Rodriguez, 2001). As governments fail to respond, or respond with violence, the third type of local/societal organization, revolutionary groups, can emerge from social movements, attempting not only to influence policy but overthrow state structures (Selbin, 1993). All three types of local/societal groups play a prominent role in the accounts to follow.

National actors: At the national level, the analytical focus is on the state as an institution. Its official status as a sovereign entity representing the nation necessitates this formal, institutional approach. Its claim (rooted in the thinking of Max Weber) to exert authority and possess a monopoly over violence within national boundaries—as dubious as it may be at times—also makes such an approach appropriate (Gerth and Mills, 1958, p. 78). While much of the analysis focuses on the state at the national level, when necessary it explores the role of local and provincial levels of government as parts of the larger state structure. This leads to a larger point: a focus on "the state" risks regarding it as an undifferentiated, monolithic institution. State actions are viewed in this book with an eye to internal state dynamics and potential divisions within state structures. Yet it can also be the case that high-profile interactions with transnational actors can lead to unity within states. One important point with regard to terminology: the term state usually refers in a general way to formal political institutions within a nation. Occasionally, the analysis will use the term "government" and "national government" when the use of the term "state" to refer to a subdivision of national authority (as in the Brazilian or Mexican state-level units) is unavoidable.

Intergovernmental organizations: This term refers to organizations that are based on national alliances, treaties, and collaboration, and that remain loyal to the spirit of agreements that have established these arrangements. It represents the sum of the multiple nations that have joined in international endeavors and is roughly synonymous with multinational organizations. The most important intergovernmental organization is the UN. Enduring groups like the Organization of American States and the Inter-American Court of

Human Rights, which remain based in the dynamics of its member states, can be labeled intergovernmental. This label also largely applies to the World Bank, the International Monetary Fund, the World Trade Organization, and the International Labor Organization.

Transnational actors: This term refers to organizations that are able to operate above and beyond national boundaries. Nation-based restrictions can constrain them, but their ability to transcend these restrictions and move seamlessly from nation to nation distinguishes them from national organizations. Their physical presence in numerous nations and their ability to use communications and transportation technology to communicate and move quickly makes them genuinely transnational. They are marked by loyalty to some ideal or economic goal beyond a national objective. Their enduring presence in a global setting makes them something more than simply an amalgamation of all the national entities in which they operate—something more than "multinational." Analysis of transnational actors in this book is informed by different global theoretical traditions: "liberal" understandings of them as generally benevolent forces operating in a setting of "interdependence" (Keohane and Nye, 1977); Marxist conceptions of them either as tools of class-based exploitation or as leaders in the anti-capitalist struggle, all acting in a global capitalist "world-system" (Chase-Dunn, 2005); or as the globally transformational, norms-based actors presented by "constructivist" scholars (Finnemore and Sikkink, 2001).

So as to avoid confusion, a series of other closely related terms are not used in this book. These include: transnational non-governmental organization, transnational social movement, transnational social movement organization, transnational advocacy network, multinational organization, and non-governmental organization. The larger goal is to provide nuanced analysis and detailed accounts to better understand how particular transnational actors can be understood as distinctive, but also as representative of influence that transcends national boundaries (Ahmed and Potter, 2006). As explained above, the general term "transnational actor" is broken down into the more specific forms of transnational networks and transnational organizations, as it is applied to each of the four transnational case studies. Furthermore, the following chapters provide detailed discussions of terms such as TNC, TDN, and THRN as they arise and examine more closely the makeup of the Catholic Church as a transnational organization.

★★★

This introductory chapter has set out the basic parameters for the book and the analytical framework which is intended to deepen analysis of transnational organizations in Latin America. Following an historical overview in Chapter 2, the book focuses on four specific transnational actors, with a chapter for each. Chapter 3 is devoted to the Catholic Church and includes case studies of

Nicaragua and Brazil. Chapter 4 focuses on TNCs and includes case studies of Bolivia and Chile. Chapter 5 provides an account of TDNs and includes case studies of Colombia and Mexico. And Chapter 6 focuses on THRNs and includes case studies of Guatemala and Argentina. Chapter 7 draws comparisons and provides theoretical conclusions. To summarize, the analysis is based on a three-tier framework for understanding complex interactions between the transnational, the national, and the local. Alongside this multi-level analysis, it also uses several theoretical lenses to more fully understand the actions of transnational groups and the forces that constrain them: the nature of institutions and networks; the impact of norms and principles; and the significance of capacity and power.

One of the primary goals of this book is to provide a fresh theoretical perspective on transnational processes that have profoundly shaped Latin America. But an even more important goal is to understand the forces that either thwart or bolster citizens as they confront power and try to improve conditions in their communities and nations. There is little question that transnational actors represent distant and often unaccountable forces in their lives. This book, in the following chapters, describes successful efforts to address and challenge transnational influence; it also points to developments within transnational groups that may empower the most marginalized Latin Americans in their struggles. In this regard, then, the details that emerge conform to both the top-down, unaccountable version of globalization and its democratic, grassroots counterpart. The remainder of the book explores the theoretical, political, and moral implications of these processes.

References

Ahmed, Shamima and David Potter, 2006. *NGOs in International Politics.* Bloomfield, CT: Kumarian Press.

Anderson, Charles, 1967. *Politics and Economic Change in Latin America: The Governing of Restless Nations.* Princeton, NJ: Princeton University Press.

Bettiza, Gregorio and Filippo Dionigi, 2015. "How do Religious Norms Diffuse? Institutional Translation and International Change in a Postsecular World Society," *UK European Journal of International Relations* 21/3, pp. 621–646.

Brysk, Alison, 1993. "From Above and Below: Social Movements, the International System, and Human Rights in Argentina," *Comparative Political Studies* 26/3 (October), pp. 259–285.

Brysk, Alison, 2000. *From Tribal Village to Global Village: Indian Rights and International Relations in Latin America.* Stanford, CA: Stanford University Press.

Centeno, Miguel Angel, 2002. *Blood and Debt: War and the Nation-State in Latin America.* University Park, PA: Penn State University Press.

Chase-Dunn, Christopher, 2005. "Social Evolution and the Future of World Society," *Journal of World Systems Research* 11/2, pp. 171–192.

Dahl, Robert, 1957. "The Concept of Power," *Systems Research and Behavioral Science* 2/3, pp. 201–215.

Darnovsky, Marcy, Barbara Epstein and Richard Flacks, 1995. *Cultural Politics and Social Movements*. Philadelphia: Temple University Press.

Evans, Peter, 2000. "Fighting Marginalization with Transnational Networks: Counter-Hegemonic Globalization," *Contemporary Sociology* 29/1 (January), pp. 230–241.

Evans, Peter, 2008. "Is an Alternative Globalization Possible?" *Politics and Society* 36/2 (June), pp. 271–305.

Falk, Richard, 1992. "Democratising, Internationalising, and Globalising: A Collage of Blurred Images," *Third World Quarterly* 13/4, pp. 627–640.

Finnemore, Martha, and Kathryn Sikkink, 2001. "Taking Stock: The Constructivist Research Program in International Relations and Comparative Politics," *Annual Review of Political Science* 4, pp. 391–416.

Galeano, Eduardo, 1997. *Open Veins of Latin America*. New York: New York University Press.

Gerth, H.H. and C. Wright Mills, 1958. *From Max Weber*. New York: New York University Press.

Hamilton, Nora, 1982. *The Limits of State Autonomy: Post-Revolutionary Mexico*. Princeton, NJ: Princeton University Press.

Jepperson, Ronald, Alexander Wendt, and Peter Katzenstein, 1996. "Norms, Identity, and Culture in National Security," in Peter Katzenstein, editors, *The Culture of National Security: Norms and Identity in World Politics*. New York: Columbia University Press, pp. 33–75.

Jones, Nathan, 2017. *Mexico's Illicit Drug Networks and the State Reaction*. Washington, DC: Georgetown University Press.

Keck, Margret and Kathryn Sikkink, 1998. *Activists beyond Borders: Transnational Advocacy Networks in International Politics*. Ithaca, NY: Cornell University Press.

Keohane, Robert and Joseph Nye, 1977. *Power and Interdependence: World Politics in Transition*. Boston, MA: Little, Brown.

Khagram, Sanjeev, James Riker and Kathryn Sikkink, 2002. "From Santiago to Seattle: Transnational Advocacy Groups Restructuring World Politics," in Sanjeev Khagram et al., editors, *Restructuring World Politics: Transnational Social Movements, Networks, and Norms*. Minneapolis: University of Minnesota Press, pp. 3–23.

Mainwaring, Scott, 1986. *The Catholic Church and Politics in Brazil, 1916–1985*. Stanford, CA: Stanford University Press.

Mainwaring, Scott, 2018. *Party Systems in Latin America*. Cambridge, MA: Harvard University Press.

Mann, Michael, 1986. "The Autonomous Power of the State: Its Origins, Mechanisms and Results," in Johan Hall, editor, *States in History*, Oxford: Basil Blackwell, pp. 182–203.

Mann, Michael, 2012. *The Sources of Social Power*. Cambridge: Cambridge University Press.

Migdal, Joel, 1988. *Strong Societies and Weak States: State-Society Relations and State Capabilities in the Third World*. Princeton, NJ: Princeton University Press.

Nye, Joseph, 2004. "The Decline of America's Soft Power: Why Washington Should Worry," *Foreign Affairs* 83/3, pp. 16–20.

Risse, Thomas and Kathryn Sikkink, 1999. "The Socialization of International Human Rights Norms into Domestic Practices: Introduction," in Thomas Risse et al., editors, *The Power of Human Rights: International Norms and Domestic Change*. Cambridge: Cambridge University Press, pp. 1–37.

Rodriguez, Ileana editor, 2001. *The Latin American Subaltern Studies Reader.* Durham, NC: Duke University Press.

Rueschemeyer, Dietrich and Peter Evans, 1985. "The State and Economic Transformation: Toward an Analysis of the Conditions Underlying Effective Intervention," in Peter Evans et al., editors, *Bringing the State Back In.* Cambridge: Cambridge University Press, pp. 44–77.

Selbin, Eric, 1993. *Modern Latin American Revolutions.* Boulder, CO: Westview Press.

Shepherd, Frederick, 1991. *State, Countryside, and External Forces in Honduras and Nicaragua (Doctoral Thesis).* Washington, DC: Georgetown University.

Sikkink, Kathryn, 2011. *The Justice Cascade: How Human Rights Prosecutions are Changing World Politics.* New York: W.W. Norton.

Silva, Eduardo, editor, 2013. *Transnational Activism and National Movements in Latin America: Bridging the Divide.* New York: Routledge.

Stepan, Alfred, 1978. *State and Society: Peru in Comparative Perspective.* Princeton, NJ: Princeton University Press.

Thomas, Clive and Kristina Klimovich, 2014. "Interest Groups and Lobbying in Latin America: Theoretical and Practical Considerations," *Journal of Public Affairs* 14/3, pp. 165–182.

Wilde, Alexander, 1987. "Creating Neo-Christendom in Colombia," Working Paper 92, Kellogg Institute for International Studies. South Bend, IN: Kellogg Institute.

2

THE RISE OF TRANSNATIONAL ACTORS

The Historical Setting

This brief historical overview of Latin America focuses on several things. First, it assesses the impact of colonialism on the form that Latin American political institutions would ultimately take. Second, it examines anti-colonial independence struggles and early forms of the Latin America nation-state to better understand the openings that might exist for transnational actors to assert their power in the roughly first 100 years of formal independence. Third, it notes, in an initial way, the different time-frames for the rise of the Catholic Church, transnational corporations (TNCs), transnational drug networks (TDNs), and transnational human rights networks (THRNs) in Latin America. Finally, it begins the process of relating details from Latin America to the larger themes of institutions and networks, principles and norms, and power and capacity, all in reference to the book's larger three-level framework of analysis.

Colonialism and Early Independence

Many historical accounts of Latin America point to the "original sin" of Spanish and Portuguese colonization of the Americas as absolutely fundamental to the future of Latin American politics—to say nothing of its impact on indigenous communities. Conditions rooted in colonialism still constrain Latin American governments' ability to perform basic functions. The application of a comprehensive and exploitative colonial system on Latin America from distant European capitals set the stage for domination by outside actors even after formal colonialism receded.

The specific form that colonialism took in Latin America accentuated this impact. Spain and Portugal came to formally control their vast colonial territories in South, Central, and North America relatively quickly. But these formal legal arrangements masked important variations in the colonial experience for indigenous Americans. Some communities were completely wiped out by violence, disease, and economic exploitation; the term genocide can be applied to these cases. In contrast, some remote areas on the Yucatan Peninsula, in the Andean highlands, in the Amazon rainforest, and in the extreme Southern Cone remained isolated. A third variation is Spanish rule imposed on large-scale civilizations in which, despite heavy losses, large numbers of the indigenous population survived, and came to account for a significant proportion of the population. A fourth variation was both a small colonial presence and only small-scale indigenous populations, with much immigration left to later, post-independence eras.

What virtually all Latin American colonial communities and future nations shared was an aloof governing elite, with few organic ties to the majority of the population. In many Latin American nations, large numbers of indigenous Americans had survived colonialism, and the colonial and post-colonial political community was far more mixed in this regard than, for example, Canada and the US. Yet, despite this diversity, Latin Americans of mixed or indigenous ancestry were disproportionately excluded from national political life when independent nations emerged. In his account of states and nationalism in Latin America, Miguel Angel Centeno argues that "the greatest threat" to the power of state elites over history "has not come from a competing elite across a border, but from the masses below." He notes that this is particularly the case in nations with significant indigenous populations. In this setting,

> the defining "ethnic war" of the continent occurred prior to state formation. The conquest and its results left deeper divisions within countries than could ever develop between them.
>
> *(Centeno, 2002, pp. 90–91)*

The relevant point for this book, then, is that the colonial experience in Latin America created the conditions for aloof, inorganic states in Latin America; the new nations were nothing more than "shards of an empire" (Centeno, 2002, p. 272). These nation-states, and the governments that ruled them, were ripe for penetration by powerful transnational forces—a penetration which had already begun several centuries earlier with the onset of colonialism.

The Catholic Church was, from the outset, a central protagonist in the application and spread of colonialism in the Americas. Catholicism was entwined with the Portuguese and Spanish crowns in a comprehensive and complex way (Burkholder and Johnson, 1990, pp. 83–97). The Catholicism emerging from the reconquest of the Iberian Peninsula was an especially intolerant and unforgiving one (Schwaller, 2011; Chapters 3 and 4). But it is also important to avoid generalizations about the Church's behavior in the Americas. It is precisely in the more humane practices of the Church that we see an early version of the global human rights struggle: Father Bartolome de las Casas's relentless efforts on behalf of indigenous Americans in the 16th century (Orique, 2009).

Conditions rooted in colonialism were largely left in place by the independence struggle of the early 19th century. It is worth briefly drawing a contrast with early efforts at independence that did not succeed. In 1780, Tupác Amaru II, who claimed ancestry from the Inca leaders who were overthrown by the Spanish, led a comprehensive rebellion of 80,000 primarily indigenous forces against the Peruvian Spanish authorities. It took many thousands of lives and came close to succeeding, until it was stamped out in 1783 (Wright, 1992, pp. 196–199). It preached a decisive break with colonialism and called for explicitly indigenous-oriented rule. Thirty years later in Mexico, two priests, Miguel Hidalgo and then José Maria Morelos, led an anti-colonial uprising, pushing for radical social reforms and the abolition of slavery. At its height, the rebellion had more than 50,000 mostly indigenous and mestizo fighters. The rebels declared independence in 1813 and established a legislature in 1814. But the colonial authorities held enough territory to continue their claim to the colony, and when the Spanish monarchy was returned to power in Europe, Spain was able to defeat the rebellion and conclusively re-establish colonial authority (Hamnett, 1986; Wright, 1992, pp. 242–243).

Mexico and Peru would not gain independence from Spain until 1821 and 1824, respectively, under leaders advocating none of the pro-indigenous radicalism of earlier independence attempts. With few exceptions, Latin American nations would emerge out of independence struggles in the 1820s led by figures who were intent on independence, but who also had strong ties to Europe. Their wars for independence had little to do with the aspirations of indigenous communities. And they failed to comprehensively break ties with Europe and European-oriented elites. After some initial attempts (described in Chapter 3), little was done to uproot the Catholic presence or the more firmly rooted Catholic cultural practices that were an important part of Latin American society. The newly independent nation-states—"shards of empire"—had few organic reasons to exist. And the new nations' borders were arbitrary, failing to reflect cultural and material differences on the ground and representing little more than the administrative units of the former empire.

Some new nations, such as Guatemala (after efforts at a unified Central America failed in 1838), Ecuador, Peru, and Bolivia, had majority or near-majority indigenous populations. Mexico's national culture gradually emerged as one that at least symbolically celebrated a syncretism that mixed European and indigenous traditions. In contrast, Colombia had less of a large-scale indigenous presence, and its status as a colonial hub led it to emphasize what was Spanish and European in its culture and political system (e.g., privileging the Catholic Church). Brazil maintained a unique and strong set of ties to Europe upon its formal independence in 1822, as the Portuguese Crown Prince Dom Pedro declared independence and he and his descendants ruled until Brazil became a republic in 1889. Nations such as Argentina, Chile, and Uruguay were marked both by smaller-scale indigenous populations and by their distance from colonial centers; their political and cultural systems would be more profoundly altered by later (largely non-Spanish) European migrations. And certain nations, such as Brazil, Chile, Uruguay, Guatemala, and other Atlantic coastal regions of Central America, were marked by a significant and growing Protestant religious presence.

Export-Based Economies, Weak Nation-States, and the Roots of Transnational Power

Despite these variations, throughout the region little sense of nationhood emerged among the people in the wake of independence, and the states ruling these nations lacked the capacity to perform even the most basic tasks of governance. The same could be said of many new nations, but several historical trends over the remaining 19th century ensured that Latin American nation-states would remain weak and superficial, and ultimately vulnerable to external, transnational actors.

The first significant region-wide trend was the national economic development strategy known as "export-led growth," with a focus on one or a few raw materials. This approach was adopted by states across Latin America during the second half of the 19th century and was effectively the first genuine effort by independent Latin American governments to fashion national economies. It involved states devoting key infrastructure, financing, resources, and support to a chosen crop, mineral, or other resource (Bulmer-Thomas, 2003). Production, extraction, and export of this item would become the engine of the national economy. In theory this would provide badly needed foreign capital and broad-based employment opportunities. It would take advantage of lucrative markets abroad in North America and Europe. The most widespread effort focused on coffee, which became the basis for national economic development across Latin America, as the region fed global demand. The best land was devoted to coffee cultivation; financial credit was disproportionately directed to large coffee farms; roads and rail lines were built to transport coffee to ports and markets; and states ensured a stable and controllable labor force for coffee growers. This process transformed the political and economic systems of many Latin American nations, especially the small Central American "coffee republics" (Williams, 1994). These efforts were matched, with some variations, in other agricultural crops, such as bananas and sugar; and with minerals, such as copper and tin.

The reality was much more conflictual and exploitative than the theory. Political power became concentrated in the hands of those who exported the key products, and the line between state and economic elites blurred and then disappeared. Providing a stable labor force for the farms and mines became an exercise in fierce oppression, as labor organizing was forbidden and work conditions were brutal, particularly given the seasonal nature of labor for most agricultural export crops. The term "neo-colonial" has often been applied to these arrangements, reflecting the extent to which a privileged class with strong ties outward to markets in Europe and North America dominated political and economic life in Latin American nations.

One important variation in this process—with implications for this book—concerns the extent to which the economy based on export-led growth remained in local hands. Certain products required significant technology and capital, and in these cases ownership of the key national economic sectors was for the most part taken over by outside firms—TNCs. This phenomenon often led to the emergence of an "enclave" economy, associated with banana cultivation, mining, and oil. In these sectors, the need for technology and capital investments favored foreign over local ownership. It is through this process that, beginning in the late 19th century and accelerating in the early 20th, we see the initial appearance of powerful TNCs in Latin America, discussed in greater detail in Chapter 4 (Twomey, 1998). On a more general level, the distortions accompanying export-led growth brought Latin American governments much closer to economic elites than to the population at large. Most of the infrastructure that was created catered to these externally oriented elites. And, in the case of enclave economies, governments welcomed powerful external actors that often functioned as a state-within-a-state, perhaps the ultimate sign of government weakness.

These developments were accompanied by a political split between Conservatives and Liberals that prevailed across Latin America for almost a century after independence, and manifested itself in entrenched national political parties and strong regional loyalties. In the most general terms, Liberals were associated with a vague commitment to political and cultural modernization, the move to export-led growth, and throwing national economies open to global markets. Conservatives were closely linked to the Catholic Church and were far more reluctant to challenge traditions handed down from colonialism. Yet the differences between the two groups should not be exaggerated. While Liberals gradually gained the upper hand throughout the region, Conservatives remained a potent force well into the 20th century: Peru, for example, was ruled by a Conservative clique during the entire decade of the 1920s (Klaiber, 1999, p. 259).

The second significant region-wide trend concerns what did not happen during the 19th century: newly independent Latin America was marked by a notable absence of conventional, interstate military conflicts. As Miguel Angel Centeno argues, nations that emerged as relatively superficial units at independence were not forced to survive and justify their existence in an atmosphere of international military competition in 19th-century Latin America. Their governments were not forced to mobilize people or resources in response to neighboring military threats. Two related outcomes emerged from this absence. The first was weak governing institutions across the region. Latin American states were able to perform few of the basic functions normally performed by states. This fundamental weakness can be seen in policy areas such as social welfare, education, policing, culture, and economic regulation as well as in the capacity to raise resources through taxation. In language introduced in Chapter 1, Latin American nations were (and continue to be) infrastructurally weak (Centeno, 2002, pp. 101–166). The second, related, outcome was that the populations in these nations felt little sense of genuinely belonging to, and viewing themselves as citizens of, their respective nation-states. Governments were not forced to win citizen loyalty because of the absence of external military threats and rivalries. And the continued weakness of states in this context made most Latin American states ineffectual in any attempt they might make to earn this loyalty (Centeno, 2002, pp. 167–216). In critical dialogue with Centeno, Cameron Thies argues that certain military rivalries, short of actual warfare, did strengthen states and nationalism in certain Latin American nations (Thies, 2005). Yet even conceding this point, Latin America has, since independence, been marked by a notable lack of conventional international military conflict, and it has weakened states and nations in the region.

In contrast, roughly the same period (and at least a century prior) was marked by consistent and ongoing international conflicts in Europe, which forced governments to mobilize resources simply in order to survive, dramatically strengthening states in the process and, at the same time, increasing nationalism among the people in nation-states. The result was much stronger government and greater nationalism throughout Europe (Tilly, 1985; Porter, 2002). No such process took place in Latin America after independence, leaving the region marked by superficial nations ruled by weak states.

The nature of the US presence in the region contributed to this state of affairs. The Monroe Doctrine, formulated in 1823, for the most part sealed off the Americas from new European influence, and had the effect of imposing region-wide stability and freezing in place most national boundaries in Latin America. Perhaps the most significant exception to this took place in Mexico in the 1840s and 1860s. The US-Mexican War of 1846–1848 demonstrated how unprepared the Mexican government was to compete militarily with the US, a rising and powerful nation-state with geographical ambitions. The result was a conventional war in which Mexico rapidly lost half of its territory (Tenenbaum, 1986, p. 79). In the 1860s, the French military's insertion of Emperor Maximilian onto the Mexican "throne" took place precisely when the US was looking inward in its own bloody civil war. The subsequent campaign to remove him is unique in the history of Latin American independence. These two historical moments were central factors in the rise of a Mexican nationalism that may be unmatched in Latin America. The rest of Latin America was—with a very few exceptions—spared conventional military conflict. This may have made the region far less deadly than Europe, but it weakened nation-states throughout Latin America.

There was a related absence of the kind of democracy in the region that might have provided governments with greater legitimacy among "citizens." It was rare that any Latin American nation would use democratic means to increase political legitimacy and constructive interactions between citizen and states. There were fleeting moments of democratic rule in Uruguay, Chile, and Mexico in the 19th century. But far more common were extended periods marked by dictatorship and corruption. The absence of democracy was significant in itself, leaving national populations with little leverage over government decisions. It also had the effect of keeping national governments aloof and disconnected from people who experienced citizenship in few meaningful ways.

The profound weakness of Latin American nation-states, both as governing forces and as national political communities, had significant implications for governments' relations outward with transnational actors. Centeno's analysis suggests that the eventual power of transnational actors may have had more to do with internal weakness than with external factors: "We might even reverse the causal order and suggest that it was the absence of war that produced a weak state, which in turn made intervention possible" (Centeno, 2002, p. 71). Following chapters explore the complex relations between internal and external factors in Latin America. But there is little question that the historical weakness of Latin American governments provided opportunities for transnational actors.

This, then, was the larger setting at the turn of the 19th century for a region marked by weak nation-states and ripe for transnational forces exerting influence—which was beginning to happen with TNCs and had happened long before with the Catholic Church. These conditions would largely prevail for several more decades, until the global Great Depression would gradually shock national governments into action. But four nations, in very different ways, provided early examples of reactions against external domination. In three of these cases, the reaction had as much to do with emerging democracy as it did with explicit stances against external domination. Under the leadership of José Batlle y Ordóñez from 1903 to 1915, the Uruguayan state established universal suffrage, launched ambitious welfare policies, took comprehensive steps against the Catholic Church, and engaged in a nationalist set of economic policies that privileged Uruguayan interests over global markets and TNCs (Fitzgibbon, 1953; Weschler, 1998, pp. 95–96). Chile began a similar democratic trajectory in 1891, and by the 1910s was marked by the emergence of a politically engaged labor movement, the middle-class Radical Party, and explicitly socialist political parties. In the 1920s, a centrist Chilean government responded to external companies' oil exploration by passing legislation to regulate and directly run portions of the emerging oil sector. Argentina moved comprehensively toward democracy under the leadership of the Union Civica Radical from 1916 to

1930, passing education, social security, and labor reforms, and creating a state-run oil company (Wilkins, 1974).

Mexico was convulsed by a series of far more violent and less democratic events during the revolution of 1910–1917. But it similarly represented a strengthening of ties between the Mexican state and the Mexican people. Nationalist, anti-external sentiment was particularly central to the revolution given the excesses of the 33-year rule of Porfirio Diáz in the decades leading up to the revolution, and US meddling during it. The Constitution stated in no uncertain terms the Mexican state's right to intervene against excessive transnational power, with numerous provisions attacking the power of the Catholic Church and, most notably, strong language about the state's control over key natural resources. Events in Uruguay, Chile, Argentina, and Mexico in the early 1900s would serve as a preview to a region-wide trend toward more assertive states and greater nationalism over the rest of the century.

Challenges to Growing Transnational Influence: An Historical Overview

In the most general terms, the decades after the Great Depression were marked by dramatic growth of transnational corporate power, the continued overwhelming presence of the Catholic Church, and, beginning in the 1970s and accelerating in subsequent decades, the emergence of THRNs and TDNs (described in greater detail in the coming chapters). These developments were accompanied by sporadically successful efforts to control, mitigate, or crowd out these transnational actors. They also took a wide variety of forms: democratic reforms, social revolutions, movements inspired by nationalism and social justice, gradual changes within the fabric of societies, collaboration with or defiance of the US government, and campaigns with multinational institutions. Some version of these efforts took place in virtually every Latin American nation, with widely varying degrees of success. In many cases, these were one-sided affairs, with unambiguous and brutal assertions of transnational power in relation to Latin American governments and citizens. In others, Latin American citizens and states were able to exert significant and surprising leverage in relation to transnational organizations. And in some cases, the Latin American people were able to work directly with transnational actors to improve their lives.

These interactions among transnational, national, and local actors are covered in greater depth in the chapters that follow. A brief account of these trends can serve as a guide to the more focused analysis to follow. The Great Depression is viewed as a watershed in Latin American history because it exposed the vulnerabilities of economies that relied excessively on global markets. Subsequent economic and political strategies formulated by Latin American leaders were designed to mitigate this vulnerability. These nationalist strategies gradually emerged before and after World War II in the form of "import substitution industrialization" (Prebisch, 1950). Efforts at greater national economic control were buoyed by growing democratization in the region. It appeared immediately after World War II that democracy was deepening its roots in Brazil, Argentina, Chile, and Uruguay. And nations such as Colombia, El Salvador, Costa Rica, and Guatemala were engaged in promising democratic reforms. Yet within several decades, tentative moves toward democracy were comprehensively reversed, with brutal dictatorships emerging throughout the region, as early as 1948 in Colombia, as late as 1973 in Chile and Uruguay, and in most Latin American nations in between. During this period, US administrations either actively connived in the destruction of democracy or did too little to keep it from happening. Many Latin American dictatorships were inspired by a "National Security" doctrine pushed by the US military, and ultimately used to target internal enemies (Weschler, 1998, pp. 113–123). Leftist regimes in Mexico and Cuba calcified into unrepresentative systems. And in the late 1970s and 1980s, Central America was swept into violent cycles of revolution, repression, and genocide, with the US again abetting the worst abuses. In an ominous development, described in Chapter 5, TDNs began to operate freely in Bolivia, Peru, and Colombia, and, more recently, Mexico, Honduras, El Salvador, and Guatemala.

A number of factors contributed to tentative moves toward democratization in the early 1980s, and then a full-blown regional democratic transformation in the late 1980s and 1990s, which came to include almost every Latin American nation. Chapter 3 discusses the role of the Catholic Church and Chapter 6 the role of transnational human rights organizations in this process. Democratization was accompanied at this time by a region-wide move toward pro-market, neoliberal policies which, among other things, led to a dramatic increase in foreign investment throughout Latin America in the 1990s. The deepening of democracy, and the backlash against a version of neoliberalism that was viewed as excessive by many Latin Americans, subsequently led to a region-wide leftist shift in the early 2000s, which came to be known as the "pink revolution." The mixed response to these leftist reforms has led to remarkable political heterogeneity in Latin America at the start of the decade of the 2020s. Latin America's two largest economies are ruled by the rightist Jair Bolsonaro in Brazil and the leftist Andrés Manuel López Obrador in Mexico. And late 2020 was marked by victories for the forces of the left as Evo Morales' allies were returned to power in Bolivia after the 2019 coup, and an overwhelming majority voted to reject the remnants of Chile's rightist constitution.

Theoretical Conclusions

This brief historical survey of Latin America provides an overview for the deeper analysis of the coming chapters. It also serves as a background for brief remarks about how the larger historical setting fits into the general theoretical structure of the book. What follows, then, are a series of points relating both the colonial history of Latin America and the first roughly 100 years of independence to key theoretical perspectives. It describes these conditions in the context of the three-level structure of analysis, clarifying relations among global, national, and local actors. And it discusses how this early history can be understood in regard to the three theoretical concerns of institutions and networks, principles and norms, and power and capacity.

The late colonial uprisings in Peru and Mexico were important examples of bottom-up, locally based groups challenging colonial power structures. What subsequently emerged with national independence in Latin America, however, represented a far different outcome. As is described in the section on power and capacity below, the new national governments had few ties to "citizens," especially in new nations with large indigenous populations. And it was only near the end of the 19th century or well into the 20th century that democratic institutions emerged in Latin American nations to encourage these ties. After independence, the transnational Catholic Church was often far more successful in influencing and gaining the loyalty of the Latin American people than were national governments.

In the first area of theoretical concern, this chapter has provided historical background for the emergence and nature of transnational **institutions and networks** in Latin America. Latin America was, under colonialism, dominated by the Spanish and Portuguese crowns. A crucial point is that the Catholic Church closely accompanied these colonial institutions, and preceded modern nations and national governments in Latin America. Chapter 3 includes close analysis of its five centuries in the region; its continued political and, especially, cultural power; and the specific forms that this organization takes as it extends its power transnationally. Transnational corporations, drug networks, and human rights networks have appeared more recently; this historical overview has less to say about their presence. But it is important to note that the larger setting of weak national states and lack of nationalism provides crucial context for understanding the form that these organizations take and how they exert their power. These issues are more fully addressed in Chapters 4, 5, and 6.

Second, theoretical discussion of **norms and principles** is, for the historical eras covered in this chapter, limited largely to the Catholic Church. Yet, coming out of late medieval Europe, the Church has also functioned as a powerful political and cultural actor in Latin America. Its preponderance means that multiple Catholic traditions have had an impact on the region: the humanitarian work of Bartolome de Las Casas is surely an early version of norms-based activity inspired by human rights. The analysis of Chapter 3 assesses the norms that drive these different traditions and the extent to which they correspond to the empowerment of different political forces. But the brutal process of dispossession under colonialism ultimately overwhelmed the work of norms-driven actors. Catholic authorities were far more likely to pursue the norm of "neo-Christendom," which would align them firmly with colonial and national political elites. The general absence of widespread nationalism in the wake of independence made appeals to norms based on national control of key resources unlikely as well. These conditions would, however, change, and the more recent rise of norms is the topic of much of the rest of the book.

Questions of **power and capacity** reveal a great deal about relations among transnational actors, states, and society during the first century of Latin American independence. Relations between state and society in Latin America coming out of colonialism departed dramatically from the Weberian model of the state as a sovereign actor enjoying a measure of dominance within national boundaries. Rather, the image of a far less powerful state as one of only many actors trying to influence society is far more appropriate to the historical Latin American setting. Figure 2.1 provides a visual representation of this state weakness; it is one of the legacies of colonialism, and the struggle for independence did little to change it. The externally oriented economic strategies and absence of conventional military conflict made Latin American state institutions even weaker in the century after independence. Governments of the new nation-states engaged in few nationalist projects that would have gained the loyalty of citizens. Formal democratic rule was fleeting, if it existed at all. And, for the most part, governments left in place many of the features of colonial Latin America, including the power of the Catholic Church and the harsh anti-indigenous political and cultural systems. The larger result of these trends was to create a vacuum for other powerful transnational actors—already filled by the Catholic Church and soon to be filled by other organizations and networks. These larger relations are depicted in Figure 2.1.

This basic weakness becomes even clearer in the context of more precise language about state strength and capacity. Many Latin American political systems in the 19th century were classic examples of governing institutions exercising "despotic" capacity. They were, for the most part, highly undemocratic. While in power, they were often able to dominate all that was narrowly political and to punish rivals for power. But they were rarely able to exert a more comprehensive kind of power which would have broadly influenced the societies they formally ruled. Whether in the form of more general efforts to increase governmental legitimacy or in more specific policy areas, such as education, welfare policy, building of communications and transportation infrastructure, or providing order and justice, these governments were largely failures or simply absent. To use Michael Mann's language, in almost every case across Latin America, the state was unable "to penetrate and centrally coordinate the activities of civil society through its own infrastructure" (Mann, 1986, p. 190). This weakness had its roots in colonialism, which in many cases set up political systems based on the systematic fear and persecution of an ethnically

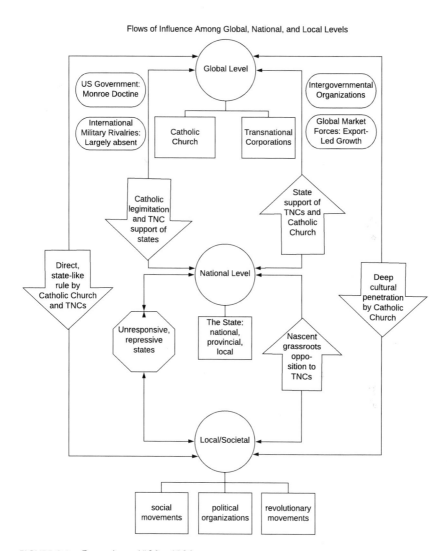

FIGURE 2.1 Overview, 1820s–1920s.

distinct group. For this reason and others, new national governments across Latin America systematically fell short in exercising genuine "infrastructural" capacity. Indeed, their race-based fear made them actively hostile to exercising this type of capacity. Thus Migel Angel Centeno argues that these states were (and remain) "highly despotic yet infrastructurally weak" (Centeno, 2002, p. 10). These conditions prevailed at the outset of independence, and remained in place for a century, as external economic strategies and the absence of international military conflict rid national governments of the need to form more meaningful relations with the societies that they ruled. And large proportions of national populations remained "citizens" in name only.

Latin American state institutions were so weak in an infrastructural sense that transnational organizations asserted, or began to assert, their own infrastructural power during the 19th century and early 20th century, as shown by the flows of influence in Figure 2.1. Chapter 3 provides an account of the long history of the Catholic Church's infrastructural capacity in Latin America. It remained very much in place with independence, and in some nations it even grew in collaboration with new national governments. Chapter 4 describes the emergence and growth of the transnational corporate infrastructure (often with strong US government support) in many Latin American nations, as these organizations often performed state-like functions. A central concern in these chapters, and in Chapters 5 and 6, is the resulting struggle over who performs these basic functions in Latin American nation-states. These three-level interactions would intensify as states grew more assertive, local movements became more influential and daring, and new transnational actors emerged. These developments are described in greater detail in the four following chapters.

This brief history sets the stage for more in-depth analysis of how powerful transnational actors have moved into the larger Latin American political setting, exerting significant influence over the domestic politics of technically sovereign nations. To use the language of the three-level theoretical framework, and to refer directly to Figure 2.1, transnational actors, at the global level, were able to bypass the state, at the national level, to directly influence Latin American societies, at the local level. This scenario represents deep external penetration of Latin American political systems and a distinctly top-down version of globalization. Additional external forces such as the US government and global economic trends tended to bolster transnational influence. The scarcity of traditional military conflict further weakened nation-states. And, given the absence of democracy, few local actors were able to constrain either national or transnational actors. In this setting, transnational influence gradually became a source of resentment and conflict across the political spectrum in Latin America. The goal of this book is to highlight these developments, and to use theoretical concepts and case studies to come to a deeper understanding of how states, citizens, and transnational actors compete for influence in Latin America.

References

Bulmer-Thomas, Victor, 2003. *The Economic History of Latin America since Independence.* Cambridge: Cambridge University Press.

Burkholder, Mark and Lyman Johnson, 1990. *Colonial Latin America.* Oxford: Oxford University Press.

Centeno, Miguel Angel, 2002. *Blood and Debt: War and the Nation-State in Latin America.* University Park, PA: Penn State University Press.

Fitzgibbon, Russell, 1953. "The Political Impact on Religious Development in Uruguay," *Church History* 22/1, pp. 21–32.

Hamnett, Brian, 1986. *Roots of Insurgency: Mexican Regions, 1740–1824.* Cambridge: Cambridge University Press.

Klaiber, Jeffrey, 1999. "Peru: Evangelization and Religious Freedom," in Paul Sigmund, editor, *Religious Freedom and Evangelization in Latin America: The Challenge of Religious Pluralism.* Maryknoll, NY: Orbis Books, pp. 253–268.

Mann, Michael, 1986. "The Autonomous Power of the State: Its Origins, Mechanisms and Results," in John Hall, editor, *States in History.* Oxford: Basil Blackwell, pp. 182–203.

Orique, David, 2009. "Journey to the Headwaters: Bartolome de las Casas in a Comparative Context," Catholic Historical Review 95/1, pp. 1–24.

Porter, Bruce, 2002. *War and the Rise of the State: The Military Foundations of Modern Politics.* New York: Free Press.

Prebisch, Raul, 1950. *The Economic Development of Latin America and Its Principal Problems.* New York: United Nations.

Schwaller, John, 2011. *The History of the Catholic Church in Latin America: From Conquest to Revolution and Beyond.* New York: NYU Press.

Tenenbaum, Barbara, 1986. *The Politics of Penury: Debt and Taxes in Mexico, 1821–1856.* Albuquerque: University of New Mexico Press.

Thies, Cameron, 2005. "War, Rivalry, and State Building in Latin America," *American Journal of Political Science* 49/3, pp. 451–465.

Tilly, Charles, 1985. "War Making and State Making as Organized Crime," in Peter Evans et al., editors, *Bringing the State Back In.* Cambridge: Cambridge University Press, pp. 169–195.

Twomey, Michael, 1998. "Patterns of Foreign Investment in the Third World in the Twentieth Century," in John Coatsworth and Alan Taylor, editors, *Latin America in the World Economy Since 1800,* Cambridge, MA: Harvard University Press, pp. 171–202.

Weschler, Lawrence, 1998. *A Miracle, A Universe: Settling Accounts with Torturers.* Chicago, IL: University of Chicago Press.

Williams, Robert, 1994. *Coffee and the Rise of National Governments in Central America.* Chapel Hill: University of North Carolina Press.

Wilkins, Mira, 1974. "Multinational Oil Companies in South America in the 1920s: Argentina, Bolivia, Brazil, Chile, Colombia, Ecuador, and Peru," *The Business History Review* 48/3 (Autumn), pp. 414–446.

Wright, Ronald, 1992. *Stolen Continents: The "New World through Indian Eyes.* New York: Houghton Mifflin.

3

THE POLITICS OF THE CATHOLIC CHURCH IN LATIN AMERICA

This chapter analyzes the impact of the Catholic Church, a transnational actor fully in place in the societies of the region well before the creation of nation-states in Latin America. It focuses on the Catholic Church because of its uniquely dominant cultural and religious position within the region. This chapter examines the Church's impact in explicit reference to the three-level analytical framework of transnational, national, and local. And it addresses each of the three theoretical concerns raised in Chapter 1: the Church's power and capacity in relation to other forces and actors in Latin America; the nature of the Catholic Church as a transnational institution; and the impact of distinctly Catholic norms in Latin America, especially the historically based norm of "neo-Christendom" and Vatican-II-inspired norms, such as a "preferential option for the poor." This chapter emphasizes the complexities and some of the limitations of the Catholic impact on Latin America. But it is important to note at the outset that the region is distinguished as much by its Catholicism as by any other cultural, economic, or political factor.

The Catholic Church in Latin America Prior to Vatican II

The Catholic Church played a central role in the conquest and colonization of Latin America. Clergy accompanied the conquistadors on their military missions, and religious structures—in the form of churches, missions, and cathedrals—were among the first physical creations of the colonizers. The Church was deeply implicated in the genocidal military and economic policies of the Spanish and Portuguese crowns. The Catholic Church performed numerous quasi-governmental functions under colonialism. It created the first schools in Latin America. Arrangements for tithing and tribute amounted to a widespread and lucrative variation on taxation. In a related role, the Church provided loans to miners, merchants, and landowners, serving a "vital economic function" and becoming "the precursor of modern banking in Latin America" (Bauer, 1983, p. 709). Huge land areas were effectively controlled by Catholic officials, beyond the direct reach of government officials. Church personnel were in charge of a series of rituals—baptism, marriage, funerals, and worship—that were central to the lives of many Latin Americans (Schwaller, 2011, p. xi).

This influence varied for a number of reasons: the basic differences between Spanish and Portuguese colonial practices (a contrast more fully explored in the Brazilian case study at the end of the chapter); which religious orders—Augustinians, Dominicans, Franciscans, Mercedarians, or Jesuits—were most present; the impact of indigenous religious traditions, which in some cases have deeply influenced Latin American Catholicism; and a more general, ongoing debate between Catholics pushing radical social justice for Latin Americans and those advocating a more severe, at times racist, approach to the region (Burkholder and Johnson, 1990, pp. 83–93). This last factor emerged immediately as Bartolomé de Las Casas became an outspoken advocate for indigenous Latin Americans and met sharp opposition in the region and in Europe (Orique, 2009). For all of this diversity, however, the larger setting was one of a controlled, hierarchical Catholic Church profoundly influencing Latin America from afar. Its influence preceded Latin American nations, and its comprehensive presence would present a genuine challenge to national governments in the region.

The Catholic hierarchy generally opposed the Latin American struggle for independence. At the same time, a figure like Miguel Hidalgo, a parish priest, could lead an increasingly radicalized independence movement in Mexico. Hidalgo was a high-profile example of widespread support of independence from lower-level Catholics based throughout the region. The euphoria of independence led to high-profile symbolic gestures of opposition to clerical influence. But these views represented only one faction within the new national elites. Catholicism's deep penetration of Latin American society made it difficult to dislodge. The independence struggle did not represent a profound break with Europe or the European-based religious structures that had been set up under colonialism (Langer and Jackson, 1988). For example, in Mexico, the radical changes pushed by Hidalgo were replaced by a far more moderate independence movement led by Agustin Iturbide, which prevailed a decade after Hidalgo's death, in 1821. Latin American leaders lacked the capacity for a full-blown effort to uproot Catholicism. This was certainly the case in the initial decades after independence as, throughout the region, new states had trouble exerting even the basic forms of power in relation to powerful societal actors.

Independent nations would take a variety of approaches to the Catholic Church over the next century. One issue that new governments had to immediately encounter was the status of colonial patronage agreements. The issue had always been a matter of tension under colonialism, as it determined control over resources and the power to make decisions regarding the Church (Cleary, 1999, p. 12). National leaders were eager to extend the same level of control with independence. Yet most "recognized that the Vatican would be unwilling to cede this power," and as a result, in an early sign of the power of the Church in newly independent Latin America, "focused their attention elsewhere" (Schwaller, 2011, p. 145). Subsequent conflicts between Latin American states and the Church were distinguished by the extent to which Liberal or Conservative elite factions achieved ascendancy. There is little question that Liberal approaches represented a greater threat to a privileged Catholic position than did Conservatives'. Yet an equally important factor was the inability of the new national governments to impose their will on powerful societal actors, given their overall weakness as leaders of new nations. A telling example of this weakness is the ecclesiastical "fueros" granted by states, which allowed the Church to function as a state-within-a-state (Fernandez, 1999, p. 130). This would gradually change in the second half of the 19th century, as Liberals pursued more comprehensive plans for reining in the Church. Yet the entrenched nature of the Catholic Church made Liberal ascendancy far from inevitable.

A few examples from the region demonstrate the dynamics of this struggle. Ecclesiastical fueros remained firmly in place in Mexico until 1857, but they, along with Church land and fees for ceremonies, came under threat from a Constitution closely associated with the Liberalism of Benito Juárez. In the following ten years, Conservatives and the Church first staged a three-year violent rebellion against the Mexican state, and then connived with Europeans who intervened and placed Emperor Maximilian in power. The successful effort to remove Maximilian was led by Juárez, and resulted in a comprehensive Liberal triumph in 1867. Yet the subsequent ostensibly Liberal rule of Porfirio Díaz, lasting until 1910, was marked by accommodation and ultimately collaboration with the Catholic hierarchy—to such an extent that Church privileges became a central target of the Mexican revolution (Fernandez, 1999, pp. 130–131). A fundamentally different set of outcomes emerged in Central America. Liberals were closely associated with the early attempts at a region-wide government and pushed numerous anti-clerical policies under Francisco Morazán in the 1830s. But the failure of unification, partly a result of Church opposition to Morazán, led to the ascendancy of Conservatism. Ecclesiastical fueros were reintroduced, and Conservatives "promptly moved to restore the Church privileges, welcome back religious orders, and declare the Church to be in charge of education, marriage, and other key aspects of social governance" (Schwaller, 2011, p. 164).

In South America, Colombia retained a strong Catholic institutional presence, a status formalized in an 1887 Concordat, which led, in Daniel Levine's words, to "complete Church-state integration." In an arrangement that remained in place until 1973, the Church received governmental financial support and operated tax-free; enjoyed autonomy from civil jurisdiction; controlled the bulk of national record-keeping; and was granted the right to exercise almost total, state-like control over specific "mission territories" (Levine, 1981, p. 71). In Argentina, the 1853 Constitution mandated that the President and Vice-President be Catholic, and the Vatican continued to appoint high-ranking clerics and directly collect fees and other revenues from parishioners (Bonino, 1999, p. 190). Chile was the South American nation that went the farthest in countering the Church during the 19th century, providing for civil marriage, pushing public education at the expense of Catholic schools, and abolishing the tithe (Poblete, 1999, p. 222). In the early 20th century, Uruguay, under the leadership of José Batlle y Ordóñez, took the strongest steps against the Church, banning religious education in public schools, removing all Catholic privileges, establishing strict separation of church and state, and engaging in "the first large-scale American experiment in the rejection of the norms and mores of a dominant Church" (Fitzgibbon, 1953, p. 31). Yet, for all of the inroads into Catholic power at the highest levels, the Latin American people remained overwhelmingly Catholic in their cultural and religious lives. The following description of Peru could apply to the rest of the region:

> The vast majority of the population...were devout and tended to reject many of the liberal innovations. As a result, especially in rural areas, the Church continued to operate as it always had: as a source of stability for the people, the one single institution that would provide guidance in changing times.
>
> *(Schwaller, 2011, p. 153)*

The Mexican Revolution represented an unprecedented threat to the Catholic Church. The 1917 Constitution provided for the expropriation of all Church wealth, banning public religious services, prohibiting the presence of foreign priests, and requiring that clerics register with local authorities. Beginning in 1926, Catholic leaders responded by supporting a three-year grassroots uprising in north-central Mexico known as the "Cristero Rebellion." The government eventually prevailed, and the outcome left the Mexican government in an extremely strong position in relation to one of the most weakened Catholic establishments in Latin America. During his rule from 1934 to 1940, Lázaro Cárdenas initially viewed the Church in the context of the nationalizations and expropriations he would pursue in key areas of the economy in the late 1930s. But he ultimately proved more conciliatory than his predecessors toward the Catholic authorities; they, in turn, realized that a uniformly hostile approach to a genuinely popular Mexican President would be politically disastrous (Michaels, 1969).

Mexico is an extreme example of the numerous forces bearing down on a once-powerful Catholic Church in Latin America. Protestantism was making inroads in Chile, Guatemala, Brazil, and other areas marked by a significant foreign economic presence or proximity to an increasingly engaged US (Sinclair, 1999, pp. 33–35). And growing economic inequality and crisis created the conditions for social movements that would take some mixture of religious, nationalist, and radical socialist forms. In the meantime, challenges to the Catholic Church at the national level grew, driven partly by a desire to assert greater national control over economic and political life in the wake of the Great Depression. The Church in Argentina initially supported Juan Perón in the 1930s, who viewed Catholic support as crucial to his nationalist agenda. But as he moved left in concert with the growing middle class and labor movements, he came into direct conflict with a generally conservative Argentinian Catholic Church (Bonino, 1999, p. 193). (Perón is often compared to Brazil's Getúlio Vargas, whose relations with the Church are discussed in depth at the end of the chapter.) Chile's Socialist and Communist parties grew but were not in a position to move against the Church until Salvador Allende's rise to power in the 1970s.

At a more general level, the Church's presence in the Latin American countryside faded during the 19th century, leading to an understaffed priesthood by the early 20th century. And those priests that did work among the people, at the more grassroots level, tended to have stronger local roots and attachments, and were less likely to follow the dictates of Rome. It was in this setting that a grassroots movement with (eventually) strong ties to the papacy would emerge in Latin America. Catholic Action had its roots in activists sponsored first by leaders in the Congregation of the Sacred Heart and then the Catholic University in Lima, Peru. Similar organizations began to emerge around Latin America, and Pope Pius XI (who led the Church from 1922 to 1939) quickly seized on the opportunity to support the groups under the larger name of "Catholic Action." Catholic Action groups were usually led and driven by the laity, in close collaboration with the local Bishop. While having some factions still wedded to Conservative allegiances of the past, Catholic Action was also marked by a new and sustained commitment to grassroots work, and spread to many remote rural areas long neglected by the Church (Schwaller, 2011, pp. 213–217). It initially stayed away from electoral politics, but the emergence of centrist or left-of-center Christian Democratic parties several decades later—most notably in Chile—had its roots in Catholic Action. Anthony Gill sees a strong relationship between the emergence of Catholic support for grassroots activity in certain nations and the existence of a strong Protestant challenge. While there are numerous factors behind the rise of Catholic Action, and later movements coming out of Vatican II, the rise of Protestantism was certainly a spur to Catholic activism (Gill, 1998).

At roughly the same time that Catholic Action was emerging, the Church unambiguously sided with forces of reaction, violence, and dictatorship in several high-profile crises. In 1932, the El Salvadoran government responded to a peasant uprising with a murderous rampage that came to be known simply as "La Matanza." The Church's close ties to El Salvador's rural elite led it to side with the government, and even directly participate in identifying alleged communists to be executed by the military. In a sermon immediately after the massacre, Padre Ravelo of the Santa Tecla community thanked God "that the evil has been yanked out at the root. God willing, it will never have life again" (Gould and Lauria-Santiago, 2008, p. 230). (The Church's support for US anti-insurgency campaigns against Augusto Cesar Sandino is described in the Nicaraguan case study.) The Catholic Church was also heavily implicated in the ten-year period (1948–1958) known as "La Violenza" in Colombia. The Church's response to the assassination of the popular leftist presidential candidate Jorge Eliécer Gaitán in 1948 was to emphasize the Church's victimization in the context of violence that consumed Bogotá. Church leaders explicitly supported the undemocratic Colombian leaders, criticized the "usurpation" of those activists who opposed the regime, and repeatedly emphasized the need for "obedience" in pastoral letters (Levine, 1981, p. 88). The Church hierarchy's response to democratic reforms in Guatemala during the late 1940s and early 1950s was one of opposition and obstruction. Top Catholic officials collaborated with the US planners who led the 1954 coup against Jacobo Arbenz, playing an extremely important political role in the countryside, and then openly celebrated his removal (Grandin, 2004, pp. 78–80). These policies reflected the Church's close ties to elites and a worldview based on "neo-Christendom" norms.

A markedly different high-profile confrontation between the Church and forces of the left took place in Cuba as Fidel Castro seized power in 1959. The regime's Marxism, and its stranglehold on political power, was ultimately seen as a threat to Catholics. At the same time, a small but significant portion of Catholic exiles became actively involved in anti-Castro activities in the US, including direct participation in the Bay of Pigs invasion. Within a year of Castro's rise to power, Catholics started leaving the island in large numbers. The regime's deep penetration of Cuban cultural and economic life left little room for an independent Catholic Church to thrive or even survive. For example, Cuba's education policies were viewed as a systematic threat to the Catholic authorities. As Margarete Crahan notes, Catholic leaders "were ill-disposed to accept a Marxist revolution in Cuba, yet their institutional weaknesses, the strength of secularism in Cuban society, and foreign links reduced their capacity to offer alternatives and be accepted as legitimate critics" (Crahan, 1999, p. 91). Throughout his rule, Castro allowed a Catholic presence in Cuba, and made formal commitments of various types to religious freedom. Yet Castro would frequently crack down on Church officials who questioned the larger goals of the revolution.

By the early 1960s, the Catholic Church's position in Latin America was affected by a wide variety of factors, all of which would come into open display in the early 1960s during the radical reassessment of the Second Vatican Council. But the ideas and practices for Vatican II did not arise in isolation. Catholic Action was an important precedent of sorts for grassroots mobilization and other local Catholic organizations engaged in activism throughout the region as well; for example, beginning in 1955, Honduran Auxiliary Bishop Evelio Dominguez explicitly supported Catholic "Radio Schools," which focused on socioeconomic justice and pioneered early versions of "concientización" among the peasantry (Richard and Melendez, 1982, p. 326). Similar organizations were at work throughout Brazil as well (Serbin, 1999, p. 209). Long before Vatican II, the chronic shortage of priests led Catholic authorities to allow a greater role for the laity in the form of study groups for lay leaders. It also led to a growing number of European and North American missionaries, who brought a renewed sense of radicalism and social justice to rural Latin America. The increasing appeal of the non-Catholic options of Protestantism (to follow Gill's argument), on the one hand, and socialism, on the other hand, added a sense of urgency to efforts to re-establish a Catholic presence. Within the hierarchy, the creation of the Conference of Latin American Bishops (CELAM) in 1955 was also closely related to questions of social justice in the region (Serbin, 1996). All these factors made significant parts of the Catholic community in Latin America uniquely receptive to the dramatic reassessment of Vatican II.

Vatican II, Repression, and Revolution

A fundamental transformation in Catholic thinking took place during Vatican II and during the Second Council of Latin American Bishops in Medellín in 1968. It is no exaggeration to say that a new set of norms on religion and social justice was introduced into Latin America not by an isolated group at the margins of political power but by an entrenched Catholic Church with a significant presence in virtually every Latin American nation. And many of these norms were formulated in precise language. Priests taking part in Vatican II focused on "immense inequalities" while advocating a "preferential option for the poor" in combatting them. Vatican II documents made explicit and repeated reference to the equality of all humans and the need for justice in this life, and specific goals such as economic equality, ending poverty, and providing education. It advocated dialogue with diverse faiths and creeds. It approved the use of local vernacular in Church ceremonies and services. It encouraged national churches to create their own liturgies for the sacraments and to look to local traditions and popular religion in doing so. An especially significant provision was an emphasis on the work of the laity, who, according to Vatican II, "share in the priestly, prophetic, and royal office of Christ and therefore have their own role to play in the mission of the whole People of God in the Church of the World" (quoted in Dodson and O'Shaughnessy, 1990, pp. 89–90).

The 1968 Medellín Council, under the auspices of CELAM, subsequently reaffirmed these ideas for a Latin American setting. In a specific effort to empower the peasantry, Medellín participants took the step of proposing new religious structures that were to become Christian Base Communities (CEBs), administered primarily by the laity. A crucial tactic in these efforts was "concientización," which had pre-Vatican roots in Latin America. In a setting marked by governmental indifference and a remote hierarchical Church, the diffusion of radical religious ideas—in the vernacular—by rapidly proliferating laity had a profound and, in some cases, revolutionary impact on the Latin American countryside. It represented a comprehensive reinsertion of the Catholic Church into some of the most geographically and politically isolated areas of Latin American society, and was a crucial factor in the rise of human rights norms in Latin America.

The impact of Vatican II and Medellín varied dramatically from nation to nation, partly because of its radical implications and partly because of the provisions it made for greater local control within the Church. In this regard, Vatican-II-inspired norms coming out of the Catholic Church were affected by power dynamics in the region. At the very highest level, top Catholic officials in nations such as Brazil, Chile, and El Salvador strongly opposed the dictatorships that emerged throughout Latin America in the 1960s, 1970s, and 1980s. In many cases, they set up formal organizations that documented and revealed human rights abuses. La Vicaría de la Solidaridad in Chile and Tutela Legal in El Salvador were among the few havens for the victims of human rights abuses during the most violent years of these nations' dictatorships. The genocidal dictatorship in Guatemala succeeded in shutting down the Catholic Archdiocese's political and human rights activities at the height of repression in 1982 and 1983 during the rule of Ríos Montt. But by the following year, under the leadership of Archbishop Juan José Gerardi, the Church played a central role in opposing the dictatorship and collaborating with victims of human rights violations (REMHI, 1999).

The Catholic hierarchy explicitly supported the "Dirty War" in Argentina in the late 1970s. The first official criticism of the regime by the Bishops' Conference did not take place until 1981, five years after the worst human rights abuses (Bonino, 1999, p. 194). In the words of the Argentinian Catholic activist and scholar Emilio Mignone,

> [T]he Argentine episcopate made a purely political choice. It allied itself with temporal power, renouncing the testimony of the Gospel which demands the denunciation of crimes and of the people responsible for them and active support of the victims, even risking persecution. The episcopate knew the truth and hid it to benefit the government of the armed forces. Between God and Caesar it chose the latter.
>
> *(Mignone, 1988, p. 71.)*

Uruguay's Catholic hierarchy was an early critic of repression in the late 1960s, but its historic weakness as a national institution enabled the dictatorship to silence and co-opt the Church during the 1970s (Goldfrank and Rowell, 2012, pp. 46–48).

At the grassroots level, the empowerment of the laity—a central theme of Vatican II—was also highly dependent on the degree of support from national and local bishops within each nation. In this regard, then, CEBs emerged in large numbers in nations like Brazil, El Salvador, Nicaragua, and Guatemala. Where there was little support from the hierarchy, barely any CEBs emerged, as was the case in nations such as Argentina and Colombia, which were dominated by conservative hierarchies. Mexico is, by most accounts, an intermediate case, with CEBs emerging in localities supported by progressive Bishops, but also explicitly prohibited in others (Camp, 1999, pp. 142–144). And in the nations marked by greatest levels of repression, Catholics who challenged the status quo were invariably the targets of government violence throughout the region. In a particularly sinister development, Catholics were the explicit focus of Guatemalan counterinsurgency campaigns led by neo-Pentecostal figures linked to the California-based Church of the Word to which Ríos Montt belonged (REMHI, 1999, p. 241). Yet collaboration among different denominational traditions also emerged to support the cause of human rights throughout the region (Bamat, 2009).

The 1979 CELAM meeting in Puebla, Mexico, came at an important moment in the history of the Catholic Church in the region. While its statements in favor of social justice were, if anything, stronger than those from Medellín a decade earlier, they represented perhaps a high-water mark in the hierarchy's support for grassroots Catholic activism. The push from below had led to tensions within the Church in many Latin American nations. And the emergence of Pope John Paul II as a global religious and political figure emboldened many leaders who had previously been reluctant to speak out against their radical fellow Christians. The Pope's anti-communism—bolstered by his close collaboration with the conservative Joséph Ratzinger (the future Pope)—hastened a backlash against radical Catholicism and liberation theology. This conflict played out most dramatically in Nicaragua and Brazil. Radical priests remained deeply embedded in the societies in which they worked. But, with significant national variations, they enjoyed far less support from the highest levels of the Church in the 1980s, suffering public admonition and official sanctions.

Democracy, Reconciliation, and the Catholic Church

As the region moved toward peace, reconciliation, and democracy in the late 1980s and 1990s, there was a general consensus that Catholics of all political persuasions needed to support the move toward more open societies. The Church's status as an independent and culturally entrenched transnational actor allowed it to play a central role in many Latin American nations' democratic transitions (Thiele and Carnes, 2018). This was emphatically the case in Chile and Brazil, as Church officials led national processes of justice and reconciliation. This was decidedly not the case in both Argentina, where the Catholic Church lost much of its moral credibility during the dictatorship, and Uruguay, where the Church was far weaker (Loveman, 1998). Instead, Catholic activists channeled their efforts outside of the Catholic hierarchy: most notably, Service for Peace and Justice (SERPAJ), an ecumenical group heavily influenced by Catholics, played a central role in opposing the dictatorships and in national reconciliation efforts in both Argentina and Uruguay. (SERPAJ is described in greater detail in Chapter 6.)

The Church's role was, if anything, even greater in nations recovering from civil war and genocide. Catholic authorities were central actors in flawed, but still surprisingly sudden and comprehensive, peace and reconciliation processes in Guatemala and El Salvador. The all-encompassing violence of these conflicts had taken the lives of courageous Archbishops in each nation—early in El Salvador's civil war with El Salvador's Archbishop Romero in 1980 and in the wake of genocide with Guatemala's Archbishop Gerardi in 1998 (Goldman, 1998). Even as the Church's commitment to revolution and radical social justice waned, it redoubled its efforts for peace and reconciliation in these two nations. And the Salvadoran and Guatemalan processes were markedly transnational in nature, with Catholics joining the UN and other global non-governmental organizations (Arnson, 1999). From almost day one of the conflict between the Zapatistas and the government in southern Mexico in early 1994, the Catholic authorities were deeply involved in efforts at mediation. Bishop Samuel Ruiz Garcia was able, based on his lengthy advocacy on behalf of marginalized citizens of Chiapas, to mediate in a way that would avoid bloodshed and facilitate a meaningful government response to the Zapatista insurrection. This mediation was far more timely than even the most well-intentioned Church efforts in previous settings of conflict in Latin America (Camp, 1999, pp. 142–143).

The early 1990s also saw heightened Catholic engagement in two of the region's most entrenched political conflicts—Cuba and Colombia. As the Cold War ended and the Castro regime lost its major international benefactor, the Church played a central role in, initially, opening Cuban civil society and pushing for provisions such as the removal of atheist provisions from the Cuban Constitutions in 1993, the dramatic easing of tensions in church-state relations in the 1990s, and Papal visits by John Paul II in 1998, Benedict XVI in 2005, and Francis in 2015 and 2016 (Kuivala, 2017, p. 28). The Church's role in efforts to end Colombia's long-running civil war is no surprise, given the Church's dominant place in Colombian politics and culture. Church officials were repeatedly called on by successive national leaders to play a central role in mediation, most notably by Álvaro Uribe in the key 2007 negotiations, and pastoral language from Colombia's Bishops has set many of the parameters for negotiations (Berkley Center, 2013, p. 6). Just as importantly, the Church has used its deep roots within Colombian society to push for peace in recent decades: "Vast social service and community networks have given faith leaders... the ability to reach into areas controlled by both leftist and right-wing paramilitary organizations, where they are often seen as honest brokers for dialogue" (Berkley Center, 2013, p. 6). Yet conservative Catholic officials have publicly protested over specific provisions in various peace treaties, and these Catholic misgivings—and those of the growing Protestant community in Colombia—were an important element in the popular rejection of a 2016 referendum to end the civil war. It also explains Pope Francis's refusal to formally endorse the peace treaty during a visit to Colombia in 2017 (Phippen, 2017).

Much of Pope Francis's worldview was formed by his experience in the Argentinian Church in the years leading up to and during the Dirty War. His acknowledged failure to protect radical priests under his authority led him to work to atone for his failure to support Catholics pushing for social justice. His background as the first Latin American Pope provided him the opportunity—indeed forced him—to devote extraordinary amounts of attention to his home region. His desire to bridge the gap that in many Latin American nations had existed between Catholic factions came out of this experience. But it was also made workable by an increasingly open political setting in the region. Coming on the heels of the "pink revolution," a generally secular move to the left in Latin America, this progressive message resonated with many in the region. Francis' stances on these and other issues should allow him to more effectively confront the legacy of Catholic sexual abuse in Latin America.

Progressive, secular norms related to gender and sexual orientation emerged in much of Latin America only as recently as the 2000s. Yet, despite the strong opposition of the Catholic Church, several Latin American governments pursued liberal social policies in the 1960s, departing from centuries of tradition. Cuba, partly because of its conflictual relationship with the Catholic Church, legalized abortion in most cases in the mid-1960s. Mala Htun points to a more surprising outcome, in which the Argentinian and Brazilian dictatorships defied the Catholic Church to liberalize policy in the area of gender and spousal equality in the 1970s and 1980s (Htun, 2003, p. 5). Several decades later, the deepening of democracy and the continued urbanization and modernization of the region have led to the emergence of norms, and a larger cultural shift, that have further challenged the Catholic Church. The movement for gay marriage has been successful in pressuring national governments to pass laws, often over the explicit objections of Catholic authorities. Argentina, Brazil, Uruguay, Colombia, Ecuador, and Mexico have all passed legislation supporting gay marriage, and over 80% of the region-wide population in Latin America lives under these laws (Díez and Dion, 2018, p. 467). Pope Francis famously responded "Who am I to judge?" when asked about homosexuality, and has not made opposition to gay marriage a priority (Pramuk, 2015, p. 83). Catholic opposition to abortion continues to prevail in much of the region, as only one nation, Uruguay, and two Mexican regions have joined Cuba in legalizing abortion (Bentancur and Rocha-Carpiuc, 2020).

What this account shows is that, regardless of the political climate in Latin America, the Church will retain a widespread presence in the region. The basis for much of its influence, and what makes it different from the other three types of transnational actors studies in this book, is its entrenched presence among the Latin American population. Based on a 2014 Pew Research Center report, 69% of the region's population identifies as Catholic, more than 3.5 times the number of Protestants. Half of the region's nations have more than 70% Catholics, and Catholics represent a plurality in every Latin American nation and a majority in all but two. Yet there are worrying trends for Catholicism as well. The Pew report points to a growth in Protestantism and shrinkage in Catholicism: 19% of respondents identified as Protestant, but only 9% had been raised that way, while 69% identified as Catholic, but a much larger proportion, 84%, reported having been raised Catholic. Protestant growth is most notable in Central America, where Honduras, Nicaragua, and Guatemala all come in at 40% or more. Uruguay's 37% figure for non-religious is more than twice as high as any other nation in the region (Pew Research Center, 2014).

Whether it will have enough influence to play a meaningful role in the region's current crises remains to be seen. The Catholic Church in Venezuela, a relatively weak group by Latin American standards, became an embattled actor during the Presidency of Hugo Chávez. The upper levels of the Venezuelan Church further marginalized themselves by openly supporting the unsuccessful coup against him in 2002 (Smilde, 2004, pp. 84–85). Chávez's subsequent concentration of power and his turn to an increasingly socialist agenda alienated the hierarchy, even as his own Christian faith and his leftist policies won over many progressive Catholics. The rise of Nicolas Maduro in the wake of Chávez's death in 2013 led to increasing confrontation between the government and the Catholic hierarchy, which has described the Maduro government as a "Marxist and communist dictatorship." At the regional level, CELAM has expressed "full solidarity with the people and Church of Venezuela" and criticized the Maduro regime as an "illegitimate and failed government." And Pope Francis has let his displeasure with Maduro be known (Phippen, 2017). In Bolivia, the strongly religious bent of the forces behind the removal of Evo Morales in late 2019 may cause significant divisions within the Catholic Church. The Constitution crafted under Morales's leadership in 2009 designated Bolivia a "plurinational" country and removed Catholicism's privileged position. The Morales government's celebration of indigenous religion did not necessarily contradict his own radical Catholicism, but it did lead to a feeling of marginalization among conservative Catholics. Jeanine Áñez, who briefly assumed the presidency in late 2019 and early 2020, and other leaders of the coup against Morales in Bolivia expressed bigoted views equating indigenous traditions with Satanism and mocking centuries of exploitation experienced by indigenous Bolivians. In the immediate wake of the coup, Morales called on Pope Francis to mediate. The Bolivian Catholic hierarchy's initial support for the coup may weaken its influence in the long run, as Morales's allies triumphed in the October 2020 election (Casey, 2019; Anderson, 2020; Young, 2020).

The Politics of Transnational Catholic Influence in Nicaragua

Compared to much of the rest of Latin America, Nicaragua was "a remote and neglected outpost of the Roman Church" (Dodson and O'Shaughnessy, 1990, p. 73). Yet the Church's early influence mirrored the divisions that have continued to plague the Nicaraguan Catholic Church. The ability of the Spanish monarchy to enforce the "New Laws" of 1542, which called for an end to the encomienda system and prohibited enslavement of indigenous Americans, was immediately tested in Nicaragua. Bishop Antonio de Valdivieso (a close associate of Bartolomé de las Casas) appealed to the Spanish authorities to punish local rulers who were flouting the laws. After a hearing in Spain, the Crown ruled in favor of Valdivieso. In defiance of Spain, the local rulers brazenly assassinated Bishop Valdivieso. The colonial authorities soon re-established control over the area, reining in the worst excesses of local rulers, but also stabilizing a Catholic presence that focused on converting natives and supporting Spanish colonialism (Foroohar, 1989, pp. 2–3). It is not an exaggeration to say that Bishop Valdivieso's spirit of justice lived on in Nicaragua.

As in much of the rest of Latin America, the upper levels of the Catholic Church sided with Spain in the Nicaraguan independence struggles. If anything, the divisions between Bishops and lower-level priests from various orders were even more pronounced, with upper-level Catholics using extremely strong language condemning the rebellion, and many priests leading armed insurrections; when rebel priests were caught, they were jailed and in a few cases executed (Foroohar, 1989, pp. 4–5). When Nicaragua ultimately gained its independence in 1824, it did so as part of the United Provinces of Central America. An initially pro-Catholic entity, it moved in a dramatically different direction with the rise to power of Francisco Morazán in 1830. His attempt to keep a united Central America together under a Liberal government, which took a series of punitive steps against the Church, failed in 1838, due in significant degree to Church opposition. Nicaragua and the other Central American nations emerged from this failed experiment with empowered Catholic churches and Conservative governments. The sordid series of events, which briefly put pro-slavery US adventurer William Walker in power in 1856 further marginalized the Nicaraguan Liberals who conspired with Walker. Nicaraguan conservatives dominated Nicaraguan politics from 1859 to 1893, signing a Concordat with the Catholic Church in 1862. This agreement recognized Catholicism as Nicaragua's official religion, gave the Church the right of censorship of written material, provided the Church a formal supervisory role in Nicaragua's educational system, and arranged for government/church collaboration in collecting tithes. In turn, the Church granted the government the right to appoint parish priests and present candidates for openings in the Bishopric (Stein, 1999, p. 177).

Conservative domination came to an end in 1893 with the rise of José Santos Zelaya, who reversed the 1862 Concordat, secularized the educational system, ended Catholicism's status as the official national religion, confiscated local Catholic wealth, and exiled priests and nuns (Stein, 1999, p. 177; Foroohar, 1989, p. 11). Zelaya eventually ran afoul of US interests and was overthrown in 1909 by an alliance of Conservative politicians and 400 US Marines, backed by the generous funding of several US companies. Nicaragua experienced almost uninterrupted US military occupation from 1912 until 1933. This intervention offended the nationalist sensibilities of many Nicaraguans, none more so than Augusto Cesar Sandino, who began a potent military rebellion against the US presence in 1927 (Navarro-Genie, 2002). The Church repeatedly expressed support for Nicaraguan government authorities during the US occupation, and as Sandino's rebellion emerged and grew, the Bishop of Granada blessed the US soldiers attempting "to finish off the bandit Sandino" (Foroohar, 1989, p. 16).

The Catholic Church also played an important role in the rise of Anastasio Somoza Garcia and the National Guard he led; Archbishop José Antonio Lezcano y Ortega argued:

> If the prelates consider the reality of the positive benefits that the guardia would bring for the Nicaraguan citizens, and relate this reality to their followers, the National Guard will certainly be more successful in meeting the goals it was created to achieve.
>
> *(Foroohar, 1989, p. 22)*

The Catholic hierarchy explicitly supported the Somoza family during its 45-year dynasty. A 1950 Pastoral Letter was typical in this regard:

> For all Catholics there is a certain exalted doctrine: all authority comes from God. God is author of whatever exists, and from the author comes the authority.... When Catholics obey the government, they do not degrade themselves, but their act fundamentally constitutes compliance with God.
>
> *(Quoted in Foroohar, 1989, p. 38)*

The first Somoza, Anastasio Somoza Garcia, successfully co-opted numerous groups, and the Catholic Church was no exception (Gould, 1990; Walter, 2000). Somoza gave Catholic Churches generous tax exemptions and allowed the Church a central educational role (Williams, 1989, p. 19). In turn, the

Catholic authorities provided a crucial source of legitimation for the Somoza dynasty (Samandu and Jansen, 1982, p. 195).

The reassessments of Vatican II and Medellín challenged the previously close relations between the Nicaraguan state and the Catholic Church. The Somoza dynasty's dominance of the political system and its close ties to the Catholic Church meant an absence of political space for progressive religious influences prior to Vatican II, going all the way back to Bishop Valdivieso in the 16th century. Progressive ideas were introduced almost entirely through transformations within the larger Catholic Church, originating not in Nicaragua but in Rome (Shepherd, 1995). The one notable exception was Ernesto Cardenal's grassroots religious community on the remote Solentiname archipelago in Lake Nicaragua, which began in 1965 (Cardenal, 1982); but its very isolation was symbolic of its removal from larger religious trends in Nicaragua. The January 1969 Pastoral Conference in Managua marked the onset of support for a progressive Church role in the countryside (Foroohar, 1989, p. 71). The Church's support for this trend was due partly to religious competition from Protestant missionaries. Renewed empowerment of the laity was viewed as the most effective way to address the shortage of clergy in the countryside (Williams, 1989, p. 49). This vacuum provided the progressive Church with a great deal of room for growth after Medellín. Dodson and O'Shaughnessy argue that these developments "were so concentrated at the base of Church and society that the advocates of change were significantly less vulnerable to pressures from either church authorities or the regime" (1990, p. 118).

It did not take long for Catholic organizing among the peasantry to cause dissent within the Church. Despite Archbishop Obando y Bravo's anti-Somoza position when he was appointed in 1970, within two years he was criticizing the "unreasoned insurrectional or armed protest" of revolutionary groups. The hierarchy then attempted to limit collaboration between the Church and the Sandinista National Liberation Front (FSLN), which had, from the outset, worked with progressive Christians (Foroohar, 1989, p. 97). Many progressives rejected these restrictions and broke ties with the hierarchy in the mid-1970s. The hierarchy's dispute with progressive Catholic groups was also evident in its response to the 1977 formation of a group of 12 moderate and radical opposition figures known as Los Doce, which included two priests, Fernando Cardenal and Miguel D'Escoto. Soon after Los Doce had publicly come out in support of the FSLN, Archbishop Obando instead announced his preference for "civilized ways" toward peace, and supported anti-Somoza groupings which excluded the FSLN (Foroohar, 1989, pp. 164–165).

At the grassroots level, the Revolutionary Christian Movement was formed in response to the government's jailing of more than 100 Catholic students in 1971. Somoza, and the National Guard he controlled, determined by the mid-1970s that CEBs in the countryside were "subversive," and they singled them out for repression (Dodson and O'Shaughnessy, 1990, p. 128). During the government-imposed state of siege from 1974 through 1977, political repression was so prevalent that churches became one of the few places of refuge. FSLN revolutionaries in Zelaya described the CEBs as "our best allies" (quoted in Williams, 1989, p. 49). The radical Church did far more than merely collaborate with the FSLN: "Churches and church schools now became focal points for organized resistance. The Christian laity began to assume specific revolutionary tasks in preparation for the general uprising" (Lancaster, 1988; Dodson and O'Shaughnessy, 1990, p. 134). Oppressive economic and political conditions deepened the commitment of the laity to dramatic change. In this setting, Catholics played a crucial role in the final effort to overthrow the Somoza regime in July 1979 (Shepherd, 1995).

Despite significant divisions within the Catholic Church leading up to Somoza's ouster, the first months in post-revolutionary Nicaragua were marked by an atmosphere of reconciliation between religious factions, evident in a November 1979 Pastoral Letter:

> If socialism brings cultural processes that awaken the dignity of our masses and gives them the strength to assume responsibilities and demand their rights, then we are dealing with a process of humanization that is convergent with the human dignity proclaimed by our faith.
>
> *(Foroohar, 1989, p. 200)*

Immediate post-revolutionary legislation established freedom of religion and outlawed words and actions that fomented religious hatred. The new government appointed four high-profile Catholics, the brothers Fernando and Ernesto Cardenal, Miguel D'Escoto, and Edgard Parrales to Cabinet-level positions. Representatives from the Association of National Clergy were formally seated in Nicaragua's new national legislature. Both these steps represented a direct threat to the Catholic hierarchy by setting up unmediated contacts between the national government and prominent, politically involved Catholics (Stein, 1999, p. 178). Christians were deeply involved in the 1980 literacy campaign, which reduced illiteracy rates from over 50% to 12% (and won international acclaim), yet many in the Catholic hierarchy viewed it merely as Marxist indoctrination of rural Nicaraguans (Foroohar, 1989, p. 201).

Opposition from the highest levels of the Catholic hierarchy soon emerged. Archbishop Obando returned from a meeting with Pope John Paul II in July 1980, declaring that Nicaragua was run by Marxists and claimed that "Christian faith and Marxism could not coexist" (Foroohar, 1989, p. 202). As politics polarized in Nicaragua with the emergence of the US-funded contra army, the hierarchy spoke out against the four priests serving in the Nicaraguan cabinet, worked to remove lower-level priests who supported the government, and failed to speak out against contra violence. When the Pope visited Nicaragua in March 1983, he publicly admonished high-level Catholics in the government, and described the idea of a "popular" Church outside of the hierarchy as "absurd and dangerous." A crucial step in this religious and political escalation was the government's 1983 decision to impose military conscription in response to contra attacks. The Nicaraguan Bishops immediately opposed it in the strongest possible language, viewing it not only in moral terms but also as an attempt by the government to insert itself into the lives of all Nicaraguans. The Pope suspended the four cabinet-level Catholics from their priestly duties in February 1984. At roughly the same time, Archbishop Obando and Pablo Vega, Bishop of Jinotega, became more overt in their support for the contra cause. Vega repeatedly traveled to Washington to lobby on behalf of the contra cause, and Obando said mass in front of contra leaders on numerous occasions. The Papacy promoted Obando to the position of Central American Cardinal in 1985 (Stein, 1999, pp. 179–180).

By the late 1980s, the Nicaraguan government was in a position of military strength in relation to the contras but in a position of political weakness in Nicaragua due to the conflict and to deteriorating economic conditions. As pressure for a negotiated end to the contra war grew, President Daniel Ortega requested that Cardinal Obando take part in talks between the government and the contras. But because of the politicization of the Catholic hierarchy, its close relations with the US, and its failure (for the most part) to speak out against human right violations by the contras against Nicaraguan citizens, the Catholic authorities were marginal actors in the area of human rights protection compared to their counterparts in the Archdioceses of San Salvador and Guatemala City (Stein, 1999, p. 178). The bulk of diplomatic work for peace and democratization was ultimately done by actors linked to regional governments, the Organization of American States, and the UN.

The ascension of the center-right (and anti-FSLN) Violetta Chamorro to power in 1990 signaled a new era for the Catholic hierarchy in Nicaragua, which strenuously supported Chamorro against Daniel Ortega. There was hope that the subsequent 1996 victory of Arnaldo Alemán, another center-right politician supported by the hierarchy, signaled a comprehensive refutation of the dramatic politicization of the 1970s and 1980s. It seemed that the fundamental threat of a government driven by socialist and radical Christian teachings had been removed, and the hierarchy could enjoy harmonious relations with popularly elected governments. But the political system was rocked by Alemán's spectacular levels of corruption and the cynical collaboration between Alemán and Daniel Ortega in 1998 to effectively rig the distribution of legislative power in their mutual interests. This arrangement would not pay off for Ortega (who was defeated for a third consecutive time in 2001) until the 2006 elections.

Daniel Ortega's electoral victory in 2006 was especially significant because it was mainly a result of Ortega's cynical overtures to the Catholic hierarchy. He and his long-time partner, Rosario Murillo, chose to marry in the Catholic Church during the campaign, in a ceremony officiated by none other than

Cardinal Obando. Ortega ran on the slogan "for the love of God, give him the opportunity to rule in peace"; and he made a high-profile commitment to support one of the most restrictive abortion laws in all of Latin America (Gooren, 2010, p. 50). Ortega won re-election in 2011 and 2016, basing his power on a combination of symbolic alliances with "pink revolution" leaders in Latin America, neoliberal economic policies, and generally good relations with the Catholic Church. (In a poignant moment, Pope Francis welcomed the four ministers defrocked 30 years earlier back into the Church in 2014.) However, Nicaragua's political stability came to a dramatic end in 2018, with nationwide protests against Ortega, concentrated in universities and churches. Jesuits at the University of Central American in Nicaragua were key actors in leading and planning the protests, and the Nicaraguan Bishops Conference was vocal in criticizing the Ortega government. Over 300 Nicaraguans died during the crackdown on the protests, and Managua's Auxiliary Bishop Silvio José Baez received multiple death threats. In late 2019, the government mounted raids against protestors gathering in churches across the nation (Weiss, 2019) Lower-level priests and laity have been split in their response: many have been moved by their radicalism to support the protestors, but a significant number, based on their links to Ortega's Sandinista Party and convinced by his expressions of Christian faith, have stood by the erstwhile socialist (Markey, 2019).

The Politics of Transnational Catholic Influence in Brazil

The analysis in this chapter so far has not dwelled on the differences between Spanish and Portuguese colonialism and their legacies. For the most part, the Portuguese crown was not nearly as engaged in colonial rule as its Spanish counterpart. The Church presence took a different form as well, as the newly formed Jesuit order was left to pursue missionary work and establish religious communities throughout Brazil. In addition, the Inquisition was never fully administered in Brazil (Serbin, 1999, p. 205). The Portuguese crown did strengthen its presence in Brazil and its control over the Church with the Pombaline reforms of the 1750s and the expulsion of the Jesuits in 1759. Yet 250 years of laxity led to extraordinary variety in Christianity's application to a sprawling and barely governed area. Subsequent diversity in Brazilian religion—a strong and varied Protestant presence, syncretism with indigenous and African traditions, and Christian ideological diversity—can be traced back to the original decentralization and laxness of the Crown and the Church's presence in Brazil (Mainwaring, 1986, p. 33).

Brazil's experience with independence was unique, in that it was primarily based on negotiations within the royal family, and was preceded by the brief transplantation of the Portuguese monarchy to Brazil. The long-term result was the creation of a second, independent monarchy with strong ties to Portugal. The presence of a monarch at the very top of Brazil's political structure meant that the nation was not subject to the Liberal/Conservative disputes that dominated much of the 19th century in the rest of Latin America. Yet the Church suffered because a monarchy, with strong ties to Portugal, was able to sustain earlier colonial reforms which exerted greater control over the Church. Being largely immune from democratic pressure, it also did not directly depend on the Church for political support. In this way, disputes over patronage were largely avoided (Mainwaring, 1986, p. 26). It therefore did little to support the Catholic presence in the countryside, which was already sparse since the expulsion of the Jesuits. The outcome of continued strong ties to Europe was, ironically, an important opening to Protestantism, as the British economic presence grew dramatically, and Protestants, enjoying the provisions of an 1824 Constitution that guaranteed freedom of religion, soon followed (Schwaller, 2011, pp. 158–162).

The global Catholic Church could not ignore Brazil, given its size and growing Protestant presence. Beginning in roughly 1850, the Papacy embarked on a process of "Romanization," through which it heightened its control over the Brazilian Church; increased training; dramatically increased the number of European priests coming into Brazil; and, more generally, initiated a modernization of the Brazilian Church (Mainwaring, 1986, p. 26). Nationalist military elements ended the Brazilian monarchy in 1889, and in 1891 stripped the Catholic Church's official status as a state religion, removed state subsidies, and secularized education. But this change in national government policy was far less significant than the sustained impact of Romanization, and the Catholic Church felt even more at liberty to pursue its initiatives coming from the Papacy. By the early 20th century, the Church had dramatically increased its presence throughout Brazil. Yet this was a European initiative meant to pull Brazilians back to traditional Catholic teachings. It also led the Church to take a stronger stance against the growing Protestant presence in Brazil (Serbin, 1999).

In 1930, the Catholic Church found an ally in the nationalist Brazilian leader Getúlio Vargas. Sebastiao Dom Leme served as Brazil's Cardinal for much of Vargas's first 15-year stint as leader of Brazil. This was a period of "intense church-state cooperation"—the kind of corporatist relations between the state and societal organizations for which Vargas became known. Both Vargas and the Brazilian Cardinal subsequently pursued an "essentially elitist and political strategy" of mutually beneficial collaboration, which represented a clear example of Catholic "neo-Christendom." Dom Leme pushed Vargas to extend the nation's ban on divorce, support religious instruction in public schools, and provide funding for Catholic secondary schools, hospitals, charities, and the building of seminaries. Leme responded with pastoral letters equating genuine Christianity with support for Vargas, and even created a Catholic Electoral League, meant to prod Catholics to vote for Vargas (Mainwaring, 1986, p. 33). When Vargas established dictatorial rule in 1937, the Cardinal responded with a circular that advocated "[b]efore everything, discipline and obedience to the Head of Government, to whom Providence has entrusted the destiny of Brazil in this hour of such heavy responsibilities" (Todaro Williams, 1976, pp. 456–457). The Church had become so deeply enmeshed in the government that "people looking for positions in the bureaucracy and minority groups seeking favors from the regime appealed first to Cardinal Leme" (Todaro Williams, 1976, p. 454). In turn, the Catholic Church "used public funds to expand Brazil's social infrastructure" in the areas of health care, education, housing, childcare, libraries, and social service provision. Thus, for example, 40% of the people in Salvador, Bahia, were receiving Catholic charity, and across the nation, religious orders tended 150,000 of Brazil's 284,000 hospital beds. Through this collaboration, "the church became a major social arm of the state" (Serbin, 1996, p. 730).

These political alignments would shift dramatically in the 1950s, 1960s, and 1970s. The key figure in this transformation was Dom Hélder Camara. As Auxiliary Archbishop of Rio de Janeiro, he helped to found the Brazilian Bishops Conference in 1952, and subsequently served as General Secretary for the group until 1964 (Mainwaring, 1986, p. 18). Hélder Camara also served as Secretary General for the 1955 International Eucharistic Congress in Rio de Janeiro, which brought Catholic officials from all over the world to Brazil. From these two positions he increased his influence as a religious thinker and activist in Latin America and throughout the world: Kenneth Serbin maintains that Hélder Camara is "arguably the most influential Latin American Bishop of the twentieth century" (Serbin, 1996, p. 723). At the same time, his experiences in these positions opened his eyes to the tremendous inequities in Brazilian society. For example, the contrasts between the opulent displays of Catholic wealth at the 1955 Congress and the poverty in nearby slums, which were obvious to his visiting peers, radicalized Hélder: "I was thrown to the ground like Saul on the road to Damascus" (Serbin, 1996, p. 748). At the 1955 gathering, he collaborated with other Bishops to form CELAM, the first such Catholic regional organization in the world. Camara's regional and global influence continued to grow as a result of his personal charisma, organizational skills, and commitment to the poor.

At Vatican II, Dom Hélder Camara is credited as being probably the most influential single participant in pushing for radical reform (Serbin, 2001, p. 136). It is thus entirely appropriate to think not only of Vatican II's impact on Brazil, but also, through the work of Dom Hélder Camara and his Brazilian colleagues, the Brazilian impact on Vatican II. His influence in global Catholic circles was matched by his influence over grassroots activism. Hélder's leadership of the Brazilian chapter of Catholic Action revitalized this organization, which became an important part of student and worker politics in the 1950s, openly radicalized in the 1960s, and served as a precursor to Brazilian CEBs. The radical turn that Catholic Action took in Brazil, in contrast to many other

Latin American nations, was a crucial factor in the emergence of a grassroots Catholic presence unmatched anywhere else in the region, evident in the numbers of CEBs and in the high-profile figures leading these efforts, most notably Paolo Freire and Leonardo and Clodovis Boff. Dom Hélder Camara's influence was thus felt on several crucial levels in Brazil: in both the radicalization coming from Vatican II and in the pressure for change coming from Brazilian society.

At the level of national politics in Brazil, the Catholic Church was slower to shed the kind of collaboration that took place during Vargas's rule. Most Bishops, including Hélder Camara, supported the 1964 coup against the leftist Goulart regime. The Church moved into strong opposition to the dictatorship only in 1968, as a new set of military rulers dramatically increased levels of repression in Brazilian society. Hélder's relocation to Olinda and Recife in 1964 marginalized him at the national level, and leadership of the still progressive Brazilian Church's efforts to defy the dictatorship fell to Paulo Evaristo Arns, who became Archbishop of Sao Paulo in 1970. Arns turned out to be a stalwart in leading human rights efforts, and his slightly more moderate political profile likely made him even more effective in pressuring the regime (Pope, 1985; Weschler, 1998, p. 12). While the levels of death and torture never reached the levels of Argentina, Chile, and Uruguay, the regime murdered hundreds of alleged subversives and engaged in widespread torture and imprisonment; it also targeted radical Catholic activists and harassed Bishops who spoke out against the regime.

In 1972, Archbishop Arns took the formal step of creating a Sao Paulo office for the Justice and Peace Commission, a global institution set up by the Vatican in 1967 (in the wake of Vatican II). The Commission came to be viewed by many Brazilians "as the last remaining social structure in which isolated individuals could join forces in defense of their interests and rights" (Pope, 1985, p. 432). Arns collaborated with secular, Jewish and Protestant activists on a clandestine effort to document the regime's widespread abuses, which resulted in the publication of "Brazil: Nunca Mais," the most comprehensive accounting of human rights violations for any of the Latin American dictatorships (a process vividly described in Weschler, 1998). A 1975 ecumenical memorial for torture victim Vladimir Herzog, presided over by Arns and attended by 8,000 mourners, is regarded as a moment that was "crucial in sparking the resurgence of an independent civil society in Brazil in the decade that followed" (Weschler, 1998, p. 13).

There was, however, a layer of complexity in the Catholic authorities' relationship with the Brazilian dictatorship that is missed with a narrative that focuses only on resistance to human rights abuses. Mala Htun's deep analysis of gender-related policies during the dictatorship demonstrates that a combination of Church-state antagonism and the dictatorship's obsession with modernizing Brazil (often in a brutal and undemocratic way) led to a series of policies that benefited women. Early in the dictatorship, the state moved to reform outdated and sexist spousal equity laws. In the 1970s, conflictual relations between the dictatorship and the Catholic Church were part of the regime's decision to push the legalization of divorce, forcing the Church to oppose a broadly popular policy initiative (Htun, 2003). The Catholic Church was such a culturally and politically entrenched institution in Brazil that, even as it took brave positions on human rights defined broadly, it was in no position to abandon more specific policies it had supported for hundreds of years.

The Catholic Church played a central role in the opening to democracy in the late 1970s and 1980s, using its moral authority and political influence to pressure the leaders of an oppressive regime. But even as Catholics were cele-brating their role in the democratic transition, the Church gradually withdrew as a political actor at the highest levels. This decision was partly the result of its great success as an anti-dictatorial force, and its intent to let more explicitly political and partisan groups run the political institutions of the new democ-racy. But it was also a sign that forces within the Church were moving against progressive Catholics in the hierarchy and at the grassroots level. Archbishop Arns was disempowered by the subdivision of the Sao Paulo Archdiocese in the mid-1980s. High-profile theologians like Leonardo Boff were sanctioned, dozens of conservative bishops were appointed, and radical priests were sus-pended and replaced. Brazil's hierarchical support for CEBs was reversed. And the Papacy reduced the independence of Archbishops and of organizations such as CELAM. But the change was not total. Many of the important post-dictatorship political actors, especially on the left, had ties to Catholic activism. Nowhere was this more evident than in the surprisingly high representation of Catholics in future President Lula da Silva's Workers' Party. A similar dynamic is at work with the continued Church support for Brazil's powerful Movement of the Landless (Serbin, 1999, p. 212).

Catholicism's partial retreat from politics has been accompanied by the growth of secularism, varieties of Protestantism, and syncretism based in Afri-can and indigenous traditions to make Catholicism a far less dominant cultural and political actor in 21st-century Brazil. Yet it continues to weigh in on the high-profile issues of the day. President Lula da Silva (who held the presidency from 2003 through 2010) butted heads with the papacy over abortion, AIDs prevention, and birth control leading up to and during Pope Benedict XVI's trip to Brazil in 2007. Yet, reflecting Lula's political realism and Benedict's desire to form a good relationship with Brazil's increasingly conservative hierarchy, the Brazilian government reached a Concordat with the Vatican in 2008 that extended the Church's role in education and administering marriages. And, in a sign of the complexity of the relationship, the Catholic Church criticized Lula's government from the left concerning its failure to deliver more fully on promises of land reform during his two terms (Gaudin, 2011). The rise of Jair Bolsonaro, who is nominally Catholic but is aligned with conservative

Pentacostal groups, has created a whole new set of tensions. Bolsonaro speaks fondly of the Brazilian dictatorship—clearly an affront to Pope Francis. Yet Francis's caution has led him to keep a low profile in the first years of Bolsonaro's administration despite their fundamental political differences. Bolsonaro has shown no such reluctance, publicly criticizing Pope Francis and, more generally, all but the most conservative Catholics. His concern about Catholic opposition, under the leadership of a progressive Pope, is a testament to the continued influence of the Catholic Church in a changing Brazil.

Theoretical Conclusions

The Catholic Church in Latin America exerts influence in a number of different ways, and it has done so for over 500 years. It established itself at the very outset of colonialism, and was a fixture in the region well before the rise of nation-states early in the 19th century. From the start, it exerted influence among the people of the region, with the national authorities, and at the highest levels of the global system, as shown in visual form in Figure 3.1. To a far greater extent than any other transnational actor, it established a pervasive presence within local Latin American societies. The following theoretical account assesses the nature of this influence at each of three levels of analysis, and in reference to institutions and networks, principles and norms, and power and capacity.

At first glance, it might make sense to view the Catholic Church in Latin America as a hierarchical organization, run mainly from the top-down and operating in a seamless way, based on decisions made in the Vatican. Yet close examination of the Catholic Church as an **institution** demonstrates that it, in Scott Mainwaring's words, "comprises more than the hierarchy," with numerous associated institutions, including the laity, operating alongside and below the top levels of the Church. This complexity brings out interesting dynamics at the global, national, and local levels. Different Catholic orders established distinctive communities and traditions throughout the region during colonialism, and conflicts between figures such as Bartolomé Las Casas and more reactionary Catholic representatives played out in often violent fashion.

These institutional relationships became even more complex with independence as distinctive traditions within the Catholic establishments of each nation led to tremendous variety throughout Latin America. This institutional complexity existed at a region-wide level as well, most notably with the actions of CELAM. This history also provides significant cases of the Catholic Church acknowledging the influence of actors in Latin America, making important concessions to local autonomy—in countless concordats and in more general policy shifts, such as the creation of Catholic Action. For all of its ideological changes, Vatican II was also significant for the new institutional arrangements it created by empowering the laity. Much of the career of the visionary and administratively savvy Dom Hélder Camara can be seen as an attempt to push

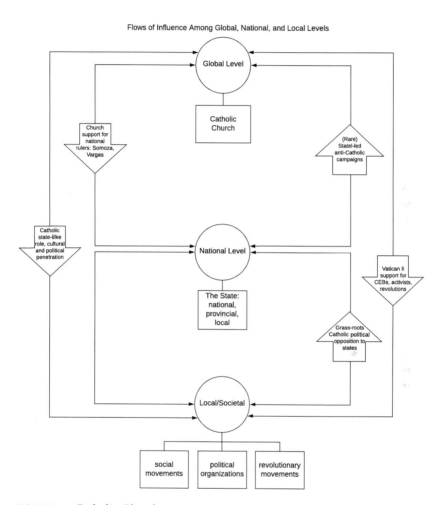

Flows of Influence Among Global, National, and Local Levels

FIGURE 3.1 Catholic Church.

the Vatican for greater autonomy in Latin America at regional, national, and grassroots levels. The origin, functioning, and continued thriving of grassroots groups—most notably the CEBs—has, in turn, been deeply influenced by local Bishops and global directives from the Vatican.

These institutional trends are also very much dialectical, in that Vatican concessions were often followed by subsequent attempts to reassert control or reinvigorate the European presence in Latin America, whether in the "Romanization" of the mid-19th century in Brazil or in John Paul II and Benedict XVI's attempts to enforce religious orthodoxy on a Church seen as straying too far to the left (and perhaps Francis's more recent moves in the opposite political direction). These different eras show the real variations in the Church's ability to seamlessly implement and impose its decisions as a transnational institution. Yet it is also worth emphasizing that the Catholic Church continues to exert an unmatched cultural influence on Latin America, often regardless of the wishes of national and local authorities. These different outcomes point to the continued power of the Catholic Church as a transnational actor, but also to the many challenges it has faced and will continue to face at the local, national, and global levels.

Analysis of **norms** espoused and implemented by the Catholic Church in Latin America must acknowledge two distinctive realities. First, the Catholic Church is an organization that is driven by norms and principles. It is naïve to ignore the history of unprincipled decisions it has made in support of genocide, exploitation, and injustice in Latin America. Nevertheless, norms, as a "standard of appropriate behavior" (Sikkink, 2011, p. 11), are at the heart of Catholicism. The great diversity of Catholic traditions and theology mean that there is genuine debate within the Church about what norms must take precedence. But every significant idea put forth by Catholic authorities is presented as coming out of normative ideas. Second, the emergence of Catholic norms in a setting like Latin America is often distinctive—and sudden. This suddenness contrasts sharply with the more typical gradual emergence of norms; accounts in Chapter 6 note that human rights norms took decades to emerge as politically significant. With historical hindsight and inside knowledge of the workings of the Church, some Catholic norms can be seen as emerging from the margins in a similarly gradual way. Yet the ability of the Catholic Church to rapidly introduce influential norms in a setting like Latin America may be unparalleled.

Most Catholic actions at the very earliest stages of conquest and colonialism were so closely aligned with those of the Spanish and Portuguese colonizers that it is difficult to speak of them as being norm-driven. As a norm, neo-Christendom dovetailed with less lofty goals to dominate Catholic thinking about political power and relations with Latin American colonial and national governments for centuries, and remains relevant to this day. The hierarchy would for centuries advocate neo-Christendom and, in this way, play a central role in legitimizing the rule of national political and economic elites. This legitimacy was crucial in a region marked by undemocratic systems and a weak sense of nationalism among populaces.

The ideas coming out of Vatican II in the early 1960s represented an introduction of dramatically new norms by an entrenched and powerful religious
organization. These norms drew on largely submerged Catholic traditions
going back all the way to Bartolomé Las Casas (and to the life of Christ). They
spoke to social justice, the empowerment of marginalized groups, and opposition to existing political structures. Given the diversity of the Church's presence in Latin America, they became the subject of intense struggle within
different Catholic communities. In some cases, earlier divisions between the
hierarchy and at lower levels became even more pronounced, as an empowered
laity pushed its interests. In others, hierarchy and laity collaborated to support
these new norms. Throughout Latin America, these new norms became an
extremely significant political reality. They came under criticism and threat
during the papacies of John Paul II and Benedict XVI, and have been more
welcome under Francis's leadership. Regardless of events at the very highest
levels, the deep penetration of Catholicism in Latin American societies meant
that the norms introduced in the 1960s have had an extraordinary impact on
politics in the region, even as they became the subject of contention.

A different dynamic has prevailed as the Catholic Church has weighed in
on an emerging set of norms related to contemporary cultural and sexual issues
in Latin America. In the 1960s and 1970s, the Church was unable to use its
position to keep undemocratic governments in Cuba and Brazil from pushing
policies related to gender and sexuality that it opposed. In the more democratic
setting of the last three decades, the Church's influence over debates about
abortion and gay marriage has been mixed: Latin America remains largely anti-
abortion, but groups pushing for gay rights have succeeded in Latin America's
largest nations. Even as it struggles with widespread allegations of abuse within
the Church, these trends demonstrate the continued strength of the Catholic
Church as a transnational organization which has deeply penetrated the societies of Latin American nations.

This chapter concludes with analysis of the **power and capacity** of the
Catholic Church, represented visually in Figure 3.1. It explicitly focuses on the
Church in relation to the state and Latin American societies, in the theoretical
context of the state-in-society approach, and state infrastructural and despotic
capacity. The larger theoretical setting is one marked by an unusually strong
non-state, societal actor, the Catholic Church, interacting with an unusually
weak set of Latin American state institutions. The result has often been direct
and unconstrained Catholic influence on Latin American societies. In a series
of key areas, spanning decades and centuries, Latin American states hobbled by
a lack of Michael Mann's "infrastructural capacity" were allowing Catholic authorities to perform functions normally filled by states. "Fueros" and "missionary zones" left the Church effectively free of government authority in many
areas of Latin America. Tithing and control of property allowed the Church to
engage in a kind of "taxation" that many weak-taxing Latin American governments could only dream of. Many governments chose to effectively contract

out education to Catholic authorities. Important rituals and record-keeping were left in the hands of Catholic institutions. Even by the mid-20th Century, a good portion of social welfare policy in Brazil was still being handled by the Catholic Church. During the Colombian civil war, the Catholic Church was the only organization that could reach into areas controlled by violent right-wing or left-wing groups to ensure safety to those working for peace.

On a less concrete level, many national governments relied on Catholic institutions and figures for political support—often expressed in fawning pastoral letters—instead of engaging in the kind of national projects that would create legitimacy on a national basis. This should come as no surprise, since a Catholic culture preceded all Latin American national cultures by centuries. And, as Centeno notes, the relatively weak states leading these nations often lacked the strength and legitimacy to supplant these cultures: states lacked the capacity and resources to do it, and there was little previous sense of national culture to challenge Catholicism at the grassroots. At a more specific level, this political support was often brazenly given in exchange for Catholic control over key functions normally performed by governments. It speaks to the cultural and political strength of the Catholic Church, as a societal actor and in relation to national cultures and Latin American state institutions.

In three notable cases, Latin American states took systematic and enduring steps against the Catholic Church. In Mexico and Cuba, the anti-Catholic campaign took place in the wake of social revolution. In Uruguay, it took place in a democratic setting already marked by Catholic weakness. The common theme in the Cuban and Mexican cases is of a thoroughgoing revolution prevailing over Catholicism in the short and medium terms, based on strong links between national governments and the social forces that put them in power. These links empowered state institutions to move against numerous powerful non-state forces, including the Catholic Church. But ultimately, these revolutionary states were unable to supplant a Catholic cultural and political tradition that both preceded and outlasted it. Less "revolutionary" events in Uruguay were more enduring because the Catholic presence was weaker to start with. In reference to Figure 3.1, the deep and direct penetration of the local/societal level by the transnational Catholic Church proved to be insurmountable to the Mexican and Cuban states in the long run, despite medium- and short-term successes against the Church. It was far less difficult for the Uruguayan state to effectively uproot a weak Catholic Church.

Probably the most interesting case in this regard is Nicaragua over the last 50 years. It resembles Mexico and Cuba in that it experienced a social revolution led by leftists. And it almost immediately came into conflict with the Catholic Church hierarchy. But the presence of radical Christians, in both the revolutionary struggle and the subsequent government, made relations between the government and the Catholic Church (and within the Catholic Church) even more fraught. In the long run, the Catholic Church prevailed. The FSLN state's decision to establish a military draft in 1983, in the context of the US-funded contra war, was a crucial factor in the FSLN's eventual defeat in 1990. The key point, in regard to the three-level analytical framework in Figure 3.1, is that the imposition of nation-wide conscription represents an ambitious political and administrative undertaking for even the strongest state institution. It was made even more so by the vehement opposition of the nation's strongest non-state institution, the Catholic Church. Subsequent events drove home this strength, with the Catholic hierarchy's role in defeating the FSLN in subsequent elections and Daniel Ortega's embrace of the Catholic Church and its social policies in 2006. Elements of the Church remain among his strongest opponents as he consolidates power and defies protests.

The greatest challenge to Catholicism as a powerful societal force will likely come not from any state institution, but from other forces within Christian and other faith traditions. Protestant denominations have made significant inroads among the faithful in every Latin American nation, and enjoy an especially widespread presence in Central America. These groups have the kind of decentralization and grassroots engagement that initially drove the growth of CEBs in the wake of Vatican II and Medellín, and they are able to offer themselves as a clear alternative to a still-hierarchical Catholic Church. The same can be said of syncretistic traditions that more accurately represent the aspirations of indigenous Latin Americans and those with African ancestry. Some reduction of the Catholic presence is inevitable, given its virtual monopoly for centuries under Spanish and Portuguese colonialism and the newly independent Latin American nation-states. This religious challenge may be far greater than that offered by any particular Latin American state.

This theoretical discussion of institutions, norms, and power and capacity highlights the thoroughgoing influence of the Catholic Church in Latin America. The three-level analytical framework shows a transnational Catholic institution that, more than any other transnational actor, has penetrated Latin American societies. Catholicism has also deeply influenced Latin American states, to the extent that the Church has often filled state-like functions. Its support has often been crucial to state legitimacy, and can be viewed as a kind of substitute for comprehensive nationalist projects in many Latin American nations. The Catholic Church's power is far from total, however. This chapter has provided examples of campaigns—led by states, often in collaboration with societal forces—to strike at Catholic privileges. Just as notable as these campaigns is the enduring influence of the Church in the face of these efforts. It is a testament to the entrenched position of the Catholic Church and the continued relevance of its principles to the people of Latin America.

References

Anderson, Jon Lee, 2020. "The Fall of Evo Morales," *The New Yorker*, March 23, 2020.
Arnson, Cynthia, 1999. *Comparative Peace Processes in Latin America*. Washington, DC: Woodrow Wilson Center.

Bamat, Thomas, 2009. "The Rights of the Poor: Christian Theology and Human Rights Practices in Latin America's Andean Region," in Frederick M. Shepherd, editors, *Christianity and Human Rights: Christians and the Struggle for Global Human Rights.* New York: Lexington Books, pp. 179–194.

Bauer, Arnold, 1983. "The Church in the Economy of Spanish America: Censos and Depósitos in the Eighteenth and Nineteenth Centuries," *The Hispanic American Historical Review* 63/4 (November), pp. 707–733.

Bentancur, Veronica and Cecilia Rocha-Carpius, 2020. "The Postreform Stage: Understanding Backlash against Sexual Policies in Latin America," *Politics & Gender* 16/1, pp. 33–51.

Berkley Center, 2013. "Colombia: Religious Actors Inspiring Reconciliation," *Religion and Conflict Case Study Series.* Berkley Center for Religion, Peace, and World Affairs, August 2013.

Bonino, José Miguez, 1999. "Church, State, and Religious Freedom in Argentina," in Paul Sigmund, editor, *Religious Freedom and Evangelization: The Challenge of Religious Pluralism.* Maryknoll, NY: Orbis Books, pp. 187–203.

Burkholder, Mark and Lyman Johnson, 1990. *Colonial Latin America.* Oxford: Oxford University Press.

Camp, Roderic Ai, 1999. "Mexico: Liberation Theology, Base Communities and Evangelical Protestantism," in Paul Sigmund, editor, *Religious Freedom and Evangelization: The Challenge of Religious Pluralism.* Maryknoll, NY: Orbis Books, pp. 139–149.

Cardenal, Ernesto, 1982. *The Gospel of Solentiname.* Maryknoll, NY: Orbis Books.

Casey, Matthew, 2019. "Old Religious Tensions Resurge in Bolivia after Ouster of Indigenous Leader," *The Crux*, November 20, 2019.

Cleary, Edward, 1999. "The Catholic Church," in Paul Sigmund, editor, *Religious Freedom and Evangelization: The Challenge of Religious Pluralism.* Maryknoll, NY: Orbis Books, pp. 11–27.

Crahan, Margaret, 1999. "Cuba," in Paul Sigmund, editor, *Religious Freedom and Evangelization: The Challenge of Religious Pluralism.* Maryknoll, NY: Orbis Books, pp. 87–112.

Díez, Jordi, and Michelle L. Dion. 2018. "New Media and Support for Same-Sex Marriage," *Latin American Research Review* 53/3, pp. 455–480.

Dodson, Michael and Laura O'Shaughnessy, 1990. *Nicaragua's Other Revolution: Religious Faith and Political Struggle.* Chapel Hill: University of North Carolina Press.

Fernandez, José Luis, 1999. "The New Legislation on Religious Freedom in Mexico," in Paul Sigmund, editor, *Religious Freedom and Evangelization: The Challenge of Religious Pluralism.* Maryknoll, NY: Orbis Books, pp. 129–138.

Fitzgibbon, Russell, 1953. "The Political Impact on Religious Development in Uruguay," *Church History* 22/1, pp. 21–32.

Foroohar, Manzar, 1989. *The Catholic Church and Social Change in Nicaragua.* Albany: State University of New York Press.

Gaudin, Andres, 2011. "Brazil's Catholic Church Slams Lula's Agrarian-Reform Record," *South American Political and Economic Affairs*, April 15, 2011. Latin American Institute.

Gill, Anthony, 1998. *Rendering Unto Caesar: The Catholic Church and the State in Latin America.* Chicago, IL: University of Chicago Press.

Goldfrank, Benjamin and Nick Rowell. "Church, State, and Human Rights in Latin America," *Religion and Ideology* 13/1 (March), pp. 25–51.

Goldman, Francisco, 1998. *The Art of Political Murder: Who Killed the Archbishop?* New York: Grove Press.

Gooren, Henri, 2010. "Ortega for President: The Religious Rebirth of Sandinismo in Nicaragua," *European Review of Latin American and Caribbean Studies* 89 (October), pp. 47–63.

Gould, Jeffrey, 1990. *To Lead as Equals: Rural Protest and Political Consciousness in Chinandega, Nicaragua, 1912–1979.* Chapel Hill: University of North Carolina Press.

Gould, Jeffrey and Aldo Lauria-Santiago, 2008. *To Rise in Darkness: Revolution, Repression, and Memory in El Salvador.* Durham, NC: Duke University Press.

Grandin, Greg, 2004. *The Last Colonial Massacre: Latin America in the Cold War.* Chicago, IL: University of Chicago Press.

Htun, Mala, 2003. *Sex and the State: Abortion, Divorce, and the Family under Latin American Dictatorships and Democracies.* Cambridge: Cambridge University Press.

Kuivala, Petra, 2017. "Policy of Empowerment: Pope Francis in Cuba," *International Journal of Cuban Studies* 9/1 (Spring), pp. 19–36.

Lancaster, Roger, 1988. *Thanks to God and the Revolution: Popular Religion and Class Consciousness in the New Nicaragua.* New York: Columbia University Press.

Langer, Erick and Robert Jackson, 1988. "Colonial and Republican Missions Compared: The Cases of Alta California and Southeastern Bolivia," *Comparative Studies in Society and History* 30/2 (April), pp. 286–311.

Levine, Daniel, 1978. "Authority in Church and Society: Latin American Models," *Comparative Studies in Society and History* 20/4 (October), pp. 517–544.

Levine, Daniel, 1981. *Religion and Politics in Latin America: The Catholic Church in Venezuela and Colombia.* Princeton, NJ: Princeton University Press.

Loveman, Mara, 1998. "High-Risk Collective Action: Defending Human Rights in Chile, Uruguay, and Argentina," *American Journal of Sociology* 104/2 (September), pp. 477–525.

Mainwaring, Scott, 1986. *The Catholic Church and Politics in Brazil, 1916–1985.* Stanford, CA: Stanford University Press.

Markey, Eileen, 2019. "When the Laity Led," *Commonweal*, October 2019, pp. 40–45.

Michaels, Albert, 1969. "The Modification of the Anti-Clerical Nationalism of the Mexican Revolution by General Lázaro Cárdenas and Its Relationship to the Church-State Detente in Mexico," *The Americas* 26/1 (July), pp. 35–53.

Mignone, Emilio, 1988. *Witness to the Truth: The Complicity of Church and Dictatorship in Argentina, 1976–1983.* Maryknoll, NY: Orbis Books.

Navarro-Genie, Marco, 2002. *Augusto "Cesar" Sandino: Messiah of Light and Truth.* Syracuse, NY: Syracuse University Press.

Orique, David, 2009. "Journey to the Headwaters: Bartolomé de las Casas in a Comparative Context," *Catholic Historical Review* 95/1, pp. 1–24.

Pew Research Center, 2014. *Religion in Latin America.* Washington, DC: Pew Research Center on Religion and Public Life, November 13.

Phippen, J. Weston, 2017. "Can the Pope Bridge Colombia's Divide over FARC? Francis's Message of Forgiveness Has Not Come with an Explicit Endorsement of the Peace Deal," *The Atlantic*, September 9, 2017.

Poblete, Martin, 1999. "Chile: From the Patronato to Pinochet," in Paul Sigmund, editor, *Religious Freedom and Evangelization: The Challenge of Religious Pluralism.* Maryknoll, NY: Orbis Books, pp. 220–234.

Pope, Clara, 1985. "Human Rights and the Catholic Church in Brazil, 1970–1983: The Pontifical Justice and Peace Commission of the São Paulo Archdiocese," *Journal of Church and State* 27/3 (Autumn) pp. 429–452.

Pramuk, Christopher, 2015. "God Accompanies Persons: Thomas Merton and Pope Francis on Gender and Sexual Diversity," *The Merton Annual* 28, pp. 71–87.

REMHI (Recovery of Historical Memory Project), 1999. *Guatemala: Never Again!* Maryknoll, NY: Orbis Books.

Richard, Pablo and Guillermo Melendez, 1982. *La Iglesia de los Pobres en America Central.* San José, Costa Rica: Departamento Ecumenico de Investigaciones.

Samandu, Luis and Ruud Jansen, 1982. "Nicaragua: Dictadura Somocista, Movimiento Popular e Iglesia," *Estudios Centroamericanos* 33, pp. 189–219.

Schwaller, John, 1986. "The Ordenanza del Patronazgo in New Spain," *Thee Americas* 42/3 (January), pp. 253–274.

Schwaller, John, 2011. *The History of the Catholic Church in Latin America: From Conquest to Revolution and Beyond.* New York: NYU Press.

Serbin, Kenneth, 1996. "Church-State Reciprocity in Contemporary Brazil: The Convening of the International Eucharistic Congress of 1955 in Rio de Janeiro," *The Hispanic American Historical Review* 76/4 (November), pp. 721–751.

Serbin, Kenneth, 1999. "Brazil: Religious Tolerance, Church-State Relations, and the Challenge of Pluralism," in Paul Sigmund, editor, *Religious Freedom and Evangelization: The Challenge of Religious Pluralism.* Maryknoll, NY: Orbis Books, pp. 204–219.

Serbin, Kenneth, 2001. ""Bowling Alone," Bishops' Biographies, and Baptism by Blood: New Views of Progressive Catholicism in Brazil," *Latin American Politics and Society* 43/4 (Winter), pp. 127–141.

Shepherd, Frederick, 1995. "Church and State in Honduras and Nicaragua Prior to 1979," in William Swatos, editor, *Religion and Democracy in Latin America.* New Brunswick, CT: Transaction Publishers, pp. 117–134.

Sikkink, Kathryn, 2011. *The Justice Cascade: How Human Rights Prosecutions are Changing World Politics.* New York: W.W. Norton.

Sinclair, John, 1999. "Historical Protestantism," in Paul Sigmund, editor, *Religious Freedom and Evangelization: The Challenge of Religious Pluralism.* Maryknoll, NY: Orbis Books, pp. 28–48.

Smilde, David, 2004. "Contradiction without Paradox: Evangelical Political Culture in the 1998 Venezuelan Elections," *Latin American Politics and Society* 46/1, pp. 75–102.

Stein, Andres, 1999. "Nicaragua," in Paul Sigmund, editor, *Religious Freedom and Evangelization: The Challenge of Religious Pluralism.* Maryknoll, NY: Orbis Books, pp. 175–186.

Thiele, John and Matthew Carnes, 2018. "Filling the Gaps in Civil Society The Role of the Catholic Church in Latin American Democratization," *Journal of Religion & Society* 2/20, pp. 1–18.

Todaro Williams, Margaret, 1976. "Church and State in Vargas's Brazil: The Politics of Cooperation," *Journal of Church and State* 18/3 (Autumn), pp. 443–462.

Walter, Knut, 2000. *The Regime of Anastasio Somoza, 1936–1956.* Chapel Hill: University of North Carolina Press.

Weiss, Laura, 2019. "Catholic Churches Are Caught in the Crossfire of Nicaragua's Political Crisis," *World Politics Review*, December 5, 2019.

Weschler, Lawrence, 1998. *A Miracle, A Universe: Settling Accounts with Torturers.* Chicago, IL: University of Chicago Press.

Williams, Margaret, 1976. "Church and State in Vargas's Brazil: The Politics of Cooperation," *Journal of Church and State* 18/3 (Autumn), pp. 443–462.

Williams, Phillip, 1989. *The Catholic Church and Politics in Nicaragua and Costa Rica.* London: MacMillan.

Young, Kevin, 2020. "The Bolivian Left's Election Win Is a Positive Sign, But It Inherits a Dire Situation," *The Guardian*, October 21.

4

THE POLITICS OF TRANSNATIONAL CORPORATIONS IN LATIN AMERICA

This chapter focuses on a highly mobile and transnationalized form of organization with a long history in Latin America. Transnational corporations (TNCs) have, for well over a century, played an outsized role in Latin American national economies. This economic dominance initially translated into overwhelming political dominance. But it has also led many citizens and policymakers to challenge the privileged economic and political position of TNCs. This chapter explores these trends as it analyzes the politics of TNCs in Latin America.

TNCs are defined by the UN Economic and Social Council as "all enterprises which control assets...in two or more countries" (UNCTC, 1978, p. 158). A recent joint effort by scholars formulated the following definition: "A multinational corporation (MNC) organizes production of goods and services in more than one country, involving the transfer of assets or intermediate products within the investing enterprise and without any change in ownership" (Jensen et al., 2012, p. 1). Scholars and practitioners are divided on whether to apply the term "multinational" or "transnational" to these global enterprises. The UN chose in the 1970s, for various political reasons, to use the term "transnational," and given the emphasis on organizations that transcend national boundaries, this book adopts this term as well.

The vastness of the topic of TNCs necessitates a series of choices for covering the topic in a single chapter. The primary concern is the politics of the transnational corporate presence in Latin America, in the context of the three-level analytical model of relations among global, national, and local/societal actors. This chapter explores questions of capacity and power as TNCs penetrate Latin American national political and economic systems. It analyzes TNCs as relatively hierarchical institutions. And it assesses the impact of norms, especially "corporate social responsibility" (CSR) and "resource nationalism," as groups attempt to use these principles to influence TNC behavior. More than any other chapter, Chapter 4 looks closely at the impact of other global actors and forces, including the US government, interstate military rivalries, intergovernmental organizations, and global economic forces, on TNCs in Latin America. The chapter concludes with case studies of Bolivia and Chile.

Given the political and scholarly attention devoted to TNCs, one theoretical debate should be addressed directly. Thoughtful investigations have come to markedly different conclusions about the overall impact of TNCs on Latin America. Scholars from the Marxist and "dependency" approaches emphasize the disproportionate political power of TNCs. For these scholars, TNCs created a larger set of relations which led to "capitalism without capital" and a set of one-sided relations among TNCs, vulnerable and co-opted national governments, and oppressed citizens. Occasionally, this exploitation would be reinforced by powerful governments (most notably the US) outside the region (Frank, 1967; Cardoso, 1979). More recent, and nuanced, versions of this approach point to "rentier" states whose economies and political systems are deeply distorted by reliance on a single product exposed to fickle global markets (Karl, 1997). A second approach, with roots in liberal and neo-liberal traditions, emphasizes the mutually beneficial nature of transnational corporate activity, focusing on equitable "interdependence" rather than exploitative "dependency." Scholars from this perspective point to the spread of wealth, technology, and enterprise, linking TNCs' presence to better overall economic performance within a nation (Gilpin, 1984). It would be naive to ignore the insights from the more radical "dependency" scenario. There are simply too many cases that fit this model. But the complex interactions among TNCs, national governments, and Latin American citizens require analysis based in multiple perspectives.

Early Transnational Corporate Dominance

Latin America was exposed to global economic forces well before the first TNCs came to the region. The formal colonial structures put in place by the Spanish, Portuguese, and other European powers presaged the kind of external economic control that would later be exercised by powerful TNCs. The decision by Latin American national leaders to adopt export-based economic strategies in the second half of the 19th century would similarly expose these national economies to global economic dynamics. But it was not until the late 19th century that TNCs would come to invest in and exert direct control over key sectors of Latin American economies.

The first wave of direct investment by TNCs took place in a variety of sectors, but one of the main initial areas was in the building of railroad lines. By 1914, a mixture of French, British, and US companies had built over 83,000 kilometers of rail lines, mostly in Brazil, Argentina, and Mexico (Coatsworth, 1979; Bulmer-Thomas, 2003, p. 105). The turn of the century was marked by significant transnational investment in the mining, extractive, and agricultural sectors, much of which used these new rail lines as transportation links. Notable in this regard were copper in Chile and Peru, and oil and a variety of mining activities in Mexico. Exxon, Royal Dutch Shell, Anaconda, Kennecott, and Alcoa were the largest early TNCs to invest in these sectors (Jenkins, 1987a, p. 5). These investments grew dramatically in the first decade of the 20th century, with huge increases in levels of extraction in the years leading up to World War One. The United Fruit Company (UFCO) quickly established its presence in Colombia, Central America, and the Caribbean after its formation in 1899, becoming the largest landowner in several nations and taking advantage of its ownership of rail lines and a large fleet of ships to corner much of the trade in fruit, especially bananas (Schlesinger and Kinzer, 1982). Other US corporations, including WR Grace, followed with investments in fruit and sugar (Jenkins, 1987a, p. 5). This period was known as a "golden age" for direct foreign investment in Latin America (Marichal, 1994, p. 8), with total foreign direct investment (FDI, including railroads) for the region reaching 179% of total gross domestic product (GDP) by 1900 and 178% in 1913 (Twomey, 1998, p. 182). The ratio of FDI to gross domestic product, known as FDI intensity, appears throughout this chapter as a measure of the foreign presence in an economy.

These early investments were part of a trend of foreign-dominated "enclave" economies that often accompanied a significant transnational corporate presence. It is worth a brief look at the Honduran case as an example of an enclave. Beginning in 1899, transnational fruit companies came to dominate the Honduran banana trade; Edelberto Torres Rivas describes how Honduras's Atlantic Coast, at this time, "for all practical purposes, was occupied by the three great fruit companies" (p. 34).

> The technical conditions of production…favored the fruit's harvest, transportation, and commercial distribution by a single enterprise. The plantation inaugurated a modern system of land occupation and productive organization that led to the industry's vertical integration as an enclave.
>
> *(p. 31)*

The outcome was a "self-sufficient and isolated sector, tied only to the foreign market." Because of the weakness of Honduran state institutions, the ports and rail lines remained primarily in transnational fruit company hands. At the local level, the company store "isolated laborers from the local market and alienated any possibility of tying the agricultural worker's consumption into the national market" (p. 35). At the global level, the companies were able to freely move profits back to the US. All of this took place in a setting of generous concessions by the national government, including tax rates of the "incomprehensible" rate of only 1% per bushel (p. 37). In the early decades of the 20th century, a series of coups was closely related to the ties different TNCs had with different government factions: "Each had a distinct set of clientelist relationships and allies inside the dominant bloc even if all sought a general stability within the class that managed the state" (Dunkerley, 1988, p. 37). The interests of the transnational companies were backed by powerful US financial institutions, and ultimately the US military, which intervened on seven separate occasions between 1903 and 1925. Torres Rivas goes on to ask the question "Could one speak, then, of the existence of a nation-state with partial political sovereignty?" (Torres Rivas, 1993, p. 39). An unavoidable part of the answer to this question is the power that was granted to TNCs within Honduran national borders, whether in isolated enclaves or in the nation as a whole.

Despite the systematic way in which key sectors came to be taken over by transnational actors in many Latin American nations, this process did not take place everywhere. Where cultivation or production required less technology, key sectors remained in local hands. This local control was most notable in economies dominated by coffee. To be sure, an elite emerged; but it was an elite based within the nation. A striking example of this localized domination is El Salvador, where (roughly) 40 families used their control of the growth and trade of coffee to dominate national political and economic life. Just as common, however, was the "enclave" model, which prevailed in nations marked by banana cultivation and extractive industries. From a broader perspective, by 1913 the main exports from Chile, Panama, Costa Rica, Honduras, and Bolivia (all accounting for over 50% of national exports) came from foreign-dominated enclave settings, and seven nations' top export was domestically controlled coffee (Bulmer-Thomas, 2003, p. 58).

The tendency toward foreign ownership was particularly marked in oil extraction. Porfirio Diaz, who ruled from 1876 to 1910, made Mexico a welcoming place to transnational oil companies. Laws passed in 1884 (and confirmed in 1909) allowed landowners to control subsoil rights and led to total foreign control of the oil industry by Royal Dutch Shell and Standard Oil, among others, initially paying almost no taxes. The US government and its ambassadorial representatives in Mexico repeatedly pressured the Mexican government on behalf of US oil companies (Meyer, 1977). Venezuela, ruled by the dictator Juan Vicente Gómez from 1908 to 1935, was not far behind. Royal Dutch Shell discovered rich oil fields in 1914, and a variety of transnational companies were drawn to Venezuela in the 1920s by massive finds. Oil became the nation's primary export in 1927, and Venezuela became the world's top oil exporter by 1929. The Vicente Gómez government set royalty rates at the extremely generous levels of between 8% and 15%. It was only after Vicente Gómez's death that laws were passed allowing labor organizations and protecting working conditions (McBeth, 2008). On a much smaller scale, Standard Oil and Royal Dutch-Shell began processing deposits in Argentina, Peru, Colombia, Bolivia, and Ecuador in the 1920's. Oil companies also set up a significant retail infrastructure in many Latin American nations for the marketing and sale of oil (Wilkins, 1974).

Foreign investment in manufacturing was initially almost nonexistent, accounting for only 6.3% of total investment in 1929 (Bulmer-Thomas, 2003, p. 158). Over the following ten years, though, TNCs, including General Electric, Goodyear, Firestone, International Telegraph and Telephone Company (ITT), Singer, National Cash Register, and numerous European companies, established roughly 200 subsidiaries throughout Latin America (Jenkins, 1987a, p. 5).

Particularly notable in this regard was the auto industry, in which Ford led the way, beginning in 1916 with a plant in Argentina and subsequent plants in Brazil, Chile, and Mexico. Ford's failed effort to create and run its own "Fordlandia" rubber plantation in the interior of Brazil in the late 1920s is the subject of Greg Grandin's evocative book (Grandin, 2009). Ford was followed soon after by General Motors and Chrysler. Most of the early TNC-owned auto factories were assembly plants, putting together pre-fabricated parts imported from the US. The only locally owned industrial activity related to automobiles in the first half of the century was in the areas of repair shops and replacement parts (Jenkins, 1987b, pp. 18–20). The second half of the century was marked by renewed foreign domination of the auto industry, with the emergence of European- and Japanese-owned plants in the 1950s, 1960s, and 1970s. Some national governments attempted to pressure the auto TNCs to locate more manufacturing plants (rather than just assembly plants) in Latin America and banned the importation of fully manufactured vehicles from outside Latin America. These attempts faltered, however. Exports of TNC brands from nations like Argentina, Brazil, and Mexico grew; Mexico became the fourth-largest exporter by 2017 and was host to some of the most technologically sophisticated plants in the world. Yet the auto industry remained firmly in foreign hands, and the proportion of parts manufactured in the region actually shrank in the 2000s (Jenkins, 1987b, p. 63; CEPAL, 2018, pp. 98–101).

Challenges to Transnational Corporate Dominance

Nationalist reaction to external economic influence has a long history in many regions of the world. It began to emerge as a political force in Latin America not long after TNCs established their presence in the region and in most cases took the form of "resource nationalism." This norm is based on the idea that "the natural resources of a country belong to the nation and exist as a national patrimony and consequently should be used for the benefit of the nation as a whole and not be exploited for private gain" (Jaffe, 2012, p. 295; Fontaine et al., 2018). The first high-profile political articulation of this idea in Latin America appeared in the Mexican Constitution of 1917, a reaction to the massive US influence over the Mexican economy. In subsequent decades, resource nationalism would emerge as the kind of norm that would influence behavior and constrain powerful actors.

After the Great Depression, national governments across the region engaged in attempts to assert national control over key sectors of the economy. One form that these efforts took was the strategy of import substitution industrialization (ISI), which eventually became closely associated with the UN Economic Commission for Latin America and its leader Raúl Prebisch (Prebisch, 1950). This movement was intended to create internal industries in sectors previously dominated by foreign interests, and had obvious implications for TNCs. It was an important factor in dramatically driving down the amount of FDI in relation to the size of national economies in Latin America. The ratio of FDI to GDP (or FDI intensity) fell from 76% in 1929 to 56% in 1938, to 17% in 1950, and all the way down to 12% in 1970 (Twomey, 1998, p. 6). This dramatic decrease was partly due to the growth of Latin American economies, but was also clearly a result of nationalist economic policies throughout the region. Peter Evans points to a "complex alliance between elite local capital, international capital, and state capital" both causing and emerging from ISI (Evans, 1979, p. 11). Variations in the alliance have helped to explain different outcomes in the region ever since the introduction of ISI. The extent to which the state favors local businesses or directly intervenes in the economy itself has important implications for TNCs in the larger Latin American nations.

A series of high-profile conflicts showed the obstacles and opportunities for Latin American states attempting to control key national resources. Lázaro Cárdenas systematically challenged the power of TNCs in Mexico during his presidency from 1934 to 1940, beginning with the expropriation of foreign-owned railroads in 1937 (Sigmund, 1980, p. 57). Cárdenas's plans to nationalize the foreign-owned oil sector proved far more contentious. In 1936, Mexican unions, newly consolidated in the government-sponsored Mexican Labor Confederation, pressured the transnational oil companies to dramatically increase wages. When the companies refused, Cárdenas began the process of expropriating the oil industry in March 1938 (Hamilton, 1982, pp. 216–240), a decision met with "an outpouring of national solidarity" (Sigmund, 1980, p. 59). Under Franklin Roosevelt, the US government was not inclined to automatically side with corporations in labor disputes, had already crafted a "Good Neighbor" policy toward Latin America, and was concerned about antagonizing its southern neighbor and providing Germany, Italy, and Japan access to copious oil supplies. The Mexican government also possessed the capacity to seize and manage the newly nationalized oil sector since it had created the state-owned Mexican Petroleum (PEMEX) oil company in 1934. Production reached pre-nationalization levels in 1939 (Sigmund, 1980, pp. 55–69). Policies based on resource nationalism proved politically popular, and, in league with oil workers, the Mexican state demonstrated the capacity to implement and administer them.

Juan José Arévalo and his successor, Jacobo Arbenz, used their legitimacy as democratically elected leaders to push a series of social reforms in Guatemala during the late 1940s and early 1950s. In 1953, under the leadership of Arbenz, the Guatemalan government proposed comprehensive land reform, which threatened large tracts of unused UFCO lands. The reformist government used the language of resource nationalism to push its case with the Guatemalan people. But the US-based company worked with the Eisenhower administration to overthrow Arbenz in 1954 and replace him with Carlos Castillo Armas, a figure far more sympathetic to US interests (Schlesinger and Kinzer, 1982). Important elements within the Guatemalan elite were quick to back the coup (Brockett, 2002). The threat to UFCO's economic interests in Guatemala dovetailed with the anti-communism of Eisenhower's Secretary of State, John Foster Dulles, and his CIA Director, Allan Dulles, both of whom had previously worked for UFCO (Immerman, 1982).

A very different outcome would emerge five years later in Cuba. Soon after the success of the revolution in January 1959, the new regime led by Fidel Castro and Che Guevara (who had witnessed the tragedy of Guatemala firsthand) began to expropriate TNCs as part of an escalating conflict with the US government. There is little question that nationalization fit with the nationalist and Marxist tendencies of the government, which, in turn, closely adhered to norms of resource nationalism. By the end of 1960, the Castro government had, in his words, seized "all Yankee property down to the nails in their shoes" (Sigmund, 1980, p. 108). Nationalization laws were passed close on the heels of CIA decisions in March to work with Cuban exiles to initiate "sabotage, economic sanctions, propaganda, and training of a Cuban exile group for possible invasion" (Sigmund, 1980, p. 105). The laws affected a huge variety of properties: US-owned cattle ranches, sugar plantations, banks, nickel plants, utilities, hotels, factories, retail outlets, and oil companies. As the nationalizations were announced, the US imposed an almost total embargo on all exports into Cuba in October 1960. Threats of US invasion, US sponsorship of military operations by Cuban exiles, and covert US anti-Castro operations were present throughout the early 1960s, and effectively placed the island on a war footing.

These confrontations over nationalization in Mexico, Guatemala, and Cuba, with their markedly different outcomes, effectively politicized relations between national governments and TNCs in much of the rest of Latin America. This politicization drove the 1962 passage of the Hickenlooper Amendment in the US Congress, which formalized the US government commitment to back US businesses in cases of expropriation. At the same time, Cuba's ability to prevail against the wishes of corporations and the US administration made the policy of nationalization a realistic option for other Latin American governments seeking to exert greater control over their national economies. (The dramatic conflict in Chile during the early 1970s is described at the end of this chapter.)

In Peru, the Velasco regime came to power in 1968 committed to national-izing key economic sectors, including Exxon's oil facilities, Grace Company's sugar plantations, ITT's communications network, Chase Manhattan's banking interests, and subsidiaries of Gulf and Standard Oil. Given the nationalist but non-Marxist nature of the Velasco regime, the Nixon administration was eager to apply a more flexible reading of the Hickenlooper Amendment and, after early protests, was unwilling to escalate hostilities over threatened expropri-ations (Stepan, 1978, pp. 259–263). The centrist Venezuelan regime of Carlos Andrés Pérez nationalized foreign oil holdings in early 1976. The only debate over the nationalization came from leftist groups that argued that the legislation did not go far enough. In the words of Paul Sigmund,

> an impeccably democratic government carried out a carefully thought out nationalization policy that respected United States security interests, offered the oil companies partial compensation and the advantages of continued contractual relationships, and maintained internal economic and political stability throughout the difficult period of transition from foreign to national ownership.
>
> *(Sigmund, 1980, p. 227)*

Brazil's rightist dictatorship took significant steps from the late 1960s to 1980s to expand the state presence and reduce TNCs' control in key economic sectors, most notably in airplane manufacturing and computer technology. Based on the argument that "national security required a national capac-ity to produce planes" (Evans, 1979, p. 219), the state created the Brazilian Aeronautical Company (EMBRAER) in 1969, and was soon providing over 80% of the company's capitalization. The government established domes-tic content requirements for plane parts, and took explicit steps to exclude companies such as Cessna. By the mid-1970s, EMBRAER had cornered a significant part of the Brazilian small aircraft market, and its 18-passenger twin-turboprop "Bandeirante" plane was enjoying brisk sales in the US and elsewhere (Hudson, 1983). Even as the state's financial interest in the com-pany has been reduced, EMBRAER has remained an important presence in Brazilian and global markets. In the computer sector, the regime engaged in delicate negotiations with US TNCs, such as Hewlett-Packard; Olivetti; and, most notably, IBM to limit their access to the domestic computer mar-ket while at the same time creating the state-owned Cobra company and empowering privately owned local companies. Emanuel Adler describes how "pragmatic anti-dependency guerrillas" in the Commission for the Coor-dination of Electronic Processing Activities (CAPRE) launched a "national computer policy" in 1975. This initiative resulted in Brazilian companies increasing their share of the computer market from zero to 67% by 1982, and effectively crowding several powerful TNCs out of the Brazilian computer market (Adler, 1986). In this way, a rightist regime pursued variations on resource nationalism in two key sectors.

In the meantime, regional efforts to regulate TNCs gained momentum. In December 1970, the Andean Pact, which consisted of Bolivia, Chile, Colombia, Ecuador, Peru, and grew to include Venezuela in 1973, agreed on Decision 24, which provided for new national agencies to regulate FDI and technology transfer, set timetables for foreign disinvestment in majority foreign-owned firms, limited profit depatriation to 14% per year, and prohibited new foreign investment in areas such as utilities, insurance, transport, advertising, and communications (Mytelka, 1979, chapter 3). Decision 24 was implemented unevenly. But it did increase local shares of TNCs, facilitate technology transfer to the Andean nations, and provide leverage for these nations in the areas of royalty payments. And it was largely non-punitive: "despite the initial hostility of American businessmen and the sometimes negative evaluations of Decision 24 made by the Andean corporate managers, it is now quite clear that Decision 24 has not been an obstacle to continued direct foreign investment" (Mytelka, 1979, p. 111).

Neoliberalism and the Reassertion of Transnational Corporate Power

In the late 1980s, a wide variety of factors would push the region in the direction of neoliberalism and market-based reforms, once again removing many obstacles for TNCs to exercise political and economic power in Latin America. This shift didn't take place suddenly, as many South American nations were recovering from dictatorships, and Central America was still reeling from genocide and civil wars. But it emerged in full force in the late 1980s and 1990s. And, for the most part, it represented a rebuke to resource nationalism. Neoliberalism's implications for TNCs were significant: with some variation from nation to nation, levels of FDI increased dramatically, as governments opened markets and reduced restrictions on TNCs. FDI intensity shot up from 9.6% to 23.4% in the 1990–2000 period, rising in Mexico and every nation in South America (Higginbottom, 2013, p. 194).

This comprehensive move toward neoliberalism led policymakers in the region to privatize many sectors of their economies. Governments chose, often with support from global financial institutions, to open up the water sector (traditionally controlled by governments) to market forces and transnational ownership. In the 1990s and early 2000s, significant portions of water systems were privatized in Argentina, Bolivia, Brazil, Chile, Colombia, Ecuador, El Salvador, Honduras, Mexico, Nicaragua, Panama, Peru, and Uruguay. The German corporation RWE-Thames and the French corporations Suez and Vivendi became the largest transnational owners of these systems. Surveys of the effectiveness of these newly privatized systems show some increased investment and improvement of quality. These successes are often linked to strong government regulation (Clarke et al., 2009). Yet there were numerous high-profile failures and many instances of dramatic, unexplained price increases (Barlow and Clarke, 2004). Increasing foreign control over a resource that many view as a right led to protests throughout the region.

The two massive regional trade agreements, the North American Free Trade Agreement (NAFTA) and Mercosur, emerged squarely in the midst of Latin America's turn toward neoliberalism. While broadly encouraging of foreign investment in the region, the two trade agreements had slightly different objectives. NAFTA, which was finalized in 1994, was pushed in concert with Canadian and, especially, US administrations intent on allowing two richer and more industrialized economies—and the TNCs based in these two economies—greater access to the less developed Mexican economy. A different dynamic was at work in Mercosur, which includes Brazil, Uruguay, Argentina, Paraguay, and Venezuela, and was created in 1991. Nations at a relatively equal level of development (with Paraguay as a possible exception) were intent on broadening their markets and empowering member economies in relation to non-member economies. In this spirit, it represented a challenge of sorts to TNCs originating outside Mercosur. There was also a spirit of encouraging companies based within each of the member nations. In this regard, Mercosur is closely associated with the rise of TNCs operating from Brazil and Argentina, and it can be viewed as incorporating both neoliberalism and ISI—but on a regional level.

Europe eclipsed the US as the largest foreign investor in Latin America in the 1990s. Figures from 1997 show Europe edging ahead of combined US/Canadian levels, with the gap growing in the following years (Higginbottom, 2013, p. 191). Spain has accounted for a significant portion of this surge, to such an extent that, in recent years, Spanish corporations alone have eclipsed US corporate levels of investment in Latin America (Toral, 2011, p. 1). Chinese investment in the region has been marked by some high-profile projects, such as $7 billion by the Chinese petroleum company Sinopec in Brazil. And speculation about a Chinese role in building a trans-isthmian canal through Nicaragua received a great deal of attention. Nevertheless, the levels of direct Chinese investment in Latin America have been lower than expected (Jenkins, 2018, p. 229). And the Chinese state is so deeply involved in Chinese global enterprises that viewing Chinese economic actors in Latin America as genuinely transnational is problematic.

Mexico and Argentina (along with Chile and Bolivia) were among the Latin American nations that pursued neoliberalism most vigorously: FDI intensity doubled in Mexico and increased more than four-fold in Argentina (the second highest rate of increase in Latin America) from 1990 to 2000. Partly as a result of pressure from multilateral financial institutions, Mexico's President Carlos Salinas de Gortari came to power committed to a neoliberal economic agenda, and was deeply involved in crafting NAFTA. Mexican privatization was accompanied by such high levels of corruption and insider dealing that Salinas and his family faced legal prosecution in subsequent years. As Salinas departed from office and NAFTA came into effect, the Zapatista movement revealed itself in early 1994 as a radical oppositional force to neoliberalism, both in southern Mexico and around the globe, with its savvy use of social media. In 1989 Carlos Menem moved quickly to open up the Argentinian economy to foreign investment and market forces. The government privatized petroleum, telephones, airlines, the postal service, nuclear plants, and electricity. Many of these industries were bought up by TNCs, which included Exxon, Royal Dutch Shell, Phillip Morris, Unilever, and the Spanish company Repsol (CEPAL, 1998, pp. 85–86). Numerous local water authorities were sold off to a combination of national and transnational companies (Clarke et al., 2009). Menem was implicated in a series of scandals, including receiving bribes from the German company Siemens for a contract to administer the national passport program. For many Argentinians, the latter scandal connected his corruption to transnational corporate influence.

TNCs and the Rise and Fall of the Pink Revolution

The details of Mexico and Argentina's (and Bolivia's) problematic experience with neoliberal economic policies help explain what came over the next several decades: a region-wide move to the left known as the "pink revolution." The rise of left and center-left regimes in almost all Latin American nations during this period did represent a dramatic break from the recent past. Figures such as Hugo Chávez in Venezuela; Evo Morales in Bolivia; Tabaré Vázquez in Uruguay; Rafael Correa in Ecuador; Néstor and Cristina Kirchner in Argentina; Michelle Bachelet in Chile; Luis Inácio "Lula" da Silva in Brazil; Ollanta Humala in Peru; Daniel Ortega in Nicaragua; and, most recently, Andrés Manuel López Obrador in Mexico led this regional movement to the left. They shared some important features: a loose allegiance to social-democratic ideals, a base in either unions or left-of-center political parties, and strong resistance to the rightist dictatorships of the 1970s and 1980s. And in some cases, most notably in Bolivia and Ecuador, they came to power as a result of radical protests against neoliberalism and its local allies.

It was in their approaches to TNCs and resource nationalism that their differences may have been just as significant as their similarities. In his comparative study of these regimes, Gustavo Flores-Macías describes as "statist" the approaches of Venezuela under Chávez, Ecuador under Correa, Bolivia under Morales, and Argentina under the Kirchners. In contrast, he categorizes Chile under Ricardo Lagos and Bachelet (and the rightist regimes of Mexico's Vicente Fox and Colombia's Álvaro Uribe) as "pro-market." Lula in Brazil, Daniel Ortega in Nicaragua, and Tabaré Vázquez in Uruguay are labeled "neutral"

(Flores-Macías, 2012, pp. 60–93). Accordingly, between 2000 and 2010, FDI Intensity was reduced from 61.8% to 35.0% in Bolivia, 39.8% to 20.1% in Ecuador, and 30.3% to 10.3% in Venezuela. The dramatic 1990–2000 increases in this ratio that occurred across the region largely remained in place or grew further in all other Latin American nations from 2000 to 2010 (Higginbottom, 2013, p. 194). Higginbottom makes this point explicitly political when he maintains that this latter group of nations "is openly collusive with foreign capital," and that the group of Bolivia, Ecuador, and Venezuela "seeks to regulate and contain the penetration of global capital" and "have sought less one-sided terms of engagement with foreign investors" (ibid, pp. 184, 195).

Each of the four "statist" examples took significant steps to rein in the power of TNCs. The Chávez government in Venezuela moved early to put the state in control of all oil production by nationalizing the French company Total and the Italian company ENI. The Chávez regime also nationalized the Mexican cement company CEMEX, the Argentinian steel maker Ternium Sidor, the Spanish coffee company Café Madrid, the Spanish bank Santander, the US rice processor Cargill, and the Hilton Hotel company. Rafael Correa in Ecuador took many of the same steps, effectively nationalizing the oil industry and mandating that 12% of oil profits must go to anti-poverty programs. The Argentinian government under Néstor Kirchner nationalized the European telecommunications corporation Thales Spectrum in 2004 and the French company administering potable water in Buenos Aires in 2006 (Flores-Macías, pp. 33–42). For all of his moderation toward TNCs, Lula did defy US-based pharmaceutical companies in his efforts to bypass patents and increase Brazilian and global access to anti-AIDs medications (Notisur, 2007). The Bolivian and Chilean cases, at the end of this chapter, provide added details of two contrasting approaches to TNCs.

Even as the Mexican leftist Andrés Manuel López Obrador was elected in 2018, the leaders of Ecuador and Bolivia have been replaced by rightists explicitly calling for neoliberal economic policies, Chávez's successor Nicolás Maduro has driven Venezuela's economy into the ground and committed serious human rights abuses in his efforts to hold on to power, and the legacy of Lula and Dilma Rousseff in Brazil is being quickly undone by corruption investigations and the extreme right-wing policies of Jair Bolsonaro. On a more specific level, the model of nations asserting themselves in relation to powerful TNCs has once again given way to a pro-market, neoliberal orientation. FDI intensity for the region grew from 33% to 48% from 2012 to 2018, with dramatic increases in Uruguay, Chile, Peru, Colombia, Brazil, and every Central American nation (CEPAL, 2019, p. 83).

Yet economic policy in the region is not moving uniformly rightward. One surprising recent outcome is the US-Mexico-Canada agreement (USMCA), which went into effect in July 2020. Despite its association with the Trump administration and the general neoliberal trends in the region, the USMCA provides for generally tougher restrictions on TNCs as they do business in the region: its environmental and labor standards are stricter, and most observers believe that the enforcement mechanisms are stronger (Swanson, 2020). And several nations have been marked by popular high-profile mobilization against TNCs and the governments associated with them. Most notable in this regard has been Ecuador, which was brought to a standstill by explicitly anti-neoliberal protests led by leftists and indigenous rights organizations in late 2019. This mobilization led to significant concessions from the rightist government. Similar forces were at work in the fall of Argentinian rightist Mauricio Macri and the rise (in alliance with Christina Kirchner) of leftist Alberto Fernandez (Tharoor, 2019). Protests in Chile and the return of Evo Morales's allies to power in Bolivia in 2020 are more closely examined in the case studies to follow. All these developments have led to speculation about new challenges to corporations and neoliberalism in the region.

Transnational activists and intergovernmental organizations have countered the trend toward unconstrained transnational corporate power by pushing the norm of "CSR." It has been pushed by organizations such as the Institute for Human Rights and Business, the Business Leaders' Initiative on Human Rights, and the Clean Clothes Campaign; Oxfam, Earthrights International, Global Witness, Human Rights Watch, Amnesty International, and Human Rights First have participated as well (Ruggie, 2013). The outcome has been a series of effective campaigns to encourage CSR, and to hold corporations accountable for human rights violations and socioeconomic injustice. Paul Haslam describes a process which "transforms the terrain on which businesses interact with other actors from one of power (where business was clearly dominant) to a terrain of (at least partial) legitimacy." This trend helps to explain high-profile cases in which local groups successfully mobilized against transnational mining companies in Peru and oil companies in Ecuador. The larger result has been a set of "emerging norms on CSR" and a "legitimacy regime" which has enabled activists to "convert the moral resources of community stakeholders into power resources at the bargaining table" (Haslam, 2007, pp. 270, 296). In 2011, the UN unanimously adopted a series of "Guiding Principles on Business and Human Rights," which have been embraced and implemented by corporations, intergovernmental organizations, human rights networks, and labor groups (Ruggie, 2013). They have begun to influence jurisprudence at the international and national levels, especially in regard to establishing minimum standards for corporate human rights performance and in influencing tort law (Glinska, 2017). In recent years, the Inter-American Court of Human Rights has begun to hear cases on corporate behavior in the region (London-Lázaro et al., 2017).

As governments around the region struggle with issues of economic dependency and development, there is some hope that these global legal and political trends will prod corporations into decisions that reflect more than their bottom lines.

The Politics of Transnational Corporations in Bolivia

Before its independence, the future nation of Bolivia played a crucial role in the colonial economy of Spain, as it provided much of the silver making its way to Spain and, ultimately, the rest of Europe. The colonial trade in silver was an early version of the intense external orientation that was to define much of Bolivia's national economic history. Building partly on the precedent of silver mining, the extraction of tin became the engine of the Bolivian economy, accounting for 41.0% of Bolivia's export earnings by 1900 and 73.8% in 1930 (Gallo, 1991, p. 33). Three dominant corporations emerged: the Patiño, Aramayo, and Hochschild companies, which collectively became known as the "Rosca." Simón Patiño became the dominant economic figure in Bolivia, and his company's rise is illustrative of how the aluminum industry began as a Bolivian enterprise, but became transnational. Patiño was gradually able to buy up Chilean- and British-owned mines, and set up processing plants in Europe and the US. He chose, in 1925, when faced with the threat of higher taxes from the Bolivian government, to formalize the company's transnationalization by incorporating in the US and moving his headquarters to the business-friendly state of Delaware. Aramayo, the second largest tin company, also had its origins in Bolivia, but formally incorporated in Switzerland in 1915 (Dunkerley, 1984, pp. 7–9).

In her analysis, Carmenza Gallo uses the term "enclave" in describing the tin industry and its place in the Bolivian political and economic system. She notes that "the tin industry was more integrated into the international market…than into the internal market" (Gallo, 1991, p. 33). Labor legislation was "minimal," with no provisions for minimum wages, workplace safety, or working hours until the late 1930s. Mining camps were "bleak and dangerous industrial outposts populated entirely by communities entirely dependent upon their employer for power, housing, food and medical care as well as work" (Dunkerley, 1984, pp. 13–14). Given the location of the tin facilities high in the Bolivian mountains, the economic and political isolation was even more pronounced than in a typical enclave setting. The Patiño Company built its own utility plants, set up its own postal service, and had its own security forces at the mines. These forces collaborated with the military to perpetrate large-scale massacres of mineworkers in 1923, 1942, and 1947 (Young, 2017, p. 16). According to Gallo, "the isolation and quasi-independence of mining camps with respect to the central government and the internal market was enhanced by the routine co-optation of local authorities by the companies' management" (Gallo, 1991, p. 36). The extreme conditions and the proximity of workers to one another in the mines led to one of the strongest and most radicalized union movements in Latin America (Dunkerley, 1984, p. 13).

Bolivia's small oil sector was initially controlled completely by Standard Oil, which began extracting in 1921. Bolivia's lack of a coastal outlet meant that oil shipments had to go through Argentina. This arrangement was crucial to the start of the Chaco War in 1932, when Argentina closed its border to Bolivia, denying this shipping access. In addition, the war was also fought over the Chaco region, which was thought to contain massive oil reserves. Two years after Bolivia's defeat in the war, during a three-year period of "military socialist government," the Bolivian government nationalized the small Standard Oil facility and created the Bolivian State Oil Fields Company (YPFB) in 1937. The regime also increased taxes on tin exports and forged strong ties with the tin workers (Gallo, 1991, p. 97). Radicalized veterans of the Chaco War pushed the state to adopt policies reflecting resource nationalism (Young, 2017, pp. 24, 28).

Two key opposition groups emerged in subsequent years. First, the political party Nationalist Revolutionary Movement (MNR) was created in 1941 by a coalition based in labor and peasant organizations, the emerging middle class, and reformist and nationalist factions in the military. Young notes that the rise of the MNR "paralleled" the emergence of resource nationalism, which had appeared as early as the 1920s as a rallying cry against the "Rosca" and, to a lesser extent, the foreign oil companies. By the early 1940s, resource nationalism had become "the most pervasive ideological force in Bolivian politics" (Young, 2017, p. 29). The military's refusal to recognize the MNR's success in the 1951 elections set off nationwide protests, strikes, and a concerted military campaign in several major cities. In April 1952, a revolutionary alliance of the MNR, the labor unions, and key factions within the military seized power (Young, 2017, pp. 29–34).

The MNR, under the leadership of Victor Paz Estenssoro, came to power with an agenda devoted to fundamental change in Bolivian society. The Bolivian Workers' Central (CBO) was created in the immediate wake of the revolution to centralize all the revolutionary worker's organizations. Dunkerley notes that the CBO was "one of the most militant trade organizations in the world" and, in the years after the revolution, "the most powerful body in Bolivian public life" (Dunkerley, 1984, p. 43). In this setting, it was no surprise that resource nationalism was a guiding principle for the new regime, and the nationalization of the tin industry became its top priority. In October, political and labor leaders announced a nationalization decree that established the state-run Bolivian Mining Corporation (Comibol) as the owner and administrator of all tin facilities previously owned by the Patiño, Hochschild, and Aramayo companies—the government takeover of the "Rosca" in its entirety. The agreement included $27 million in compensation to the companies. The US government was convinced by able diplomatic work from the Bolivians that the new regime did not represent a communist geopolitical threat (Young, 2017, pp. 53–56).

The new state-run arrangements proved immediately problematic. Comibol had to struggle to provide the same kind of technological development that a far-flung TNC would have had access to. It also became marked by mismanagement, bureaucratization, and politicization. These problems took only a few years to become a matter of major political contention, and almost immediately brought the long-term future of the state-run tin sector into question. The first steps toward an opening up of the Bolivian economy to TNCs did not take place with tin, but rather in the oil sector. The 1955 New Petroleum Code, originally drafted by a US firm and known as the "codigo Davenport," set extremely generous provisions for foreign oil exploration and investment (Young, 2017, pp. 62–63). Gulf Oil came to dominate the Bolivian oil industry, accounting for over 80% of oil production by the late 1960s. Gulf would, however, once again fall prey to a regime inspired by resource nationalism, as its Bolivian holdings were expropriated during the short-lived rule of General Alfredo Ovando Candía in 1969. In early 1970, Bolivia joined in Decision 24 of the Andean Pact, which (as noted previously in this chapter) represented a regional effort to increase leverage over TNCs (Mytelka, 1979, pp. 29–38; Dunkerley, 1984, p. 128).

During the 1970s, encouraged by international banks and by rising oil and tin prices, the Bolivian government borrowed heavily. As commodity prices fell in the 1980s, Bolivia was marked by massive government debt, hyperinflation and a collapsed currency, and daily strikes by the still-powerful labor movement. None other than Victor Paz Estenssoro and the MNR, central actors in the 1952 revolution, came to power in 1985 and quickly initiated the New Economic Policy, a high-profile and early case of a "structural adjustment program" imposed by international financial institutions. It dramatically reduced government spending, calling for the privatization of state-owned enterprises, tagging the Bolivian currency to the US dollar, and encouraging TNCs to invest. Yet foreign investment only materialized in large numbers with a second set of MNR-backed policies launched in 1993, under the leadership of Gonzalo Sánchez de Lozado (known as "Goni"). These policies led to dramatic increases in foreign investment: Bolivia's FDI intensity rose from 21.1% in 1990 to 61.8% in 2000, the highest in the region (Higginbottom, 2013, p. 194). State-owned airlines and railroads, electricity, and hydrocarbon and telecommunications companies were sold off to a mixture of US, Italian, Argentinian, Brazilian, and Chilean TNCs. In 1999, the state privatized the Cochabamba water system and sold it to a consortium led by Bechtel, the huge US-based construction company. In virtually all privatized sectors, new transnational ownership moved to quickly slash jobs; the railroad company, for example, reduced its workforce by 80% (Kohl, 2004, pp. 903–904).

Foreign ownership was only one of many factors in protests that dominated Bolivian politics in the early 2000s. But the huge foreign economic presence reminded many Bolivians of their vulnerabilities to forces beyond their control (Dangl, 2007, p. 45). And the rise of indigenous rights activism became closely linked to issues of economic justice and foreign economic control. In this setting, TNCs would become a target for mass-based protests.

Resource nationalism was central to these actions, and the protests added a grassroots element to its larger economic argument. Not for the first time in Bolivian history, there was a perception among many on the left and within the military that government policy toward TNCs had offended national pride. The military, for example, viewed the sale of the railroads to a Chilean company as a threat to national security and an insult to Bolivian honor (Kohl, 2004, p. 899).

It would be two "wars" against the government and its collaboration with TNCs that would set Bolivia in a markedly different direction over the next decade. In response to dramatic increases in water prices levied by the Bechtel-controlled water company, the people of Cochabamba formed the Committee to Defend Water and Life in early 2000, and mounted protests that repeatedly shut down the city. The government initially responded with violence, but then quickly gave in to public pressure by terminating the water contract with Bechtel. Flush from victory, protestors led by Evo Morales and Felipe Quispe fought against water laws that had allowed the sale to Bechtel—"an easy target as it symbolized the worst of neoliberalism—the privatization of water, a gift from the heavens and the essence of life" (Dangl, 2007; Kohl, 2006, p. 318). This struggle over water would prove crucial to the emergence of coordination among increasingly successful water-rights groups across Latin America (Dupuits, 2019). In 2003, the "gas war" also focused explicitly on the government's relations with TNCs. In the wake of oil privatizations, the government had contracted with a consortium that included Exxon, British Gas, British Petroleum, the Spanish firm Repsol, and the French firm ELF to build a pipeline through Chile exclusively for export, a tendentious decision given Chile's status as a traditional geopolitical enemy and the revelation that new standards for negotiation had reduced the royalties to the state from 50% to 18% (Kohl, 2004, p. 904, 2006, pp. 319–320). Anti-globalization activists, military nationalists, veterans of the Chaco War, union leaders, and coca growers formed an explicit alliance in July 2002. Nationwide protests in early 2003 led to the deaths of 80 people at the hands of the military. But the protests grew to include hundreds of thousands of people across Bolivia, and Goni was forced to resign and flee to the US in October 2003 (Dangl, 2007, pp. 145–151).

Carlos Mesa assumed power and, over the next two years, gradually moved to ally himself with the business community and transnational interests. In a March 2005 speech he criticized nationalist proposals for a hydrocarbon law: "Brazil has told us, Spain has told us, the World Bank, the United States, the International Monetary Fund, Great Britain, and all of the European Union: Bolivians, approve a law that is viable and acceptable to the international community" (quoted in Spronk and Webber, 2007, p. 37). But Mesa's words defied an emerging, grassroots movement based on resource nationalism. He chose to resign in June 2005, and in December, Evo Morales and his Movement Toward Socialism (MAS) party won 54% of the vote in national elections, twice that of the nearest contender and the first absolute majority for a candidate since Bolivia's return to democracy in 1982.

Near or at the top of Evo Morales's agenda was a set of policies to exert greater state and popular control over key resources and economic sectors. Indeed, both the protests leading to Evo's rise and his platform as he took power closely resembled the norm of resource nationalism, defined as a "collective action master frame that merges nationalist and anti-imperialist ideologies with natural resource-based demands" (Kohl and Farthing, 2012, p. 225). In a symbolically important act, on May 1, 2006, the government placed banners at Bolivia's gas stations, oil refineries, and natural gas fields with the message "Nationalized: Property of Bolivia." Yet, if the term "nationalization" is taken to mean the complete government takeover of an industry or company, the banners were misleading. It became clear that the Morales government was intent on gaining control of the hydrocarbon sector, but through majority ownership and negotiating more favorable terms with the TNCs, a process described as "negotiating nationalization." In most cases royalty level agreements with transnational companies rose to 50% for the Bolivian state, one of highest levels in Latin America, and a central reason that the Morales government was able to provide funding for ambitious social initiatives without falling into ruinous debt. For the most part, transnational hydrocarbon companies, including BP, British Gas, Exxon, Total, and Repsol, resigned themselves to this arrangement and came to a relatively harmonious working relationship with the Morales government. YPFB, down to a few hundred employees in the wake of the earlier waves of privatizations, grew dramatically, and became an important actor and collaborator in the Bolivian hydrocarbon sector (Botham, 2008).

The Morales administration passed laws explicitly banning water privatization and set up the Interinstitutional Water Council (CONIAG) to facilitate collaboration among the state, grassroots organizations, and businesses, and as a barrier to transnational corporate control of water. By 2012, the Morales administration fully or partially nationalized three tin mines owned by the Swiss Glencore company. And on May 1, 2012, the government expropriated the national electric grid from the Spanish company Red Electrica (Farthing and Kohl, 2014, p. 75). Figures on total foreign investment reflect the general thrust of government policy toward TNCs under Morales: FDI intensity declined from the extremely high 2000 level of 61.8% to 41.8% in 2007, and then to 35.0% in 2010. From 2012 to 2018, these levels remained more or less constant in the low and mid-30s, a higher level than Ecuador, Argentina, and Venezuela (CEPAL, 2019). The tolerable, or even harmonious, relations between the government and numerous TNCs in the wake of "negotiated nationalism" allowed the companies to continue to make money in Bolivia and provide sustained prosperity for broad sectors of the Bolivian populace. Yet these arrangements also allowed the regime to remain mostly faithful to the norm of resource nationalism—although not enough to entirely silence critics from the left.

It was initially unclear whether the 2019 ouster of Evo Morales was just one more chapter in the struggle over control of the Bolivian economy or simply reflected disputes at the very highest levels of Bolivian politics. The violence and racism of the coup plotters and their nod to neoliberal economic policies (and even the Trump administration) were met by widespread protests at the hands of Morales's supporters (Anderson, 2020). These protests, and the successful campaign of Morales ally Luis Arce, led to the MAS' decisive electoral victory in October 2020 and a likely return to the policies of the previous 15 years. It appears that the model for relations among the people, the Bolivian state, and TNCs crafted by Morales will remain in place (Young, 2020).

The Politics of Transnational Corporations in Chile

When copper was first mined in a rudimentary form in Chile during the second half of the 19th century, it was controlled by domestic interests, and Chile became the world's leading exporter of copper. But, as easily accessed ore was exhausted, global business interests came to enjoy a decisive advantage in gaining access to Chilean copper (Moran, 1974, pp. 20–22). Through rapid investment from a variety of US interests, the US companies Kennecott and Anaconda came to control all large-scale mining in Chile by 1923, accounting for between 80% and 90% of Chilean copper production, in what became known as "Gran Minería" (Sigmund, 1980, p. 136). Driven by the foreign-dominated copper sector, Chilean FDI Intensity rose to the second highest level in the region in 1929 and 1938 (Twomey, 1998, p. 6).

In his broad study of TNCs, Rhys Jenkins singles out copper in Chile as "a classic enclave sector" (Jenkins, 1987a, p. 181). Theodore Moran notes that the transnational companies' control of technology and capital "placed the companies in a strong position to expect, or demand, generous initial concessions from the Chilean government" (Moran, 1974, p. 23). The government initially failed to tax transnational copper company profits at all, with a 6% rate introduced in 1922, an additional 6% in 1925, and again in 1934 (Sigmund, 1980, p. 136). Even with these modest increases, only 16% of the profits from copper production remained in Chile in 1930 (Vernon, 1970, p. 125). The companies controlled every step of the process of mining, refining, and transporting copper. Conditions in the mines were harsh, and there was initially little regulation moderating company treatment of workers. Communities adjacent to the Anaconda-owned Potrerillos mine were marked by "repression, paternalistic ideas and total control" of the workforce, based on factors such as the company store and compulsory company identification cards. The company built and controlled rail networks connecting the mine, nearby towns, and the port, avoided paying local taxes, and did little to aid municipal projects such as water systems, while systematically segregating Chilean workers from their higher-paid US counterparts (Vergara, 2003, pp. 391, 393). Silicosis, a classic symptom of unsafe working conditions in mines, was so prevalent that it, more than any other labor-related concern, was "the central subject of all workers' demands" (Vergara, 2005, p. 730; Montano, 2019).

A number of factors slowly came together to constrain the power of the transnational copper companies in Chile over the following decades. Chile had a strong democratic tradition, and the Radical, Socialist, and Communist parties had close ties with workers' organizations. Just as important was the emergence of nationalist politics in opposition to the copper companies, and as a response to the vulnerabilities exposed by the Great Depression and the resulting shrinking of external markets. The result was the gradual emergence of a resource nationalism norm that would be a central part of Chilean politics even through the Pinochet dictatorship. Beginning in the 1930s, the government and nationalist business interests "created an entire institutional framework around the protection and promotion of its industrial manufacturing sector," based on the spirit of ISI and the imperative of finding alternatives to transnational economic power (Bucheli and Salvaj, 2018, p. 406). In 1938, the state created a national development corporation (CORFO) and increased taxes on the copper companies. This policy, and others, brought on increases in the Chilean share of copper profits from 16% in 1930 to 28% in 1940 and 58% in 1950 (Vernon, 1970, p. 125). The state created the Copper Office in 1955, and then the Copper Corporation of Chile (CODELCO) in 1966.

TNCs established themselves as important actors in other parts of the Chilean economy, including the oil and telecommunications sectors. These companies were, from the start, challenged by Chilean nationalists. In response to imminent TNC oil exploration in Chile in 1928, the legislature passed a law suspending the authority of the president to grant oil concessions and providing the national government substantial sums for exploration of its own (Wilkins, 1974, p. 443); in 1934, it created the Chilean Petroleum Company (COPEC) (Bucheli and Salvaj, 2018, pp. 407, 409). ITT gained control of 78% of the Chilean telecommunications market in 1927. ITT would periodically become the target of protests when rate hikes, determined in collaboration with the state, were seen as overly steep. Political parties from across the political spectrum attacked ITT, culminating in a formal Congressional debate in 1962 about the company's future in Chile (Bucheli and Savaj, 2018, p. 412).

In the 1964 elections, both the left-of-center Christian Democrats and the leftist coalition ran on high-profile platforms of dramatically curtailing the power of TNCs in Chile, reflecting widespread popular support for resource nationalism. The victorious Christian Democrats, under the leadership of Eduardo Frei, pledged to pursue a policy of "Chileanization" in the copper sector and outright nationalization in other sectors. This party was buoyed by the support of the US government, which viewed it as a non-communist vehicle for reform in Chile. Frei backed off on initial pledges to nationalize telecommunications and gas distribution. But because of copper's prominent role in the economy and considerable pressure from the left for nationalization, Frei moved quickly to "Chileanize" Kennecott, assuming a 51% interest in the company, and, after revelations about secret negotiations with the companies radicalized Chilean public opinion, did the same with Anaconda in 1969. This arrangement set the stage for more dramatic steps in the 1970s (Moran, 1974, pp. 121–146).

Salvador Allende, leading the leftist Popular Unity coalition, won the 1970 elections with an unambiguous platform of nationalization. Radomiro Tomic, the Christian Democratic candidate, was also a strong advocate for national-izing the copper industry. Allende's stance, and the shift from US support for the Christian Democratic government to open (and covert) antagonism toward Allende, led to politicization and polarization around a series of issues. But there was broad consensus within Chile in support of full nationalization of the copper companies and resource nationalism more generally. In July 1971, the Chilean Congress unanimously approved a decree for the transfer of ownership of all foreign-owned copper mines to CODELCO, which, based on formulas for past "excess profits," included no compensation for the TNCs (Sigmund, 1980, p. 153, passim).

In the context of the Chilean state's unanimous declaration of its political will to take over the copper sector, it is important to step back and assess the technical capacity to do so and to keep it running as a viable economic enter-prise. Raymond Vernon's in-depth study of Chilean copper traces the steps toward nationalization in the decades leading up to the nationalization decision of 1971: "During that period they developed the skills necessary to mine cop-per, smelt it, refine it, and by the early 1970s they possessed the capacity to carry out all the operations of production on a larger scale of their own" (Vernon, 1974, p. 3). This capacity would ultimately prove more significant than political considerations in maintaining a state role in the copper sector.

Soon after taking power, the Allende government began the process of na-tionalizing whole sectors of the Chilean economy. Among the companies whose Chilean facilities were seized were Bethlehem Steel, Ralston Purina, Coca Cola, General Electric, Pfizer, Dupont, Dow Chemical, Ford, and General Motors (Sigmund, 1980, pp. 155–160). In some instances, transnational compa-nies were seized as strikes were being carried out by workers with strong ties to the Socialist and Communist parties. The nationalization of ITT was especially fraught, not because of government overreach but because of the company's role in the early CIA-led conspiracy against Allende, which sped the widely supported decision to nationalize the firm in September 1971. In sharp contrast, foreign oil companies affiliated with the Chilean state company COPEC were spared nationalization, even as many other oil-related transnational compa-nies (such as Dow Chemical) were expropriated. Formal ties to a state-owned company provided political cover, while conspiracy with the US government virtually assured nationalization (Bucheli and Salvaj, 2018, p. 412). Non-US transnational companies also tended to receive gentler treatment, since the Al-lende government was depending on Latin American and European credits to weather an economic crisis (Sigmund, 1980, p. 164).

In a setting of national polarization and economic crisis, the Allende government was overthrown on September 11, 1973, and one of Latin America's most democratic nations was plunged into a prolonged military dictatorship. Nationalization policy was not the only factor in the coup of 1973. But it would also be foolish to downplay the significance of the decisions by the Allende government to expropriate the wealth of companies with a transnational reach. That these companies could, in the early 1970s, look to an aggressive, anti-communist US government to support their interests in Chile may have been crucial.

The Chilean dictatorship led by Augusto Pinochet systematically clamped down on Chilean civil society, committed widespread human rights abuses, and pursued neoliberal policies during its decade and a half in power. But a closer examination of the Pinochet dictatorship, with a focus on its relations with TNCs, brings out important complexities in its policies. There was little question that, in the wake of what was viewed by the dictatorship as a failed socialist experiment, the military government would prioritize the interests of business. But this was not the only priority, and there were important divisions among economic nationalists, radical internationalists (the "Chicago Boys), and economic pragmatists as well as different factions within the state and the military (Silva, 1993).

The Pinochet regime took quick and high-profile steps to provide compensation to ITT, Kennecott, and Anaconda for expropriations prior to 1973. In 1974, it issued a decree putting in place tax concessions, subsidies, tariffs, and repatriation policies designed to attract foreign investment. Chile withdrew from the Andean Pact in 1976 (Mytelka, 1979, p. 73). The new 1980 Constitution and the 1983 Mining Code unambiguously put TNCs on an equal legal footing with state-run and national businesses, and provided a setting which systematically favored property rights and the private sector (Nem Singh, 2010, p. 1421). But several factors led the regime away from comprehensively favoring TNCs in the 1970s and early 1980s. First, in the years immediately after the coup, the military prevailed over free-marketers in its insistence on CODELCO's continued role, put a General in charge of the state-run company, and set up a system in which proceeds from CODELCO would go directly to military (Nem Singh, 2010, p. 1422; Haslam, 2016, p. 1155). Second, despite the welcoming policy environment, TNCs were slow to rush into Chile in the wake of the coup. Politically connected national business interests moved into this vacuum. The result was a roughly eight-year period in which Chilean-owned "conglomerates" emerged in virtually every sector of the economy (Fernández Jilberto, 2004, pp. 192, 190). In this more conservative, pro-business guise, a form of resource nationalism survived. This approach did not provide a lasting blueprint for Chilean prosperity, however, as it led to a profound economic crisis in the early 1980s.

Beginning in 1985, with the lessons of the economic crises of both the early 1970s and the early 1980s on their minds, Chilean economic planners pursued policies that catered to TNCs and led to "the overall denationalization and globalization of the Chilean economy" (Silva, 1993, p. 555; Fernández Jilberto, 2004, p. 199). The government was acutely aware of the failure of local, Chilean interests to invest in diverse economic sectors, and looked to international capital. The "transnationalization" of the economy happened rapidly during this five-year period. By 1988, 13 of the 19 largest privatized public companies came under control of transnational companies. A common strategy was for transnational companies to gain a controlling interest in the Chilean privately owned "conglomerates" that had emerged in the late 1970s, "transnationalizing" the privatization and market concentration that had taken place ten years earlier (Fernández Jilberto, 2004, p. 198).

A vast political transformation took place in Chile at the end of the 1980s, as courageous activists and politicians took steps to end a decade-and-a-half of repression, and once again establish Chile as a genuine multi-party democracy. Yet the commitment to neoliberal policies with a strong transnational orientation remained firmly in place. In post-Pinochet Chile, democratization did not result in resource nationalism. This orientation comes out most clearly in FDI Intensity figures. In 1990, the ratio of FDI to GDP stood at 48.1%, over double that of any other nation in South America. It rose to 60.8% in 2000 and to 76% in 2010 (Higginbottom, 2013, p. 194), and 102% in 2016 (CEPAL, 2019). At a purely electoral level, Chile can be included as one of the nations that were part of the "pink revolution" in Latin America in the past two decades, with Socialists controlling the Chilean presidency from 2000 to 2010 and from 2014 to 2018. But Ricardo Lagos and Michelle Bachelet heightened the Chilean commitment to internationalizing its economy. Flores-Macías, in his comparative study of "pink revolution" governments, places Chile at the most free-market end of the spectrum (Flores-Macías, 2012, chapter 2). Chile, led by socialists, has chosen foreign investment over resource nationalism in the 21st century.

The list of transnational companies operating in Chile is long, and includes such household names as Royal-Dutch Shell, Nestle, Exxon Mobil, Unilever, Phelps Dodge, General Motors, Coca Cola, and Johnson & Johnson. Transnational companies came to either dominate or hold significant market shares in virtually every sector of the Chilean economy. They dramatically increased their presence in the oil, automobile, sugar, beer, electricity, airlines, steel, telecommunications, banking, chemical, paper, and forestry sectors. The Aylwin government kept the 1974 Foreign Investment Statute and the 1983 Mining Code firmly in place. Both the Christian Democrat governments of the 1990s and the Socialist governments of the 2000s were noted for their "institutional stability and openness to foreign capital" (Nem Singh, 2010, pp. 1422, 1414). CODELCO continues to control some of the largest copper mines in Chile and has expanded its operations to three new large-scale mines. But the presence of transnational companies in the copper sector has increased even more dramatically, with 14 new large private mines commissioned since 1990 (Lagos, 2017). By 2018, the private, internationalized copper sector came to account for almost 70% of copper produced in Chile (Leiva, 2019, p. 136).

Chile's system for exploiting and developing water resources was privatized during the Pinochet regime, and has become the subject of significant contention, especially among indigenous communities (Prieto, 2015). The government's approach to managing facilities for providing water to the Chilean populace as a utility has been more complicated. Prior to 1981 and throughout much of Chilean history, local public institutions provided water services to urban areas. This continued to be the case until 1999, even though a water code described as "the most free market-oriented water code in the world" was passed in 1981 (Bauer, 2004, p. 1). In 1999, a consortium led by Spanish and French TNCs bought 51% of the shares in the Santiago municipal water service. Numerous other systems were sold to Chilean business interests and transnational companies. The new systems mostly met ambitious goals for providing clean water to virtually the entire urban population at levels unmatched in the rest of Latin America. The government had in place a strong system for regulating private companies and provided subsidies for poor Chileans. Madeline Baer argues that

> the strong state capacity to govern the water sector in the public interest by embedding reforms in state interventions explains the relative success of the Chilean water sector and the fulfillment of the minimum criteria for the human right to water.
>
> *(Baer, 2015, pp. 163–164)*

Despite these successes in the area of water services, there have been recent protests against opening up to international market forces what many Chileans believe should be a fundamental right (Gallagher, 2016).

Chile has moved so far in the direction of welcoming transnational investment that it is tempting to view it as an example of neoliberalism run amok. And the 2010 Copiapó mine collapse, which received massive global media coverage, seemed to confirm every preconception about the dangers posed by under-regulated transnational copper companies (Tobar, 2014). Fernández Jilberto describes a "neo-liberal technocracy" of former Pinochet officials: "These so-called 'men of the privatizations' are made up of former ministers, former sub-secretaries, former executives of the former public companies, former officers and generals of the armed forces and last but not least relatives of the dictator himself" (Fernández Jilberto, 2004, p. 202). In the worst kind of fraudulent "revolving door" between public and private interests, it was this group that oversaw the transactions that internationalized the Chilean economy, and put much of it in the hands of TNCs.

Yet a closer examination of the relation among TNCs, the government, and Chilean social forces reveals the extent to which the transnational presence in Chile, as pervasive as it is, has been, in turn, influenced by the Chilean political system. TNCs have become such a central part of Chilean economic life that a large portion of the political left and the government bureaucracy has become closely associated with their presence. However, the state-run mining company CODELCO continues to survive and thrive alongside an increasingly internationalized copper sector.

> Both Codelco and the private sector have benefited from the natural creation of a mining technology cluster, from the competition for management and worker skills, from different styles of administration, investing and operating, and from diverse environmental and social corporate policies.
>
> *(Lagos, 2017)*

In a variation on this relationship between the Chilean state and TNCs, the Chilean version of water privatization, even as it has sold off water interests to national and international companies, has for the most part succeeded in effectively providing water to its citizenry. It has done so through a "strong regulatory framework," "strong state capacity," and by "embedding reforms in state interventions" (Baer, 2015, pp. 163–164).

The cushioning of neoliberal policies that favor TNCs has also been achieved on a more general political level by the Chilean state. This approach could be seen several decades earlier, as the Pinochet regime gave in to widespread protests over its initial decision to dismantle a highly successful state-run milk provision system, keeping the program in place and, partly as a result, ensuring low Chilean levels of infant malnourishment to this day (Weil, 2017). Successive socialist regimes took a similar approach in the 21st century: in 2002, the Lagos government initiated the Chile Solidarity policy, which targeted the poorest 5% of the population, roughly one million Chileans, with an array of social services; in 2007, the Bachelet government initiated "Chile Grows with You," a program which has succeeded in providing the most marginalized Chileans access to the national early education and health systems; and in 2018, the Chilean legislature passed a law guaranteeing free college education to the poorest 60% of Chileans (Carneiro et al., 2014; Milman et al., 2018). These policies did little to steer ostensibly socialist leaders away from their commitment to a neoliberal economic strategy that empowered TNCs. But they are symptomatic of a kind of pro-TNC approach that is not immune to influence from the Chilean political system, and is also indebted to social-democratic principles of generous welfare provisions.

Processes at the global level have also influenced transnational corporate behavior in Chile. Chile was the first Latin American nation to join the UN Global Compact and the Global Reporting Initiative in 2001, an important intergovernmental effort in the area of CSR. Beckman and her collaborators describe a "virtuous relationship cycle" in which TNCs, encouraged and pushed by both local and transnational NGOs, adopt recognized CSR standards, which, in turn, pressures local businesses to do the same. In this way, CSR standards are "imported" by external companies. A "network of stakeholders," which includes local and transnational activists, unions, government officials, and community organizations provides the political incentive for the companies—both local and transnational—to sustain their commitment to CSR (Beckman et al., 2009).

Fernando Leiva's account of the Chilean copper companies' response to reductions in global prices and anti-corporate protests in the early 2010s is worth quoting at length: "Chile's strategic mining sector has become a key site where local and foreign transnational capital alongside center-left epistemic communities are... actively engaging local organizations, government agencies, civil-society entities and academic institutions" in mining-related projects. Leiva's distinctly critical perspective leads him to conclude that the ultimate goal for these efforts is "producing political technologies to deter, deflect, and ultimately defeat community resistances to megaprojects in mining, lumber and cellulose, hydropower, energy, and infrastructure," and in this way to "open up new spaces for extractivism" by TNCs (Leiva, 2019, pp. 145–146, 136). Given the history of TNCs in Chile, it is naive to dismiss Leiva's conclusions. Yet it is also possible to interpret his description of this extensive collaboration in a more neutral way, in the context of competitive Chilean democracy, two decades of only occasionally interrupted center-left political rule, genuine moves toward CSR, and more than a few examples of effective state control or regulation of key economic sectors.

In a paradoxical way, this may be precisely the lesson of the protests of 2019 and 2020, and the successful campaign to fully overturn the 1980 Chilean Constitution. As noted above, the 1980 Constitution was highly undemocratic, and served as an important instrument in Chilean pro-TNC, free-market economic policies. Constitutional reforms in 2005 eliminated many of its authoritarian political features. One of the main themes of protests leading to the 2020 referendum was economic inequality; the constitutional provisions that continued to privilege private economic interests, including TNCs, quickly became a central focus for the referendum campaign (Alarcon, 2020). The pressure for this change came from social movements outside the mostly pro-neoliberal political parties. The referendum for constitutional change prevailed by a margin of 78–22%, setting the stage for a constitutional convention. There is little question that the disproportionate role of TNCs in the economy—and in specific areas such as health care, education, and pensions—will be a central focus of the delegates to the convention (Bonnefay, 2020). Chile's highly democratic political system will most likely make genuine attempts to rein in the immense power of TNCs.

Theoretical Conclusions

This concluding section focuses on the politics of TNCs in Latin America through reference to institutions and networks; power and capacity; and norms. It does so in the context of the three-level analytical structure, which explores interactions among global, national, and societal/local levels.

TNCs are, indeed, coherent **institutions** that transcend national boundaries. Idiosyncratic features determine exactly how coherent TNCs are in a global setting. But they remain largely hierarchical organizations with the capacity to implement decisions taken in distant headquarters. They have always been more physically mobile than the Latin American workers, governments, and political organizations with which they interact. The early model was of TNCs seamlessly owning and operating facilities in Latin America, as represented in Figure 4.1. In many cases, these companies were able to either effectively bypass or co-opt national state institutions with their operations in Latin America. This model still applies to some extent in the region. But the political relationships among TNCs, states, and societies have become more complex, constraining these companies. TNCs are seldom completely immune from local pressures and concerns, but it generally was not until the threat of nationalization emerged that states succeeded in significantly changing corporate behavior. It is only in this context that, for example, TNCs agreed to "Chileanization" in the 1960s without pulling out of the nation in defiance. The same dynamic was at work during Evo Morales's "negotiated" approach to influencing and controlling TNCs in Bolivia. These dynamics are more closely explored in the following section on TNCs and the "state-in-society" approach.

At the national level, a key consideration is the extent to which states can provide sufficient institutional effectiveness to offer alternatives to transnational corporate control of key economic sectors of national economies. The record has been decidedly mixed in this regard. But there have been numerous cases in which state institutions have proven able to influence and take over sectors previously under the control of transnational companies. State-run enterprises in a number of nations—notably oil in Mexico, computers in Brazil, and copper in Chile—have all managed to thrive, or least survive, in a setting of global economic competition. Just as significant have been the many cases in which efforts by national institutions have failed because of institutional shortcomings. And larger political factors, explored in subsequent sections, are often crucial to this effectiveness.

For all the concern with TNCs' economic and political power, principles and **norms** are an important part of the analysis in this chapter. They have become significant as they have been introduced to, or imposed on, TNCs by groups trying to influence or control them. The norm of CSR represents a highly principled response to transnational corporate power in the Latin American setting. CSR is a norm precisely because it has become, or is in the process of becoming, "the shared expectations or standards of appropriate behavior accepted by states and intergovernmental organizations that can be applied to states, intergovernmental organizations, and/or nonstate actors of various kinds" (Khagram et al., 2002, p. 14). This transformation has not been total, of course. But it has begun to change the behavior of powerful TNCs, which

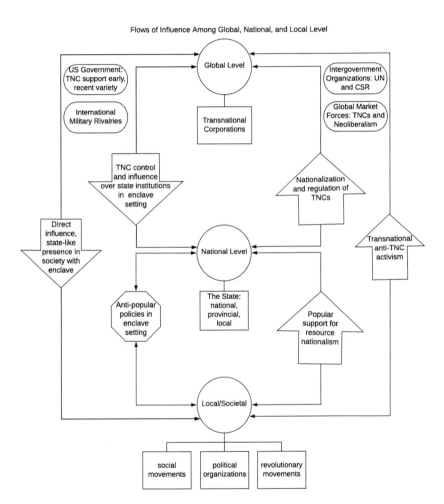

FIGURE 4.1 Transnational Corporations.

have in many cases formally committed to it. In Chile, for example, even as levels of FDI have soared, commitment from TNCs combined with pressure from local and global actors has made CSR a political reality. At the global level, both transnational activists and intergovernmental organizations such as the UN and the Inter-American Court of Human Rights have played a crucial role in pushing CSR and accountability. Their important role in implementing this norm at the global level is reflected in Figure 4.1.

"Resource nationalism" gained political currency in Latin America as a result of extreme levels of external economic domination and penetration. It gradually became a meaningful norm as governments, and the citizens and organizations supporting them, considered taking steps against this penetration. The subjects of these actions were most often TNCs. This economic nationalism emerged in a Latin American region that, as Miguel Angel Centeno argues, had for the most part been marked by an historical absence of nationalism. This economically nationalist norm has been associated mostly with the political left: Cárdenas in Mexico, Arbenz in Guatemala, Castro in Cuba, and Allende in Chile; and more recently with Chávez in Venezuela, Correa in Ecuador, and Morales in Bolivia. But there have been numerous more centrist and rightist examples as well, a sign of its political transcendence. The norm of resource nationalism has repeatedly come up against the power of transnational corporations and entrenched global market forces, an explanation for its fleeting and cyclical appearances. The extent to which governments and local groups were able to act on it in an enduring way at the expense of TNCs is placed into theoretical context in the coming section.

The following theoretical treatment of **power and capacity** begins with extreme and largely unconstrained cases of transnational corporate power in Latin America. In these cases, TNCs were able to impose their virtually unchallenged power in two ways. First, they penetrated nation–states and created enclave settings in which their control over production and workers was almost total. Second, they were able to exert disproportionate influence over national state political systems in order to create and bolster these enclave settings. They did this either by co-opting and controlling governments or (often in alliance with the US government) removing those that displeased them. As depicted in the three-level model in Figure 4.1, TNCs were able to either bypass or control the national state in creating the enclave, and directly exploit the resources and labor of Latin American societies. The weakness of the state at the national level ensured that interactions between TNCs and society were highly exploitative, and that the flow of global influence ran largely from the top-down. In the context of the state in society approach, the struggle in these cases between the state and an extremely powerful societal actor (with a global reach) was one-sided. The state institutions that allied themselves with transnational corporate power were able to exert a kind of political dominance, but it was short term and undemocratic, and closely resembled Michael Mann's "despotic" capacity.

State institutions were, in the long term, stunted by this external domination, and were unable to develop sustained democratic interactions with the societies that they ostensibly ruled. In this type of setting, it was often the TNCs that exerted the type of infrastructural capacity normally reserved for states. The companies created a kind of alternative infrastructure, not for governing and national development, but for extracting resources and transporting them to global markets.

But by the mid-20th century, relations among TNCs, states, and societies in Latin America began to shift. The largely top-down dynamic was supplemented by pressures originating at the national and societal levels, symbolized by the arrows pointing upward from the state and society in Figure 4.1. Resource nationalism became a rallying cry to states across the region in the wake of the Great Depression. In some cases, nationalism and pressure for radical socioeconomic change came from society as well, in the form of social movements and revolutionary activity. Power relations among TNCs, states, and societies had shifted enough so that these nationalist efforts emerged as challenges to the status quo. Other efforts by centrist and rightist regimes constrained TNCs while privileging internal, national business interests. And regional intergovernmental efforts, by the Andean Pact, met with some success in constraining TNCs in the 1970s. From the state in society theoretical perspective, these explicit confrontations represented state-led challenges to powerful societal actors, with mixed outcomes. These nationalist economic policies were deeply influenced by the capacity of Latin American states to carry them out and to win popular support from their societies for these anti-corporate steps. At the local/societal level, support from labor organizations and revolutionary movements was often crucial to initial steps taken against TNCs. Yet a deeper, more lasting infrastructural capacity was required for success in increasing the state role in the economy and, more specifically, operating the newly state-run companies. In this area, many, but not all, Latin American states were constrained by their infrastructural weakness in coordinating and running the key sectors of their national economics.

The late 1980s and 1990s were marked by the reassertion of powerful global economic forces. Whether as a response to general economic trends or to externally imposed structural adjustment programs, states throughout Latin America retrenched from the economic nationalism of earlier decades. Global economic forces, represented in Figure 4.1, came to more directly affect Latin American societies. On a more specific level, TNCs were able to buy up key sectors of national economies. For roughly a decade, the seemingly relentless power of global market forces seemed to triumph over the power of national states, regardless of the political orientation of specific governments. The excesses of neoliberalism and the maturing of Latin American democracies eventually provoked a strong but varied response throughout the region in the early 2000s. But the "pink revolution" did not represent a region-wide rebuke of neoliberal economics and corporate dominance. Rather, governments with legitimacy brought on by their electoral triumphs and links to left-of-center parties and organizations offered a variety of strategies for dealing with transnational economic power. The experiences of Chile and Bolivia show the dramatically different strategies of two largely successful cases. Chile's neoliberal, pro-corporate policies were cushioned by relatively generous government welfare policies; competent management of existing state-run companies; and, in some cases, effective regulation of TNCs—all these factors were the result of the Chilean state's infrastructural capacity. Along similar lines, Bolivia's innovative "negotiated nationalization" won over many TNCs. The state's capacity to administer these policies, and channel the proceeds from them, led to both dramatic economic growth and increased equity in Bolivia.

Both the Chilean and Bolivian cases demonstrate the significance of the state's capacity to push the interests of citizens in the context of transnational corporate power. A more ambitious approach might equate genuine state infrastructural capacity with a comprehensive ability to control and prevail over a powerful transnational actor. This has become a less realistic proposition in the 21st century. The delicate balance among local, national, and transnational forces accomplished in Chile and Bolivia has momentarily served the people of these nations well. The balance was accomplished partly because of the increasing capacity of the Chilean and Bolivian states to reach down, manage, regulate, and influence conditions in their respective societies. Events in 2020 in both nations may ultimately empower those forces that hope to equitably balance the interests of TNCs and the Chilean and Bolivian people.

Conventional interstate military conflicts have been few and far between since Latin American independence. Yet these conflicts, or the imminent threat of them, have occasionally had important implications for TNCs operating in the region, a factor incorporated in the global level in Figure 4.1. In Mexico, Lázaro Cárdenas and his allies gained leverage over transnational oil companies in the late 1930s, due to the Roosevelt administration's concerns over German, Italian, and Japanese access to Mexican oil. Both the 1937 nationalization of Bolivian oil and events leading up to the 1952 Bolivian revolution (and subsequent expropriation of transnational tin holdings) were deeply influenced by the legacy of the Chaco War and driven by radicalized veterans of the war. The Castro government in Cuba was emboldened by the threat of US military intervention to deepen its nationalization policies to virtually every sector of the economy in the early 1960s. And the nationalist, anti-US backlash provided widespread popular support for these actions. Resource nationalism became an important norm throughout Latin America; it was especially prevalent in nations affected by traditional interstate rivalries.

A final key point in this chapter concerns the power and engagement of the US, a scenario incorporated into the global level in Figure 4.1. In the case of TNCs, US policy was an absolutely crucial factor early in the 20th century, as, until the late 1930s, US interests and those of US-based TNCs closely aligned.

The US government intervened repeatedly—often with the military—to defend US corporate interests in Latin America. Beginning in the late 1930s, the motivations behind US government policy toward US corporations in Latin America became more complex, as US President Franklin Roosevelt refused to intervene on behalf of US oil companies in Mexico (or, in a less high profile case, in Bolivia a year earlier). As the cases of Guatemala in 1954 and Chile in 1973 show, this did not end US intervention on behalf of US-based TNCs in Latin America. Even as these interventions took place, the US was choosing not to intervene in roughly contemporaneous cases elsewhere in Latin America. And corporate concerns played almost no role in the massive, but less direct, interventions in Central America in the 1980s. It is also notable that a relatively hawkish George W. Bush administration took no direct action (with the partial exception of Venezuela in 2002) against the leftist "pink revolution" regimes, and that the Trump administration has not intervened in ongoing conflict in Venezuela. Ironically, it was during the Obama administration that factions of the US State and Defense Departments connived with those overthrowing Honduras' leftist leader Manuel Zelaya in 2009 (Johnston, 2017).

The evolution of power and capacity, institutions, and norms has led to a wide variety of outcomes in relations among TNCs, states, and societies in Latin America. In many regards, TNCs remain ascendant, as the most recent leftist political wave in Latin America made only a few inroads into their power. But in a positive development, these companies seem to have genuinely engaged in—or at least not sabotaged—Chilean and Bolivian efforts to make their economies more equitable and inclusive. What might be less subject to the seemingly inevitable swing of the political pendulum from left to right and back is the new transnational and multinational effort to increase transnational corporate accountability. This global initiative may ultimately prove more enduring than developments at the national and societal level in Latin America, as empowered local and transnational activists prod TNCs to take steps that broadly benefit Latin Americans.

References

Adler, Emanuel, 1986. "Ideological Guerrillas and the Quest for Technological Autonomy: Brazil's Domestic Computer Industry," *International Organization* 40/3 (Summer), pp. 673–705.

Alarcon, Daniel, 2020. "Letter from Santiago: Chile at the Barricades," *The New Yorker*, October 12, 2020.

Anderson, Jon Lee, 2020. "The Fall of Evo Morales," *The New Yorker*, March 23, 2020.

Baer, Madeline, 2015. "Private Water, Public Good: Water Privatization and State Capacity in Chile," *Studies in Comparative International Development* 49, pp. 141–167.

Barlow, Maude and Tony Clarke, 2004. "The Struggle of Latin America's Water," *NACLA Report on the Americas* 38/1 (July-August), pp. 15–20.

Bauer, Carl J., 2004. *Siren Song: Chilean Water Law as a Model for International Reform*. Washington, DC: Resources for the Future.

Beckman, Terry et al., 2009. "The Emergence of Corporate Social Responsibility in Chile: The Importance of Authenticity and Social Networks," *Journal of Business Ethics* 86, pp. 191–206.

Bonnefay, Pascale, 2020. "'An End to the Chapter of Dictatorship': Chileans Vote to Draft a New Constitution," *New York Times*, October 26.

Botham, Kathryn, 2008. "Bolivia's Legal Gamble: Negotiating Nationalization," *Wisconsin International Law Journal* 26/2 (Summer), pp. 507–550.

Brockett, Charles, 2002. "An Illusion of Omnipotence: US Policy toward Guatemala, 1954–1960," *Latin American Politics and Society* 44/1, pp. 91–126.

Bucheli, Marcelo and Erica Salvaj, 2018. "Political Connections, the Liability of Foreignness, and Legitimacy: A Business Historical Analysis of Multinationals' Strategies in Chile," *Global Strategy Journal* 8, pp. 399–420.

Bulmer-Thomas, Victor, 2003. *The Economic History of Latin America since Independence*. Cambridge: Cambridge University Press.

Cardoso, Fernando Henrique, 1979. *Dependency and Development in Latin America*. Berkeley: University of California Press.

Carneiro, Pedro et al., 2014. "Tackling Social Exclusion: Evidence from Chile," Working Paper No. 2014:3, Uppsala University, Department of Economics, Uppsala.

CEPAL, 1998. *Foreign Direct Investment in Latin America and the Caribbean 1998*. New York: UN/CEPAL.

CEPAL, 2018. *Foreign Direct Investment in Latin America and the Caribbean 2018*. New York: UN/CEPAL.

CEPAL, 2019. *Foreign Direct Investment in Latin America and the Caribbean 2019*. New York: UN/CEPAL.

Clarke, George et al., 2009. "Has Private Participation in Water and Sewerage Improved Coverage? Empirical Evidence from Latin America," *Journal of International Development* 21/3 (April), pp. 327–361.

Coatsworth, John, 1979. "Indispensable Railroads in a Backward Economy: The Case of Mexico," *The Journal of Economic History* 39/4 (December), pp. 939–960.

Dangl, Benjamin, 2007. *The Price of Fire: Resource Wars and Social Movements in Bolivia*. Oakland: AK Press.

Dunkerley, James, 1984. *Rebellion in the Veins: Political Struggle in Bolivia, 1952–1982*. London: Verso.

Dunkerley, James, 1988. *Power in the Isthmus: A Political History of Modern Central America*. New York: Verso.

Dupuits, Emilie, 2019. "Water Community Networks and the Appropriation of Neoliberal Practices: Social Technology, Depoliticization, and Resistance," *Ecology and Society* 24/2, pp. 20–45.

Evans, Peter, 1979. *Dependent Development: The Alliance of Multinational, State, and Local Capital in Brazil*. Princeton, NJ: Princeton University Press.

Farthing, Linda and Benjamin Kohl, 2014. *Evo's Bolivia: Continuity and Change*. Austin: University of Texas Press.

Fernández Jilberto, Alex, 2004. "Neoliberal Restructuring: The Origin and Formation of Economic Groups in Chile," *Journal of Developing Societies* 20/3–4, pp. 189–206.

Flores-Macías, Gustavo, 2012. *After Neoliberalism? The Left and Economic Reforms in Latin America*. Oxford: Oxford University Press.

Fontaine, Guillaume et al., 2018. "Explaining a Policy Paradigm Shift: A Comparison of Resource Nationalism in Bolivia and Peru," *Journal of Comparative Policy Analysis: Research and Practice* 20/2, pp. 142–157.

Frank, Andre Gunder, 1967. *Capitalism and Underdevelopment in Latin America*. New York: Monthly Review Press.

Gallagher, Daniel, 2016, "The Heavy Price of Santiago's Privatised Water," *The Guardian*, September 15, 2016.

Gallo, Carmenza, 1991. *Taxes and State Power: Political Instability in Bolivia, 1900–1950*. Philadelphia: Temple University Press.

Gilpin, Robert, 1984. *US Power and the Multinational Corporation*. New York: Basic Books.

Glinska, Carol, 2017. "The Ruggie Framework, Business Human Rights Self-Regulation and Tort Law," *Nordic Journal of Human Rights* 35/1, pp. 15–34.

Grandin, Greg, 2009. *Fordlandia: The Rise and Fall of Henry Ford's Forgotten City*. New York: Picador.

Hamilton, Nora, 1982. *The Limits of State Autonomy: Post-Revolutionary Mexico*. Princeton, NJ: Princeton University Press.

Haslam, Paul, 2007. "Is Corporate Social Responsibility a Constructivist Regime? Evidence from Latin America," *Global Society*, 21/2, pp. 265–299.

Haslam, Paul, 2016. "Overcoming the Resource Curse: Reform and the Rentier State in Chile and Argentina, 1973–2000," *Development and Change* 47/5, pp. 1146–1170.

Higginbottom, Andy, 2013. "The Political Economy of Foreign Investment in Latin America: Dependency Revisited," *Latin American Perspectives* 40/3 (May), pp. 184–206.

Hudson, Rexford, 1983. "The Brazilian Way to Technological Independence: Foreign Joint Ventures and the Aircraft Industry," *Inter-American Economic Affairs* 37/2, pp. 23–43.

Immerman, Richard, 1982. *The CIA in Guatemala*. Austin: University of Texas Press.

Jaffe, Amy Myers, 2012. *Beyond the Resource Curse*. Philadelphia: University of Pennsylvania Press.

Jenkins, Rhys, 1987a. *Transnational Corporations and Uneven Development: The Internationalization of Capital and the Third World*. New York: Methuen.

Jenkins, Rhys, 1987b. *Transnational Corporations and the Latin American Automobile Industry*. Pittsburgh: University of Pittsburgh Press.

Jenkins, Rhys, 2018. *How China Is Reshaping the Global Economy: Development Impact in Africa and Latin America*. Oxford: Oxford University Press.

Jensen, Nathan et al., 2012. *Politics and Foreign Direct Investment*. Ann Arbor: University of Michigan Press.

Johnston, Jake, 2017. "How Pentagon Officials May Have Encouraged a 2009 Coup in Honduras," *The Intercept*, August 29.

Karl, Terry, 1997. *The Paradox of Plenty: Oil Booms and Petro-States*. Berkeley: University of California Press.

Khagram, Sanjeev, James Riker and Kathryn Sikkink, 2002. "From Santiago to Seattle: Transnational Advocacy Groups Restructuring World Politics," in Sanjeev Khagram et al., editors, *Restructuring World Politics: Transnational Social Movements, Networks, and Norms*. Minneapolis: University of Minnesota Press, pp. 3–23.

Kohl, Benjamin, 2004. "Privatization Bolivian Style: A Cautionary Tale," *International Journal of Urban and Regional Research* 28/4 (December), pp. 893–908.

Kohl, Benjamin, 2006. "Challenges to Neoliberal Hegemony in Bolivia," *Antipode* 38/2, pp. 304–326.

Kohl, Benjamin and Linda Farthing, 2012. "Material Constraints to Popular Imaginaries: The Extractive Economy and Resource Nationalism in Bolivia," *Political Geography* 31, pp. 225–235.

Lagos, Gustavo, 2017. "Mining Nationalization and Privatization in Peru and in Chile," *Springer, Pontificia Universidad Catolica de Chile* (November). www.researchgate.net/publications

Leiva, Fernando, 2019. "Economic Elites and New Strategies for Extractivism in Chile," *European Review of Latin American and Caribbean Studies* 108 (July-December), pp. 131–152.

Londono-Lázaro, Maria et al., 2017. "The Inter-American Court of Human Rights and Multinational Enterprises: Towards Business and Human Rights in the Americas?" *The Law and Practice of International Courts and Tribunals* 16/3, pp. 437–463.

Marichal, Carlos, 1994. *Foreign Investment in Latin America: Impact on Economic Development, 1850–1930.* Milan: Universita Bocconi.

McBeth, Brian, 2008. *Dictatorship and Politics: Intrigue, Betrayal, and Survival in Venezuela, 1908–1935.* Notre Dame: University of Notre Dame Press.

Meyer, Lorenzo, 1977. *Mexico and the United States in the Oil Controversy, 1917–1942.* Austin: University of Texas Press.

Milman, Helia Molina et al., 2018. "Scaling Up an Early Childhood Development Programme through a National Multisectoral Approach to Social Protection: Lessons from Chile Crece Contigo," *British Medical Journal* 12/3, pp. 1–7.

Montano, Rosario Margarita Vasquez, 2019. "Organización obrera y políticas laborales en las minas de cobre de México y Chile, 1900–1940," *Región y Sociedad* 31, pp. 1–23.

Moran, Theodore, 1974. *Multinational Corporations and the Politics of Dependence: Copper in Chile.* Princeton, NJ: Princeton University Press.

Mytelka, Lynn, 1979. *Regional Development in a Global Economy: The Multinational Corporation, Technology, and Andean Integration.* New Haven, CT: Yale University Press.

Nem Singh, Jewellord, 2010. "Reconstituting the Neostructuralist State: The Political Economy of Continuity and Change in Chilean Mining Policy," *Third World Quarterly* 31/8, pp. 1413–1433.

Notisur, 2007. "Brazil Breaks HIV Drug Patent after Failed Negotiations with Pharmaceutical Giant Merck," *Notisur*, p. 1.

Prebisch, Raúl, 1950. *The Economic Development of Latin America and Its Principal Problems.* New York: United Nations.

Prieto, Manuel, 2015. "Privatizing Water in the Chilean Andes: the Case of Las Vegas de Chiu-Chiu," *Mountain Research and Development* 35/3, pp. 1–17.

Ruggie, John, 2013. *Just Business: Multinational Corporations and Human Rights.* New York: WW Norton.

Schlesinger, Stephen and Stephen Kinzer, 1982. *Bitter Fruit: The Story of the American Coup in Guatemala.* New York: Doubleday.

Sigmund, Paul, 1980. *Multinationals in Latin America: The Politics of Nationalization.* Madison: University of Wisconsin Press.

Silva, Eduardo, 1993. "Capitalist Coalitions, the State, and Neoliberal Economic Restructuring: Chile, 1973–1988," *World Politics* 45/4 (July), pp. 526–559.

Spronk, Susan and Jeffery Webber, 2007. "Struggles Against Accumulation by Dispossession in Bolivia: The Political Economy of Natural Resource Contention," *Latin American Perspectives* 34/2 (March), pp. 31–47.

Stepan, Alfred, 1978. *State and Society: Peru in Comparative Perspective.* Princeton, NJ: Princeton University Press.

Swanson, Ana, 2020. "As New NAFTA Takes Effect, Much Remains Undone," *New York Times*, July 1.

Tharoor, Ishaam, 2019. "The anti-neoliberal wave rocking Latin America," *Washington Post*, October 29.

Tobar, Héctor, 2014. *Deep Down Dark: The Untold Stories of 33 Men Buried in a Chilean Mine and the Miracle that Set Them Free.* New York: Picador.

Toral, Pablo, 2011. *Multinational Enterprises in Latin America since the 1990s.* New York: Palgrave MacMillan.

Torres Rivas, Edelberto, 1993. *History and Society in Central America.* Austin: University of Texas Press.

Twomey, Michael, 1998. "Patterns of Foreign Investment in the Third World in the Twentieth Century," in John Coatsworth and Alan Taylor, editors, *Latin America in the World Economy Since 1800*, Cambridge, MA; Harvard University Press, pp. 171–202.

UNCTC (United Nations Centre on Transnational Corporations), 1978. *Transnational Corporations in World Development: A Re-examination.* New York: United Nations.

Vergara, Angela, 2003. "Company Towns and Peripheral Cities in the Chilean Copper Industry: Potrerillos and Pueblo Hundido, 1917–1940s," *Urban History* 30/3, pp. 388–407.

Vergara, Angela, 2005. "The Recognition of Silicosis: Labor Unions and Physicians in the Chilean Copper Industry, 1930s–1960s," *Bulletin of the History of Medicine* 79/4, pp. 723–748.

Vernon, Raymond, 1970. "Foreign Enterprises and Developing Nations in the Raw Materials Industries," *American Economic Review* 60, pp. 125–143.

Weil, Jael Goldsmith, 2017. "Using Critical Junctures to Explain Continuity: The Case of State Milk in Neoliberal Chile," *Bulletin of Latin American Research* 36/1, pp. 52–67.

Wilkins, Mira, 1974. "Multinational Oil Companies in South America in the 1920s: Argentina, Bolivia, Brazil, Chile, Colombia, Ecuador, and Peru," *The Business History Review* 48/3 (Autumn), pp. 414–446.

Wilson, Jeffrey D., 2015. "Understanding Resource Nationalism: Economic Dynamics and Political Institutions," *Contemporary Politics* 21/4, pp. 399–416.

Young, Kevin, 2017. *Blood of the Earth: Resource Nationalism, Revolution, and Empire in Bolivia.* Austin: University of Texas Press.

Young, Kevin, 2020. "The Bolivian Left's Election Win Is a Positive Sign, But It Inherits a Dire Situation," *The Guardian*, October 21.

5

THE POLITICS OF TRANSNATIONAL DRUG NETWORKS IN LATIN AMERICA

This chapter focuses on transnational drug networks (TDNs), the most violent, and least subject to moral or legal standards, of all the transnational actors appearing in this book. Their history as transnational actors in Latin America is relatively recent. But in a short time, they have transformed and laid waste to large areas of the region. As is the case with the three other transnational actors, analysis in this chapter focuses on networks and institutions, norms, and power and capacity in order to understand how TDNs function at the local, national, and global levels.

Groups creating and delivering mind-altering substances have a long history in Latin America, as colonial authorities engaged in the export of tobacco and, even earlier, the large-scale civilizations of central Mexico and the Andes took advantage of abundant supplies of a variety of hallucinogens. The relatively new nations of Latin America exported coffee and the coca that would be part of the legal trade of cocaine at the end of the 19th century and early 20th century. But it would not be until the second half of the 20th century that first marijuana and then cocaine would be produced transnationally in large quantities as illicit products. And it would not be until the final quarter of the 20th century that Latin American transnational networks would emerge as dominant actors in the global trade in cocaine, marijuana, heroin, and other illicit drugs. The specific nature of this trade, and of the actors taking part in it, has been transformed by the changing policies of governments inside and outside Latin America.

In this regard, it is important to be clear about the content of this chapter. Focus on the networks that produce, transport, and market illicit drugs takes priority over a more general concern with the global drug trade. It is impossible to ignore the demand for drugs in the US (and other areas outside Latin

America). This chapter's analysis will take seriously Latin American claims that the root of the pathologies associated with the global drug trade are based primarily in the drug-consuming habits of North Americans and others outside the region. Yet the main analytical focus will be on processes related to production and trafficking within Latin America.

Popular representations of the drug trade bring to mind images of large-scale economic and political coordination at the national and global levels. But close scrutiny shows that in response to anti-drug policies, drug organizations have become fragmented and embattled. And even when large-scale organizations were predominant, for example, the Colombian "cartels" in the 1980s, the trade in which they participated was still decentralized, and they depended on other organizations, in other nations, over which they had only indirect influence. In this regard, it makes most sense to refer to these actors as **transnational drug networks**. The further distinction between "territorial" and "transactional" drug networks is discussed in the Mexican case study.

The trade itself has remained transnational in nature, and its key actors have acted beyond the authority of individual nation-states. They enjoy a lucrative trade from markets which are often geographically distant; the proceeds often dwarf the resources available to governing institutions in their nation-states. Most successful efforts to stamp out or constrain drug networks extend beyond the boundaries of a single nation, given the likelihood of what Bruce Bagley describes as the "balloon" effect, in which successful anti-drug efforts in one nation lead to its reemergence in another (Bagley, 2013). (This has also been referred to as the "whack-a-mole" pattern.) These global efforts have usually taken the form of bilateral collaboration between individual Latin American nations and the US. They have generally not been led by empowered global anti-drug intergovernmental organizations, although the UN has been an important actor in setting the terms for the eradication-based strategies pushed by the US.

This account is not limited to one particular form of drug. Heroin, marijuana, and, more recently, methamphetamine and synthetic opioids have been an important part of the trade coming out of Latin America. But any account of the Latin American drug trade must begin with cocaine, for two main reasons: cocaine was the primary export crop as the inter-American drug trade was established and grew; and most cocaine on global markets originates in Latin America. The type of cocaine and its legal status in key markets is also crucial. Decisions to illegalize it in the US are particularly significant in this regard. It is also important to emphasize and clarify the different steps in the process of creating cocaine and other drugs to lucrative markets. In the most general terms, the key steps are growing, processing, transporting, and marketing/selling. Virtually all growth and processing of cocaine take place in Latin America, primarily in the three nations of Peru, Bolivia, and Colombia (and previously to a smaller extent in Chile). Political factors have led to important variations in each nation's share of growth and processing. But physical inaccessibility and the Andean climate have made these nations the almost exclusive settings for growing coca. Most processing—through which the coca plant is transformed into cocaine—also takes place near growing locations in small-scale laboratories. Fluctuating policies from governments inside and outside the region have led to significant changes in transportation routes within Latin America over the past 75 years. Finally, the majority of cocaine is marketed and consumed outside Latin America, although the Latin American share has grown in recent decades.

In the most general terms, other forms of illicit drugs are less exclusively associated with Latin America, as the early steps of their creation—most notably their growth—are less dependent on conditions unique to Latin America. But, primarily because of the presence of powerful drug networks and the proximity to lucrative US markets, Latin America is also marked by large-scale and growing trade in marijuana, heroin, methamphetamines, and synthetic opioids. The illicit Latin American trade in marijuana was, prior to the 1970s, more significant than cocaine, only to be overshadowed by it more recently.

Legal Drugs and Early Developments in the Illegal Drug Trade

Much of what is described above applies in the most general terms to a system that emerged beginning in 1947 and became entrenched in 1973. Yet it was not inevitable that eradication would dominate global efforts to control drug use. For example, cocaine was a legal product with genuine medical potential in the decades surrounding the turn to the 20th century. Coca was mostly grown for export in Peru, German pharmaceutical companies were eager to promote it, and it had a strong market among US medical consumers. But, beginning in roughly 1905, successive US administrations became globally active in pushing an eradicationist agenda, resulting in the League of Nations' categorization of cocaine as a narcotic substance (Gootenberg, 2012, p. 162). After World War II, the US used its dominant global position to push both unilaterally and especially through UN for de-legalization and eradication. The UN created the Commission on Narcotic Drugs in 1947 which pursued a strong eradicationist approach that was formalized in a 1961 UN treaty. The US pushed the primary coca-growing nations at the time toward eradication: Peru's government pledged to do so in 1948 and, after a decade of instability owing to the 1952 revolution, the Bolivian government did so in 1961.

These efforts did not entirely eliminate the trade, however, and what was grown and processed tended to flow through two routes: the Caribbean, as Cuba became a hub for cocaine trafficking; and Chile. These routes were subsequently cut off by Castro's revolution in 1959 and by Pinochet's rise in 1973. It is worth emphasizing the extent to which the Castro revolution uprooted the drug trade in general, isolating the nation from most forms of legal and illegal global commerce. Castro's revolution resulted in the deep penetration and tight control of a Cuban society previously overrun by various illicit activities (Sáenz Rovner, 2008). In the following decades, renewed US efforts at eradication and the resulting dispersion disrupted the trafficking infrastructure that had been in place, and set the stage for a dramatic transformation in the global drug trade (Gootenberg, 2007).

This change was driven partly by the policies of the Nixon administration. At the most general level, his policies, the first real incarnation of a "war on drugs," heightened the US commitment to ban and eradicate drugs coming from Latin America. But the "war" focused mostly on marijuana (which Nixon saw as a cultural threat) and heroin. Nixon policies succeeded in breaking up European-Latin American heroin networks in the early 1970s just as demand for cocaine in the US grew dramatically (Marcy, 2010, p. 12). Cocaine was given room to thrive even as general US policies became more punitive. At the same time, eradication successes several decades earlier in Bolivia and Peru had led to a "restructured" system: Colombia became a hub for both producing and trafficking cocaine, and the first real TDNs, often referred to as "cartels," emerged in the late 1970s (Gootenberg, 2012). This process, and its impact in Colombia, is described in detail in the case study at the end of this chapter. But developments in Colombia had important implications for the rest of the region, as drug trafficking routes from Colombia through the Caribbean and Florida grew and solidified, and levels of imports into the US grew dramatically.

Prior to this period, the political impact of the drug trade was marginal in most Latin American nations, even those hosting major coca-growing efforts. In this regard, it is understandable that the US was able to prevail on Peruvian leaders in 1948 and Bolivian leaders in 1961 to move against coca interests. By roughly 1980, however, the power of drug-related interests was such that they challenged the authority of nation-states. It was in this setting that one could begin to see different patterns of relations between strong and growing trans-national drug interests and states that were regarded as relatively weak within their national boundaries. The extreme version of this relationship, and one that closely resembles the kind of transnational penetration described in other chapters of this book, is described by Robert Bunker and John Sullivan as one in which the drug organization functions as a "criminal state successor," creating a "criminal enclave, parallel state or polity—essentially ruling a physical or lawless zone" (Bunker and Sullivan, 2010, pp. 34–36). Yet, especially when the US government becomes deeply involved, significant variations in relations among TDNs, states, and Latin American societies can emerge.

The Rise of Transnational Drug Networks

Several key developments in the 1980s and 1990s further transformed the drug trade (many of which are described in the Colombian and Mexican case studies at the end of this chapter). The Reagan administration accelerated the militarization of the war on drugs. Demand for cocaine grew, especially in its highly addictive "crack" form, heightening anti-drug efforts. Reacting to the brazen inroads made by drug traffickers in southern Florida, the Reagan administration succeeded in destroying trafficking routes from Colombia through the Caribbean and along Florida's south and west coasts. Later in the 1980s, US authorities were able to pressure the leaders of Peru and Bolivia to take meaningful steps against the growth and processing of coca (McClintock, 1988). The leaders of both nations were susceptible to pressure, given their extraordinary levels of financial indebtedness to global creditors, and they were forced to take punitive, politically difficult steps. Bolivia's transformation was particularly notable, in that it had been effectively functioning as a "narco-state" in the late 1970s and early 1980s, and without US pressure, it might have become the kind of hub for drug activity that Colombia became in the 1980s and early 1990s (Breinen, 2015).

A less savory side of US foreign policy intruded into, and contradicted, these efforts in the 1980s. The overwhelming imperative of overthrowing the Sandinista regime in Nicaragua led to extensive US collaboration with organizations and governments heavily implicated in the drug trade. Some of the reporting and debate on this collaboration became heavily politicized because of its links to larger arguments about Reagan administration policy in Central America and its link to drug consumption in the US. What is beyond dispute is that US officials worked with elements of the Nicaraguan contras and Panama's Noriega government to collaborate in drug-running efforts intended for the US market. Noriega's Panama was also an important center for drug-related money laundering (Dinges, 1990; Kornbluh, 1997; Marcy, 2010, pp. 106–115, 142–150). This initial Central American contribution to the drug trade would, in a different way, dramatically expand in later decades.

Anti-drug efforts in Peru begun in the 1980s were accelerated by the Fujimori government in the 1990s (also driven by important events in Colombia described at the end of this chapter). His decade of authoritarian rule was marked by several significant triumphs against the drug trade. His successful campaign against the Shining Path insurgency weakened a central actor in the countryside which had, by the 1990s, become "more of a cocaine cartel than an ideological movement," and with US-supplied radar technology, he shut down the "air bridge" through which drugs had been transported to Colombia (Breinen and Rosen, 2015, p. 230). The Bolivian leader Hugo Banzer collaborated with the US to aggressively pursue eradication during his rule from 1997 to 2001. Anti-drug efforts were so zealous and indiscriminate during this period that dozens of Bolivian coca farmers were killed and hundreds were injured (Farthing and Kohl, 2014, p. 132). In a significant example of the "balloon" effect, these developments in Peru and Bolivia shifted a great deal of growing and processing to Colombia in the 1990s. Yet the successful anti-drug efforts in Colombia stretching from the late 1980s through the mid-2000s weakened or destroyed the large-scale Colombian organizations, and led to still another example of the "balloon" effect, pushing a significant amount of drug activity back to Bolivia and Peru—Peru once again became the world's leading cocaine producer early in the 21st century (Breinen and Rosen, 2015, p. 233). Colombia's decline as a hub for growing and trafficking led to a dramatic shift in drug routes to the Central American isthmus. By 2010, roughly 90% of drugs coming into the US were trafficked through Central America and Mexico (Aravena, 2015).

The small Central American nations of Honduras, Nicaragua, and Guatemala were in no position to stand in the way of this relentless trafficking. They became key stops for storage and transshipment of drugs, offering an "unchecked path" to Mexico and ultimately US markets (Marcy, 2014, p. 3). Central American nations' weak political institutions were simply swamped by the drug trade and the violence accompanying it. An added element was the growth of criminal gangs. These groups have strong ties to each of these nations, and even to regions and towns. But they are also highly transnational, in that they, for the most part, originated when the US began expelling large numbers of Central American criminals in the 1990s and 2000s, a number that eventually rose to over 300,000 (Farah, 2012, p. 56). Their relationships with TDNs have always been a matter of debate, but the consensus is that, while starting as foot soldiers and escorts for the organizations, the larger gangs, most notably MS-13, have assumed a position more as "partners." The Los Zetas and Sinaloa organizations from Mexico have formed the strongest ties with Guatemalan and Honduran gangs, respectively. And recent reports demonstrate strong ties between Mexican drug networks and politicians at the highest levels of Central American politics (Avalos, 2020). Whatever the exact nature of their collaboration is, there is little question that Central American gangs have become a crucial part of TDNs.

Entire regions of these Central American nations became controlled by gangs working in collaboration with the TDNs. Aravena describes "failed zones," which "lack the presence of the state, and illegal actors determine the rules" (Aravena, 2015, p. 280). The TDNs flush with drug money "easily buy off the poorly paid police and judges in Central America" (Marcy, 2014, p. 20). In Honduras, for example, entire communities have formed loyalties to representatives of the drug trade because of their economic impact, strategic investments in public works, and ability to "provid[e] public services that the state is often unable to supply" (Kolb, 2012). And the gangs often levy unofficial taxes on businesses and services. Through this extortion and the profits of the drug trade, these gangs have grown dramatically. Honduras, El Salvador, and Guatemala now play host to roughly "80,000 members whose primary loyalty is to the gangs rather than any state" (Farah, 2012, p. 60). These three Central American nations have had, for the entire decade of the 2010s, among the highest death rates in the world. As the TDNs have become entrenched through more firmly established relations with Central American gangs, social organizations that might counter them have little hope of help from the state, and can be easily marginalized or stamped out. For example, one rural community's attempt to organize in Guatemala for greater access to electricity in a gang-controlled area was ignored by the state, and community leaders were then systematically murdered (Molenaar, 2017). Some leaders of the military and civil society groups that fought in the violent conflicts of the 1980s transitioned to democratic, peaceful politics. But a far greater proportion joined the gangs or filled illegal and often violent functions in the transnational drug trade (Bagley, 2015, p. 10).

Nothing was closer to Evo Morales's heart than a new approach to coca and the drug trade when he came to power in 2005. He rose to political prominence in Bolivia through his leadership of the coca farmers', or "cocaleros," organization and he pushed the idea "coca no es cocaine." He was also aware of the failed efforts of Bolivian regimes that were, on the one hand, too close to the drug trade or, on the other, too close to punitive US efforts at eradication. His opposition to the US-supported policy of eradication was "the point where leftist activism and cocalera interests converged" (Breinen, 2015, p. 220). He gradually eliminated eradication campaigns in the key producing areas of Yungas and Chapare. These campaigns were replaced by a "cato" program through which farmers were allowed a limited amount of coca on land already under cultivation, with a ceiling placed on total acres under coca cultivation in specific regions and nationally. He expelled the US Drug Enforcement Agency (DEA) from Bolivia in 2008 and immediately began lobbying the UN to reverse key parts of its 1961 treaty that declared coca to be an illicit substance, ultimately succeeding in 2013 (Farthing and Kohl, 2014, p. 133). These policies struck a nationalist and populist tone with many Bolivians, who viewed it as a matter of national sovereignty and respect for the common person—chewing coca is not only an indigenous custom, but it is also looked down on by much of the lighter-skinned Bolivian elite (Breinen, 2015, p. 211).

A crucial factor in these initiatives was the Morales government's reliance on "social control" and collaboration with the cocalero unions in regulating coca production and enforcing government policy. Under this system, coca farmer organizations staffed compliance offices (funded by the EU) visited farms, and informed anti-drug police about excess coca who then eradicated it. Farthing and Kohl note that "[w]here unions are strong, cohesive, and committed to the MAS," Morales's party, "social control has shown considerable success"; satellite technology has increased the unions' and government's ability to monitor farmers' adherence to the limits (Farthing and Kohl, 2014, pp. 136, 137). In his analysis of "forms of intermediation" in the drug trade, Bruce Bagley singles out Bolivian coca growers' associations as playing an important role by filling a vacuum that was filled by illicit organizations in other nations

(Bagley, 2015, p. 9). At the same time, the Morales government has eschewed a militarized anti-cocaine policy, both a cause and result of strained ties with successive US administrations. Bolivia's efforts to encourage legal consumption, form stronger ties with farmers, and collaborate with the cocalero organizations has led to better relations with Bolivia's own anti-drug police, which, as a result, enjoyed budget increases during Morales's second term. Increase in demand for cocaine in the US and in Bolivia's neighbors has meant that, for all of these successes, cocaine exports from Bolivia have increased over the past 15 years (Farthing and Kohl, 2014, p. 140). But there is little doubt that these increases would have had a far more malign impact within Bolivia, if the government had not engaged in its innovative approach to coca and cocaine.

Morales's triumph in getting the UN to revise its approach to coca is one of a very few examples of meaningful global intergovernmental or transnational efforts to constrain or change the transnational drug trade. This chapter highlights some successes in national and binational efforts to constrain or destroy groups engaged in the transnational drug trade. But almost none of this has happened at the multinational level. Bowing to US pressure, the UN has rarely departed from its original commitment to eradication, with the notable exception of its concessions to Bolivia in 2013. At the regional level, the Inter-American Drug Abuse Control Commission is merely "embryonic," and relies primarily on voluntary compliance (Horwitz, 2015).

A final crucial concern in Latin America is the growth of demand within the region for cocaine, methamphetamine, heroin, and other illicit substances in recent decades. While this trend is not a central concern in this study of transnational drug networks, it has enabled trafficking organizations with a smaller transnational reach to meet regional needs even as they are crowded out of the markets in North America. In this regard, Brazil's rise as the world's third largest market for cocaine has been a boon for growers in Bolivia and the hundreds of "cartelitos" in Colombia.

The Politics of Transnational Drug Networks in Colombia

A series of factors, some already discussed, made Colombia host to some of the world's most powerful TDNs in the 1980s and early 1990s. These networks rose—and fell—due to a complex mix of local, national, and global factors. One can look to Colombian political institutions, Colombian geography, and Colombian economics to explain the rise of drug trafficking. However, external factors, such as the global demand for drugs, the legacies of economic dependency, and the vagaries of US government policies, are also a crucial part of any complete understanding of drugs in Colombia.

Colombia's insertion into this illegal drug trade began at a small scale, with the growth of marijuana for both internal consumption and export in northeastern coastal areas emerging as early as the 1940s. Colombia only became a notable contributor to the global market for marijuana in the early 1970s, but the timing—during the Nixon administration's "war on drugs"—and its proximity to US markets made Colombian anti-drug policy a priority for US planners. It was in this setting that the Colombian government pursued a marijuana eradication policy in collaboration with the US and, in 1978, took the politically important step of forging an extradition agreement with the US. These policies dramatically reduced the export of Colombian marijuana. Those involved in the trade quickly looked for a more lucrative product for their already established illicit network. The rise of Colombian cocaine export was rapid, and it would not be long before large-scale Colombian drug networks would emerge (Restropo, 2015, pp. 141–145). Their rise was made easier by the weakness of the Colombian state.

The Colombian state had a historically weak presence in the countryside, and Colombia's successive administrations from the 1980s through the 2010s pursued neoliberal economic policies that shrank the state's presence in the national economy. While it may be an exaggeration to view the fight against drug traffickers as a "neoliberal trojan horse," Colombian economic strategy weakened the state's ability to perform basic functions and provide services to the population, providing instead a low-taxing, free-market set of policies. More recently, while much of the rest of the region was moving left during the "pink revolution," Colombia responded to pressures from the IMF in 2003 with a series of reforms and austerity measures that reduced the funds available to state institutions (Paley, 2015). The effect was to make it even easier for drug interests to corrupt government officials.

From the start, cocaine trafficked from Colombia was a transnational product: it was intended largely for export markets; and the coca that would be processed into this cocaine was initially grown mostly outside Colombia. At first, two large organizations based in the Colombian cities of Medellín and Cali arose in the late 1970s and early 1980s to oversee the transnational trafficking of cocaine. (Smaller-scale groups also emerged in Bogotá and along the Caribbean coast.) These groups gradually set about creating transnational intelligence networks; private security forces; and transportation networks for ground, air, and sea. They established relations with coca growers and processors in Peru and Bolivia. They set up drug distribution networks in the major markets throughout the US. And they worked diligently to infiltrate national and local political institutions (Restropo, 2015, pp. 138–140). The Medellín network was viewed as far more violent, while Cali worked much more assiduously to co-opt the state and infiltrate and distort the political process. Dramatic increases in US demand and the Colombian government's extradition agreement with the US raised the political and economic stakes considerably. The drug networks immediately exerted significant political influence: using their resources to bribe public officials and, on some occasions, even placing individuals in key political positions. Pablo Escobar was briefly a member of the Colombian legislature.

Far more typical, though, was a much bloodier approach that dominated and traumatized Colombian politics through 1991 (Thoumi, 2012, pp. 975–980).

This violence swept through Colombian society, as death rates in Medellín grew from an annual rate of 730 in the early 1980s to 5,300 in the late 1980s (Gootenberg, 2012, p. 167). And much of this violence was focused on high-profile representatives of the Colombian state. Some of the most notable examples were the 1984 assassination of Justice Minister Rodrigo Lara-Bonilla; the systematic murder in the late 1980s of leftists and former guerrillas who had put down their arms to join the Patriotic Union political party; and the murder of liberal politician and presidential front-runner Luis Carlos Galan in 1989. From 1979 to 1991, more than 100 Colombian judges were assassinated. In response to this violence, specifically Galan's murder, the government of Virgilio Barco declared a state of emergency. The years of 1989 through 1991 were marked by systematic "narco-terrorism" and violent government responses (Restropo, 2015, p. 141).

At the height of their power, the Medellín and Cali drug networks exerted state-like authority in Colombia. They effectively captured parts of the state, especially in remote areas and in the cities of their origin. They provided their own (brutal and non-neutral) version of law and order and conflict resolution. Serena Simoni's innovative work shows that women were significant participants in this process within the network (Simoni, 2018). While their practice of providing largesse to communities they dominated was self-serving and fell far short of comprehensive state-provided welfare policies, they were able to marshal considerable resources to buy the loyalty of local populations. The Medellín network initiated a "Medellín without Slums" housing program for the poor, created lighting and sewage systems for communities, built 80 lighted sports stadiums, and erected schools and churches around the nation. The group's method was "to send teams into the poor neighborhoods to consult with residents and determine which projects they thought would be of most benefit to them" (Filippone, 1994, p. 337). The Cali network engaged in similar projects, but on a smaller scale, and tended to focus more on using resources to corrupt local and national officials (Crandall, 2001).

Through at least the late 1980s, the Cali and Medellín networks controlled key steps in the global trade of a lucrative product and in overseeing trafficking networks that extended from Colombia throughout Latin America and North America. These trafficking networks initially ran along the gulf coast, through various Caribbean islands, and into Miami and the west coast of Florida. The US DEA smashed these networks in the mid-1980s with air and naval interdiction operations (Gootenberg, 2012, p. 168). The Cali and Medellín networks adjusted by redirecting trafficking through Central America and Mexico. This change would eventually contribute to the weakening of the Colombian networks. But they initially made the shift from a position of strength. The Medellín network took the initiative to coordinate trafficking with the emerging

Mexican groups in the late 1980s, setting up a system through which Mexico would serve as a "trampoline for Colombian cocaine." This arrangement would pay Mexican traffickers $1,000 per kilo entering the US. The Medellín network would then reacquire the cocaine inside US borders and use its own network to market and distribute it inside the US (Marcy, 2014, pp. 3–4).

But this dominance was relatively fleeting: the Medellín and Cali networks were able to function as powerful transnational actors for not much more than a decade. The power of the Medellín group was dramatically diminished even before the death of Pablo Escobar in 1993, and it disappeared as a significant actor after that. The Cali network began to supplant Medellín as early as 1990, taking advantage of efforts by US and Colombian authorities to crack down on the more violent and high-profile network. But the nature of Cali's role in the trade demonstrated the emerging obstacles to the Colombian organizations operating as genuinely transnational networks. The Cali network, too, suffered "rapid dismantling" by the government in 1995 (Peceny and Durnan, 2006, pp. 105–106). And the networks' influence as drug traffickers had begun to wane well before their destruction.

For all of the nationalist outrage over extradition and the US presence, US logistical, financial, and political support for the government was crucial in its ability to destroy these networks. There are numerous vivid accounts of the massive US role in these dramatic efforts (Bowden, 2001). Yet developments within Colombia were also important. The new 1991 Constitution provided a far more viable framework for establishing order and punishing drug traffickers, as did more specific policies such as the creation of a system for confidential prosecution of drug interests. In the most general terms, it took a binational effort—involving the tremendous technological and military resources of the US government and Colombian reforms—to wipe out these TDNs. This success did not, however, remove or even notably reduce the drug trade in and out of Colombia (Thoumi, 2012).

The destruction of the Medellín and Cali networks dramatically reduced the overall Colombian role in trafficking drugs northward. But this reduced role was already being forced on Colombian networks prior to their downfall. An embattled Medellín network was forced in the early 1990s to relinquish its distribution networks inside the US to Mexican traffickers (who had previously returned cocaine to the Medellín network after it crossed into the US). The initial arrangements between Cali and Mexican traffickers in 1990 contained no provisions for distribution in the US. And as the Medellín and Cali networks faced extinction at home, Mexican trafficking organizations were quick to fill the vacuum. William Marcy, whose account is based partly on previously classified US communications, is worth quoting at length:

> In 1996, Juárez cartel leader Carrillo Fuentes called for meetings across
> Central America between Colombian and Mexican traffickers. In those

meetings, the Mexicans told the Colombians that they must give up their U.S. drug markets. The Colombians could transport cocaine from the Andean region, but could carry it only as far as Mexico, where the Mexicans paid them in cash. Carrillo Fuentes then controlled the transport and distribution of cocaine into the United States and assumed control over U.S. markets. Reeling from the break-up of the Medellín and Cali cartels, the decentralized Colombian cartels were in no position to oppose the Mexicans and, in many respects, preferred to leave the responsibility of moving cocaine into the United States up to them.

(Marcy, 2014, p. 6)

Due to both domestic and global developments, a new array of forces related to the drug trade emerged within Colombia. All this took place in the context of Plan Colombia put forth by President Pastrana and adopted as a framework by the Clinton Administration and then the Bush Administration (Marcy, 2010, pp. 232–238). In what Bruce Bagley describes as the "cockroach" effect, the groups fragmented and became far more decentralized in nature. It is estimated that between 200 and 300 Colombian "cartelitos" emerged by the early 2000s. The nature of the drug-trafficking organizations was also, ironically, affected by increases in Colombian coca cultivation—a result of Bolivia and Peru's successful efforts at interdicting the coca grown in their nations in the late 1980s. Just as cocaine trafficking by the large Colombian cartels was increasingly threatened, Colombia was emerging as the top coca producer in the world. Decentralization and increased cultivation weakened TDNs and strengthened the groups controlling large areas in the Colombian countryside: the right-wing paramilitaries and especially the left-wing Revolutionary Armed Forces of Colombia (FARC). It is no coincidence that the FARC's control over drug production—and the vast amount of money it could provide—grew dramatically, as it was formally ceded land by the government as part of the "distension zones" that lasted from 1998 to 2002 and covered a huge proportion of Colombian territory. The larger effect was to tip the balance of power toward the paramilitaries and the FARC, and "put the traffickers at a disadvantage since they had to buy cocaine from them" (Peceny and Durnan, 2006; Thoumi, 2012, p. 978).

Colombians continue to be important actors in the global drug trade. And Colombia's move in the direction of peace and increased stability, and away from "narco-terrorism," is an important development. Power has been decisively transferred away from large-scale networks to, on the one hand, more fragmented and smaller "cartelitos" and, on the other, paramilitaries and rebel groups. Indeed, even as the high-profile networks were destroyed, corruption remained very much in place. The more nationally based networks, in collaboration with right-wing paramilitaries, "systematically penetrated virtually all public institutions" in the 2010s, in a process that became known as "parapolitica" (Restropo, 2015, p. 145). For all its continued weakness and corruption, the Colombian state has increased its leverage over drug networks within its national boundaries. The era of powerful transnational actors coming out of the drug trade in Colombia was relatively brief, spanning the 1980s and early 1990s. The Cali and Medellín networks were supplanted by more locally and nationally based organizations within Colombia. It is also crucial to note that the smashing of these powerful organizations was done by the Colombian state, but only in collaboration with the far more powerful US government. Finally, these developments do not represent the end of powerful TDNs in Latin America. Rather, far-flung TDNs are still very much alive, based in Mexico, and active throughout Central America and northern portions of South America.

The Politics of Transnational Drug Networks in Mexico

The emergence of drug networks in Mexico is the result of complex interactions between local, national, and global forces. Drug trafficking had its origins in Mexico as its national economy became closely linked to the US economy in the late 19th and early 20th centuries. The initially legal market for products such as marijuana, opium, and cocaine was transformed by the rush in the US to ban mind-altering substances. The outcome in Mexico was the emergence of black markets and cross-border drug distribution channels in marijuana and opium as early as 1916, and later, in whiskey. This activity was concentrated in states and regions that have remained central to the drug trade to this day (Recio, 2002). The end of US prohibition ended much of the alcohol-related illegal activity; but the flow of illicit drugs continued at a low level, and an important precedent had been established. The system that emerged in the 1930s, and that was dominated by the Institutional Revolutionary Party (PRI) for over half a century, provided the kind of stability and partial legitimacy that effectively placed constraints on trafficking organizations in Mexico. Successive PRI administrations tolerated the drug trade in a working relationship between the governments and drug interests, and certain regions, states, and localities were marked by drug-related corruption (González, 2009; Grillo, 2011). But there was little chance of drug organizations running roughshod over Mexican society and dominating the Mexican state during most of the PRI era (CRS, 2019, p. 10).

The Mexican political system began to simultaneously open up and decentralize in the 1980s just as the drug trade accelerated in Latin America. It continued to do so in the 1990s and 2000s, as the epicenter of the trade moved north from Colombia to Central America and Mexico. The issue of cause and effect in this case is complex; but a more open and decentralized system provided Mexican trafficking organizations genuine political opportunities just as demand was increasing and a vacuum was emerging in the transnational drug world. PRI-supported political reforms provided the political space for opposition parties to emerge and placed greater power in the hands of state and local governments, increasing the number of possible points of penetration for the drug networks. Growing electoral competition at all levels of government removed the stability that had constrained drug networks and increased opportunities for corruption.

This is a point explored by Guillermo Trejo and Sandra Ley, who studied the outbreak of inter-network wars and political violence in Mexico from 1990 to 2006. They focus on cases in which power changed hands at the level of Mexican states, and find a significant increase in drug-related violence:

> after six decades of one-party rule, subnational electoral democratization and the alternation of political parties in state gubernatorial power led to the breakdown of informal government protection networks and motivated drug lords to create their own private militias to protect themselves against potential attacks from rival cartels and from incoming opposition authorities.
>
> *(Trejo and Ley, 2018, p. 902)*

The drug networks viewed a new governor's replacement of personnel at the top and middle levels of state police and prosecutorial offices—who "had provided informal protection for drug cartels under one-party rule" until the late 1980s—as a threat. States marked by changes in political party rule experienced far greater levels of drug-related violence. Trejo and Ley note increased violence in the first years of new gubernatorial administrations, "when old personnel had been removed and new security policies had not yet been implemented" (Trejo and Ley, 2018, pp. 902, 903). These specific trends were part of a larger process through which, in Nathan Jones's words, Mexican drug networks were able to "graft" themselves onto Mexican political institutions at local, state, and national levels (Jones, 2017, pp. 19–40).

A series of neoliberal economic policies first launched in the late 1980s during the Salinas presidency, and sustained by subsequent administrations, also weakened the Mexican state. They reduced tax revenue, lessened the state's commitment to social policies and national infrastructure, and opened up the national economy to global trade. These policies led to dramatic moments of national economic trauma—most notably the devaluation of the Peso in 1994—and to what several observers have described as "state fragility" (Rosen and Kassab, 2017; Jones, 2018). The general retreat of the state provided an opportunity for drug organizations. Reduced taxation left government at local, state, and national levels strapped for resources, and even more vulnerable to bribery and corruption. The North American Free Trade Agreement ended protections to small Mexican farmers and exposed them to competition from large US growers. The result was widespread rural unemployment, which ultimately made participating in the drug trade an attractive option for many Mexicans.

Mexican TDNs were emerging as an increasingly powerful political and economic factor as these political and economic changes were taking place. The drug trade was enriching them. And, with the fall of the large-scale Colombian TDNs, the Mexican networks were coming to control more of the steps in the transnational drug trade. It is worth recalling how Mexican organizations were acting merely as couriers for drugs crossing the US border in the late 1980s. Within a decade, they had come to control trafficking routes through Central America, had effectively removed the Colombian networks from Mexico, and had set up their own distribution networks in the US (Marcy, 2014, p. 6). The larger shift in power from Colombia to Mexico was especially evident in the cocaine trade. By the early 2000s, however, drug trafficking had also been transformed by the greater variety of drug offerings. Mexican networks were able to play a central role in the heroin, methamphetamine, and synthetic opioid trade, gaining market share not only from other Latin American organizations but also from groups based in the US. Mexican TDNs controlled virtually every step of the trafficking of marijuana grown within Mexico (although US markets are threatened by steps toward legalization). They controlled the growth and trafficking of heroin coming from Guatemala and Mexico, and made significant inroads into a US meth market that had initially been dominated by US producers. Mexican TDNs were also able to traffic fentanyl into the US, although much of the supply chain originated in China (CRS, 2019, pp. 12–14). Drug networks have also expanded into human trafficking and petroleum theft and sales (Jones and Sullivan, 2019).

The first comprehensive effort to combat the drug networks at a national level took place during the Felipe Calderón presidency (2006–2012). Early in his administration, Calderón and President Bush crafted the Merida Initiative, which committed the US to provide over $1.4 billion and assume "shared responsibility" with the Mexican authorities for fighting the drug networks. On both sides of the border, the language of war was used to describe anti-drug policy, and the effort became known as "Calderón's War" in Mexico. Previous Mexican leaders had been reluctant to leave themselves open to nationalist criticisms of too closely collaborating with their northern neighbor. Calderón assigned the military a central role, sending whole battalions to the areas of greatest drug organization activity. He also collaborated with the US in extraditing high-profile drug figures. Calderón had isolated successes. He worked with local authorities to make certain urban areas, most notably Mexico City, far safer. And his "kingpin" strategy succeeded in removing key high-level figures while seriously weakening some networks (Flannery, 2013). But the drug trade continued to grow as more and more trafficking was routed through Mexico. Levels of violence reached unprecedented heights during his six-year term: at least 60,000 Mexicans died in violence related to the drug war from

2006 to 2012. Thus, in response to Calderón's strategy, networks which might previously have opted to "evade" or "corrupt" Mexican authorities, to use John Bailey and Matthew Taylor's typology, chose instead to "confront" the Mexican state (Bailey and Taylor, 2009). Precise measurement is impossible, but thousands of these deaths were attributable to government forces (Fisher and McDonnell, 2018).

After six years, the violence unleashed as a result of Calderón's focus on combatting the drug trade made him an extremely unpopular figure, and Enrique Peña Nieto (of the PRI) won the 2012 election partly because he offered a vague alternative which effectively deprioritized the anti-drug campaign. But levels of violence remained high, at certain points even eclipsing the levels of the Calderón years. In a continuation of the "kingpin" strategy, the government remained committed to pursuing high-level figures, including, most notably, Joaquín "El Chapo" Guzmán of the Sinaloa cartel, who was captured in 2016 and extradited to the US.

Roughly 12 years of a militarized government response (aided by billions of US dollars) to the drug organizations transformed Mexican TDNs, as did developments within the drug trade. The networks became more fragmented, as the very top levels of the most powerful networks suffered disproportionately from the government's military efforts. Immediately prior to the onslaught of the Calderón government, as the Mexican drug networks had established dominance in the Americas, four groups controlled most of the drug trade: the Gulf Cartel, the Tijuana/Arellano Félix Organization, the Sinaloa Cartel, and the Juárez/Vicente Carillo Fuentes Organization. These networks fragmented in the face of concerted governmental efforts, aided by US assistance and the threat of extradition. Within several years, the US DEA estimated that these groups had fragmented into at least seven separate organizations. A 2019 Congressional Research Service report put the number at nine—with Los Zetas and the Jalisco New Generation Cartel (CJNG) as especially significant new actors—although it acknowledges the number could be as high as 20 (CRS, 2019, p. 14). Each of the four original networks has survived in some form, but has more challengers and a smaller share of total trafficking. Analysts also note that strong ties between networks and particular states and key ports have allowed numerous networks to coexist (uneasily) in different parts of Mexico (Jones, 2018, pp. 28–32).

In their work on Mexico, Nathan Jones and Peter Reuter make an important distinction between "territorial" and "transactional" drug networks in Mexico (Jones, 2017; Reuter, 2009). Territorial networks are linked to specific regions and states in Mexico, and are far more focused on controlling entire areas, explicitly challenging the government, and imposing order and taxing the areas they control. This type of network is generally more centralized and relies heavily on large-scale extortion and bribery. The Gulf Cartel and Los Zetas are examples of territorial networks. Transactional networks are most focused on trafficking drugs, which in their calculations does not require control of geographical areas. They are less centralized, engage in violence only when necessary for a specific purpose, and use selective corruption, generally aimed at high-level officials. The Sinaloa network and the remnants of the Arellano Félix organization are examples of this type of network (Jones, 2017, pp. 143–145). Given their high profile and their claims to territory, territorial networks are far more likely to be the target of government anti-drug campaigns than transactional networks (Jones, 2017, p. 39). It is worth emphasizing that as networks adapt to new threats and opportunities, their makeup and approach can change dramatically. And despite these variations, both types are decentralized enough that they can still be viewed as networks rather than as seamless organizations. But they do have different implications for TDNs' relations with the state, a topic discussed in greater detail at the end of this chapter.

Fragmentation and adaptation have not meant the demise of Mexican networks as powerful transnational actors, as was the case in Colombia. The best example of this continued global reach is the relatively new CJNG, which emerged out of the fragmentation of the Sinaloa network beginning in 2010. Since then, the CJNG has used the tactic of "adopting orphan" criminal cells which had been cut adrift from centralized groups by the government's "kingpin" strategy (Jones, 2018, p. 24). Over the past decade, it has grown to become, by most accounts, the largest drug network in Mexico, with a presence in all 32 Mexican states. The CJNG has been able, to a certain extent, to do what no Colombian network could: "reconsolidate" drug networks (Jones, 2018, p. 20). From this position, the CJNG has been able to accomplish a number of things. Within Mexico it has been able to "corrupt and confront the state at a high level." To the south, it is in a powerful position from which to continue displacing Colombian traffickers in the cocaine source region, and has extended its collaboration with (and perhaps control over) Central American gangs and drug groups. To the north, it is augmenting its already significant trafficking networks within the US. And to the east and west, it has the capacity to use higher profits and controls of ports to further market penetration in Europe and Asia (Jones, 2018, p. 32). The CJNG continues to function as a powerful, far-flung TDN, evident in its brazen June 2020 attack on the Mexico City chief of police in an up-scale neighborhood near the Paseo de la Reforma.

Anti-drug campaigns have done little to dislodge drug organizations from within Mexican society. And this is not because the Mexican state is a particularly weak institution by Latin American standards; the state presence grew during the PRI era, as it formed strong ties with key societal groupings. But in recent decades, the state has shown little capacity to systematically counter the pull of powerful drug networks with a significant degree of allegiance from Mexican society—even as these organizations commit atrocities against Mexican citizens. In this regard, Roderic Ai Camp's descriptions are worth quoting at length:

> Socially, drug cartels have exerted an important impact on the culture. They are sophisticated in marketing themselves and in providing economic assistance to nonprofit institutions and governmental

> projects in poorer, rural communities…Many drug traffickers have been romanticized in popular musical ballads known as narcocorridos in concerts and on the radio…[M]any Mexicans actually view drug cartels in a positive light, from being Robin Hood-type criminals to producing economic opportunities, employment, and good works in their communities.
>
> *(Camp, 2020, p. 189)*

In a 2017 survey, over 30% of Mexican respondents claimed that drug trafficking generates progress in the communities where they live. Fully 36% of respondents agreed that "drug traffickers do more public works in communities than governments" (Camp, 2020, p. 189). Calderón's abysmally low approval ratings at the end of his term, and the public's rejection of his party's candidate in the 2012 election, very much reflected these sentiments.

Self-defense organizations have emerged in numerous Mexican communities, often in opposition to drug cartel violence, but just as often over community frustration over the government's failure to provide safety. At the height of violence during the Calderón administration, these organizations operated openly in 13 states and 68 municipalities (Asfura-Heim and Espach, 2013). But these efforts frequently regressed to arbitrary exercises of power and human rights violations. More than a few of these organizations either originated as or became front organizations for the cartels. Several large-scale TDNs actually got their start as self-defense organizations. Beginning in 2014, the government engaged in a comprehensive effort to regulate and collaborate with them, which ultimately led to their disbanding (Aranda, 2018).

More promising has been some indigenous communities' responses to the threat of drug networks. Drug networks frequently target indigenous communities, as they are often located along trafficking routes, possess key natural resources, or are physically and politically removed from the reach of the state. In their study, Ley, Mattiace and Trejo point to groups that have succeeded in protecting themselves from drug cartels, even as they distance themselves from government authorities. The conditions for success are very specific; however:

> [T]he communities that are able to resist narco conquest are those that have a history of social mobilization in which indigenous movements have played a key role in connecting communities, developing translocal bonds of trust and solidarity, and expanding village-level indigenous customary laws and traditions into regional ethnic autonomy regimes.
>
> *(Ley et al., 2019, p. 182)*

Marginalized Mexican communities have been able "to construct mechanisms of internal control and external protection that enable indigenous communities to deter the narcos from corrupting local authorities, recruiting young men into their ranks, and imposing rule through force." The authors also point to "normative motivations" that, based on local traditions, serve as a "source of honor" for those who actively oppose the drug organizations. These organizations have done what numerous national governments in Latin America have not been able to do: create "a parallel policing and judicial regional system... that has largely contained the narcos" (Ley et al., 2019, p. 183). Finally, the Catholic Church worked to connect local organizations with groups such as the Guerrero Council of 500 Years of Indigenous, Black, and Popular Resistance and the Network of Indigenous Communal Authorities, effectively making them part of a "continent-wide movement" for indigenous rights (ibid, p. 187).

It is highly likely that President López Obrador and his MORENA party, based as it is in the more marginalized groups of Mexican society, would applaud these efforts and see them as a model for dealing with TDNs. But, as he triumphed in 2018, he inherited the same Mexican state that has a distinctly mixed record in opposing, collaborating, and conniving with these networks. His focus on government corruption in his campaign is clear evidence that he is aware of the obstacles to genuine transformation in the Mexican drug policy. His proposal for a new quasi-military national organization to fight the networks is not that different from an ultimately failed proposal by his predecessor Peña Nieto. His near-pacifist comments about high-profile clashes with drug networks—most notably over the imprisonment and subsequent release of El Chapo's son in late 2019—do represent a departure, but seem not to offer any hope of a meaningful government strategy. López Obrador is, in the wake of Calderón's debacle, the second president in a row to deprioritize the government's struggle against the cartels. Whether this represents irresponsibility or an innovative approach to an intractable problem is a question that will no doubt be answered by the end of his term.

Theoretical Conclusions

The transnational drug trade has profoundly influenced the political and economic systems of northern South America, Central America, and Mexico over the past 50 years. TDNs have played an important role in this process, but their status has been precarious and they have been forced to adapt in response to sustained and often violent efforts to extinguish them. These networks are the most flamboyant and fearsome of the transnational actors studied in this book. Yet individual networks tend to be embattled, short-lived, and under constant threat from governments and rival organizations. Their almost completely illicit status makes it both easier and more difficult for them to survive and thrive as a transnational actor in Latin America. The final section of this chapter assesses the significance of institutions and networks, norms and principles, and power and capacity to understanding TDNs in Latin America, all in the context of the three-level analytical structure.

Above all else, the status of transnational drug organizations as **institutions and networks** in Latin America has been profoundly influenced by the illicit nature of the global drug trade. Decisions made by powerful global actors, including the US government and the UN, determined that international trade in products such as cocaine, heroin, and marijuana (not tobacco and, for the most part, alcohol) would be illegal on a global scale. This illegality has, of course, provided the larger set of opportunities for TDNs, closing off the trade to legal, official economic and political groups. Yet it has also required transnational drug organizations to face all-out, and often violent, responses from some governments whose citizens are affected by their operations. The global scope of the drug trade necessitates that these networks be transnational in scope. An early version of this was the transnationality of the cocaine trade. Subsequent changes in all steps of the drug trade through Latin America and into the US, the rise of new illicit substances (or the growing popularity of old ones), and the anti-drug campaigns of governments created entirely new conditions for the drug trade. Transnational networks had to adapt or face extinction, the clear lesson of the contrast between the early Colombian-dominated and the current Mexican-dominated systems.

These factors have led to a wide variety of relationships within and among the various organizations taking part in the drug trade. At the peak of their powers, the Cali and Medellín "cartels" were relatively coherent, far-flung organizations, operating as far south as Bolivia and as far north as US markets. Yet even these organizations more closely resembled networks than seamless hierarchical organizations. They never directly controlled the farmers who grew the coca, especially those in Peru and Bolivia. And after the routes through the Caribbean were ended, they depended on Mexican groups to transport drugs across the US border. An important part of their networks were their corrupt government collaborators in various states. The Mexican networks' rise to dominance implied a further restructuring. From the start, networks based in Mexico were far less centralized, whether they were, territorial or transactional in nature. Both versions were less centralized than their predecessors in Colombia. Yet this distinction does have important implications for TDN relations with the Mexican state, as transactional networks are less likely to directly confront the state and, in turn, less likely to be targets of high-profile actions by the state.

Further south, the trade has recently been marked by fragmentation into "cartelitos" in Colombia, and tremendous violence and instability along the Central American trafficking routes. Many Mexican networks have fragmented as well, further complicating relations with Central American gangs and drug organizations. Yet the rise of heroin, methamphetamine, and synthetic opioids—for which a high proportion can be grown or processed in Mexico—has led to greater Mexican control over key steps in the trade. For all the coercive power in the hands of illicit organizations controlling a trade in lucrative products, the complex and decentralized nature of the drug trade makes these transnational networks among the most subject to economic and political factors beyond their control.

Analysis of the impact of **norms and principles** on TDNs must begin with the crucial decisions taken in the early 20th century and immediately after World War II to emphasize eradication over any alternative approach to the global drug trade. The norm—to stretch the term—of eradication, and the subsequent rise of an almost entirely illicit drug trade controlled by brazenly illegal groups, ruled out any significant influence for the kinds of global norms that would constrain powerful actors in other issue areas. Global intergovernmental organizations, most notably the UN, committed themselves to eradication. One outcome of this decision was to comprehensively weaken global efforts to control a trade—and all of its deadly outcomes—which operated completely outside domestic and international law. The subtle and growing power of norms in areas such as corporate behavior and human rights, often based on using laws and regulations as leverage, is almost nowhere to be found when assessing transnational drug organizations. In this setting, for example, victims of drug-related violence have no genuine recourse to norms-based appeals at the national or global level, although one notable exception is the norm-inspired success of indigenous Mexican communities in defying drug networks at a local level. The larger struggle against these organizations has taken a very different form, and is based primarily in the power-based calculations of Latin American states and especially different US administrations.

A crucial initial point when discussing **power and capacity** in regard to TDNs is the extent to which they have penetrated Latin American national political systems. This point comes through clearly in the three-level analytical structure depicted in Figure 5.1. The element of external penetration makes this political usurpation even more comprehensive, as a transnational organization with global resources and leverage gained from an independent external existence can more fully dominate a national government and society. This is especially likely, given the historical weakness of Latin American states. The brief histories of Colombia and Mexico, and additional details from Bolivia, Peru, and the Central American nations, are replete with cases of TDNs exercising direct, government-like powers in Latin American nations. The concept of the "captured state" or the "criminally-possessed state" fully applies to the Latin American political systems caught up in the transnational drug trade.

One of the cruel ironies of this penetration is that it was made easier by the democratization of Colombia and especially Mexico. These are simply more open and, in the case of Mexico, more decentralized systems. Even the weakened and fragmented Colombian "cartelitos" of the 2000s were still able to deeply penetrate the national political system, leading to widespread political scandals. In Mexico, decentralization led to many more potential points of

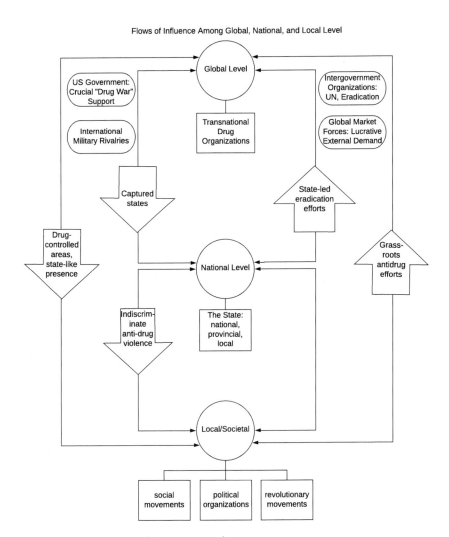

FIGURE 5.1 Transnational Drug Networks.

contact, and drug networks used their resources to corrupt subnational states and municipalities. Electoral competition at all levels removed the stability that, under PRI domination, had kept the drug networks in check. The outcome was a temporary weakening of the state in relation to powerful TDNs. And the euphoria of peace and democratization in the northern triangle of Central American nations was, within a decade, replaced by comprehensive external domination at the hands of TDNs in league with local organizations.

The "state-in-society" approach is well equipped to analyze the interactions of powerful TDNs with Latin American states and societies. These transnational networks exert direct influence within Latin American societies, and genuine leverage over the governments that would either defy or collaborate with them. But this outsized influence does not mean that influence runs in entirely one direction. These final few paragraphs of the chapter are devoted to analyzing instances of both transnational domination by drug networks and successful efforts by governmental or societal groups to counter this domination.

The rise of the transnational drug organizations and the moments of failure in government efforts to combat them show all the weaknesses of Latin American states. One of the great ironies of these anti-drug efforts is that they employ the language of war. In many historical eras and regions of the world, mobilization for wars has been the spur to systematic strengthening of state institutions and growth in state capacity, which in the long run empowered states in relation to non-state and transnational actors. As depicted in Figure 5.1, the "drug wars" in Colombia and Mexico (and earlier in Bolivia as well) were carried out by governments in comprehensive collaboration with a powerful outside patron. The US provided much-needed technological, financial, and economic support, and in many ways led the effort with a massive commitment of resources and military firepower. In each case, the Latin American state was marked by weakness: Bolivia was, at precisely the same time as its anti-drug efforts in the 1980s, dramatically weakening state institutions with an externally imposed structural adjustment program; Colombia, a historically weak state, continued to pursue low-tax, market-based policies throughout the "drug war"; in response to economic crises and external pressure, the Mexican state pursued one of the more dramatic neoliberal turns in all of Latin America beginning in the 1980s, reducing the state's role in the economy and society.

The distinction between infrastructural and despotic capacity can provide genuine insight into these developments. The warlike approach of these governments had the effect of privileging despotic capacity, in that states used the more coercive parts of the state and emphasized violence over negotiation with societal groupings. As they adopted this approach, they also pursued anti-state neoliberal policies, and relied on an outside benefactor, the US, to fund the bulk of the anti-drug effort. In the language of state capacity, the state's ability to "reach down and centrally coordinate" its national society was, with the exception of narrowly militaristic initiatives, being systematically reduced as the drug war was heating up. Despotic capacity was being emphasized just as infrastructural capacity was being reduced. In this regard, Nathan Jones's reference to reductions on the Mexican government's taxing capacity in his analysis of the drug war in Mexico brings out an important connection between falling state infrastructural capacity and the growing power of TDNs. The perception in polling that drug networks were more successful at providing social benefits to Mexican citizens than the Mexican government is a stinging indictment of state infrastructural capacity in the midst of a deadly struggle against the drug trade. A similar connection can be made between the continuing drug trade in Colombia and the FARC's control of vast areas of land at the turn of the century. The state's weakness as a societal actor allowed the transnational drug trade to thrive, even after the stronger Medellín and Cali networks had been replaced by the more fragmented "cartelitos."

Collaboration with the US strengthened Latin American government efforts to stamp out elements of the transnational drug trade, leading to victories in the short and medium terms against powerful transnational drug organizations. Yet the long-term outcomes have been more fleeting. These long-term failures are closely related to a continued state infrastructural weakness in nations such as Bolivia, Colombia, and Mexico, and even more so in the small, vulnerable nations of Central America. In other eras and regions of the world, war-related initiatives have forced states to raise resources and mobilize citizens to fight external enemies, leading to increased state infrastructural capacity. The central US role in the drug war as an external benefactor has let Latin American governments off the hook, ridding them of the responsibility of forging alliances with their own citizens in obtaining resources and support for a "war" against drug networks. This outcome can be seen in the area of taxation and control of resources, as Nathan Jones argues. It can also be seen in the area of justice. Providing a neutral and effective arena for legal justice is a basic function for a government. Yet extradition to the US was a crucial tactic in the efforts against TDNs in both Colombia and Mexico. Reliance on the US for adjudicating and enforcing the most difficult cases has relieved Colombian and Mexican authorities of the need for the difficult reforms that would address issues of widespread corruption in the judicial system, and force the government to make the changes and provide the resources that would make it more difficult to bribe and intimidate the state's legal representatives.

There are scattered examples of Latin American governments curbing the power of TDNs' power by reaching down into society, working with organized groups, and displaying some level of infrastructural capacity (viewed in Figure 5.1 as increased collaboration between national and local levels, in opposition to transnational networks). Probably the earliest version of this occurred in Cuba when Fidel Castro, in the wake of the revolution, routed entrenched drug interests as he deeply penetrated society by seizing control of the economy and creating mass organizations linked to the communist party. A more recent and democratic version of this process took place in Bolivia under Evo Morales, as organized coca growers (still officially led by Morales even after he became president) worked closely with the government to monitor coca growth and restrict its use for cocaine processing. While these policies did not dramatically reduce the flow of illegal cocaine out of Bolivia, they did provide coca farmers with a level of stability and safety from the drug organizations. These examples demonstrate that strong ties between governments and social movements can strengthen state capacity and constrain transnational drug organizations.

Furthermore, the outcome of efforts by grassroots organizations to take matters into their own hands, as a response to mistreatment by both government officials and drug organizations, can reveal a great deal about relations among societal forces, states, and transnational actors, as depicted in Figure 5.1. The experience of loosely defined "self-defense forces" in Mexico is sobering, and a clear sign of the malignant power of TDNs. Yet a far more positive set of outcomes has been associated with groups formed in indigenous Mexican communities, which, with the assistance of indigenous and Catholic transnational organizations, have survived to push for their interests and to reject pressures from drug organizations. The FARC in Colombia may initially seem to be a very different, far less virtuous case, as it engaged in widespread drug trafficking in areas which it controlled. Nevertheless, this revolutionary group had significant leverage over weakened Colombian drug organizations in interactions that involved growing and trafficking coca and cocaine, due to its entrenched position among the rural population. These grassroots efforts effectively constrained the power of TDNs.

The most important lesson of this chapter is that TDNs exert a comprehensive and deadly influence over much of Latin America. Demand for highly addictive and illegal substances enriches TDNs and exerts the kind of political pull that can overwhelm the efforts of governments and communities. The drug trade continues, even as specific TDNs rise and fall.

TDNs fit the model of a powerful group that transcends national boundaries, hems in governments, and spreads violence and mayhem among Latin American populations, even as some groups benefit from the lucrative drug trade. All this takes place with the primary purpose of transporting a product to meet the needs of addicts outside the region. Yet close study reveals real complexities in relations among TDNs, states, and societies in Latin America. National governments have—often in league with the US—succeeded in weakening and destroying key actors in the drug trade. And, in rare cases, citizens and grassroots organizations have prevailed over TDNs. But, despite these successes, of all the transnational actors examined in this book, drug networks are the least subject to norms and laws—at the local, national, and global levels—that would improve conditions for the people affected by them. The efforts that have worked against them are often only slightly more righteous than the evils they are trying to stamp out. It's unlikely that a more worthy set of tools will emerge in the near future to combat transnational drug networks.

References

Aranda, Salvador M., 2018. "'We Are Men of War': Self-Defense Forces, Paramilitarism, and Organized Crime on the Mexican Periphery," *The Global South* 12/2, pp. 148–165.

Aravena, Francisco, 2015. "Democracy, Security, and Organized Crime in Central America," in Bruce Bagley and Jonathan Rosen, editors, *Drug Trafficking, Organized Crime, and Violence in the Americas Today*. Gainesville: University of Florida Press, pp. 276–292.

Asfura-Heim, Patricio and Ralph Espach, 2013. "The Rise of Mexico's Self-Defense Forces," *Foreign Affairs* 92/4, pp. 143–151.

Avalos, Hector Silva, 2020. "Arrests Could Strengthen Links between Tony Hernández and Sinaloa Cartel in Honduras," *Insight Crime*, June 18, 2020.

Bagley, Bruce, 2013. "The Evolution of Drug Trafficking and Organized Crime in Latin America," *Sociologica, Problemas e Practicas* 71, pp. 99–123.

Bagley, Bruce, 2015. "Introduction. Drug Trafficking and Organized Crime in Latin America and the Caribbean in the Twenty-First Century: Challenges to Democracy," in Bruce Bagley and Jonathan Rosen, editors, *Drug Trafficking, Organized Crime, and Violence in the Americas Today*. Gainesville: University of Florida Press, pp. 1–26.

Bagley, Bruce and Jonathan Rosen, editors, 2015. *Drug Trafficking, Organized Crime, and Violence in the Americas Today*. Gainesville: University of Florida Press.

Bailey, John and Matthew Taylor, 2009. "Evade, Corrupt, or Confront? Organized Crime and the State in Brazil and Mexico," *Journal of Politics in Latin America* 1/2, pp. 3–29.

Bowden, Mark, 2001. *Killing Pablo: The Hunt for the World's Greatest Outlaw*. New York: Atlantic Monthly Press.

Breinen, Marten, 2015. "Bolivian Drug Policy under the Morales Administration," in Bruce Bagley and Jonathan Rosen, editors, *Drug Trafficking, Organized Crime, and Violence in the Americas Today*. Gainesville: University of Florida Press, pp. 203–222.

Breinen, Marten and Jonathan Rosen, 2015. "The Vicious Cycle: The Resurgence of Drug Production and Drug Trafficking in Peru," in Bruce Bagley and Jonathan Rosen, editors, *Drug Trafficking, Organized Crime, and Violence in the Americas Today*. Gainesville: University of Florida Press, pp. 223–238.

Bunker, Robert and John Sullivan, 2010. "Cartel Evolution Revisited: Third Phase Cartel Potentials and Alternative Futures in Mexico," *Small Wars and Insurgencies* 21/1 (March), pp. 30–54.

Camp, Roderic Ai, 2020. *Politics in Mexico: The Path of a New Democracy*. Oxford: Oxford University Press.

Crandall, Russell, 2001. "Explicit Narcotization: U.S. Policy toward Colombia during the Samper Administration," *Latin American Politics and Society* 43/3 (Autumn), pp. 95–120.

CRS (Congressional Research Service), 2019. *Mexico: Organized Crime and Drug Trafficking Organizations Updated December 20, 2019.* Washington, DC: Congressional Research Service.

Dinges, John, 1990. *Our Man in Panama: How General Noriega Used the United States and Made Millions in Drugs and Arms.* New York: Random House.

Farah, Douglas, 2012. "Central American Gangs: Changing Nature and New Partner," *Journal of International Affairs* 66/1 (Fall/Winter), pp. 53–67.

Farthing, Linda and Benjamin Kohl, 2010. "Social Control: Bolivia's New Approach to Drugs," *Latin American Perspectives* 37/1, pp. 197–213.

Farthing, Linda and Benjamin Kohl, 2014. *Evo's Bolivia: Continuity and Change.* Austin: University of Texas Press.

Filippone, Robert, 1994. "The Medellín Cartel: Why We Can't Win the Drug War," *Studies in Conflict and Terrorism* 17, pp. 323–344.

Fisher, Steve and Patrick J. McDonnell, 2018. "Mexico Sent in the Army to Fight the Drug War. Many Question the Toll on Society and the Army Itself," *Los Angeles Times*, June 18, 2018.

Flannery, Nathaniel, 2013. "Calderón's War," *Journal of International Affairs* 66/2 (Spring/Summer) pp. 181–196.

González, Francisco, 2009. "Mexico's Drug Wars Get Brutal," *Current History* 108 (February), pp. 72–76.

Gootenberg, Paul. 2007. "The "Pre-Colombian" Era of Drug Trafficking in the Americas: Cocaine, 1947–1965," *The Americas* 64/2 (October), pp. 23–37.

Gootenberg, Paul, 2012. "Cocaine's Long March North, 1900–2010," *Latin American Politics and Society* 54/1 (Spring), pp. 159–180.

Grillo, Ioan, 2011. *El Narco: Inside Mexico's Criminal Insurgency.* New York: Bloomsbury Press.

Horwitz, Betty, 2015. "The Role of the Inter-American Drug Abuse Control Commission: Confronting the Problem of Illegal Drugs in the Americas," in Bruce Bagley and Jonathan Rosen, editors, *Drug Trafficking, Organized Crime, and Violence in the Americas Today.* Gainesville: University of Florida Press, pp. 369–394.

Jones, Nathan, 2017. *Mexico's Illicit Drug Networks and the State Reaction.* Washington, DC: Georgetown University Press.

Jones, Nathan, 2018. "The Strategic Implications of the Cártel de Jalisco Nueva Generación," *Journal of Strategic Security* 11/1, pp. 19–42.

Jones, Nathan and John Sullivan, 2019. "Huachicoleros: Criminal Cartels, Fuel Theft, and Violence in Mexico," *Journal of Strategic Security* 12/4, pp. 1–24.

Kolb, Ana-Constantina, 2012. "Outgunned: The Honduran Fight against Transnational Cocaine Traffickers," *Columbia SIPA Journal of International Affairs*, November 26.

Kornbluh, Peter, 1997. "Crack, Contras, and the CIA: the Storm over 'Dark Alliance,'" *Columbia Journalism Review* 35/5, pp. 33–40.

Ley, Sandra, et al. 2019. "Indigenous Resistance to Criminal Governance: Why Regional Ethnic Autonomy Institutions Protect Communities from Narco Rule in Mexico," *Latin American Research Review* 54/1, pp. 181–200.

Marcy, William, 2010. *The Politics of Cocaine: How US Foreign Policy Has Created a Thriving Drug Industry in Central and South America.* Chicago, IL: Lawrence Hill Books.

Marcy, William, 2014. "The End of Civil War, the Rise of Narcotrafficking and the Implementation of the Merida Initiative in Central America," *International Social Science Review* 89/1, pp. 1–36.

McClintock, Cynthia, 1988. "The War on Drugs: The Peruvian Case," *Journal of Interamerican Studies and World Affairs* 30/2–3 (Summer–Autumn), pp. 127–142.

Molenaar, Fransje, 2017. "Power Short-Circuited: Social Movement Organisation under Cartel Rule in Rural Guatemala," *Journal of Latin American Studies* 49/4 (November), pp. 829–854.

Paley, Dawn, 2015. "Drug War as Neoliberal Trojan Horse," *Latin American Perspectives* 42/5 (September), pp. 109–132.

Peceny, Mark and Michael Durnan, 2006. "The FARC's Best Friend: U.S. Antidrug Policies and the Deepening of Colombia's Civil War in the 1990s," *Latin American Politics and Society* 48/2 (Summer), pp. 95–116.

Recio, Gabriela, 2002. "Drugs and Alcohol: US Prohibition and the Origins of the Drug Trade in Mexico, 1910–1930," *Journal of Latin American Studies* 34/1 (February), pp. 21–42.

Reuter, Peter, 2009. "Systemic Violence in Drug Markets," *Crime, Law, and Social Change* 52/3 (September), pp. 275–284.

Restrepo, Elvira Maria, 2015. "Colombia and Its Wars against Drug Trafficking," in Bruce Bagley and Jonathan Rosen, editors, *Drug Trafficking, Organized Crime, and Violence in the Americas Today*. Gainesville: University of Florida Press, pp. 139–160.

Rosen, Jonathan and Hanna S. Kassab, eds., 2017. *Fragile States in the Americas: Security in the Americas in the 21st Century*. New York: Lexington Books.

Sáenz Rovner, Eduardo. 2008. *The Cuban Connection: Drug Trafficking, Smuggling, and Gambling in Cuba from the 1920s to the Revolution*. Chapel Hill: University of North Carolina Press.

Simoni, Serena, 2018. "Queens of Narco-Trafficking: Breaking Gender Hierarchy in Colombia," *International Affairs* 94/6, pp. 1257–1267.

Thoumi, Francisco, 2012. "Illegal Drugs, Anti-Drug Policy Failure, and the Need for Institutional Reforms in Colombia," *Substance Use & Misuse* 47, pp. 972–1004.

Trejo, Guillermo, and Sandra Ley, 2018. "Why Did Drug Cartels Go to War in Mexico? Subnational Party Alternation, the Breakdown of Criminal Protection, and the Onset of Large-Scale Violence," *Comparative Political Studies* 51/7, pp. 900–937.

6

THE POLITICS OF TRANSNATIONAL HUMAN RIGHTS NETWORKS IN LATIN AMERICA

Transnational human rights activism has a long history in Latin America. The global injustices of colonialism left the Latin American victims of human rights abuses with little recourse at the local level. Witnessing these injustices, Father Bartolomé de las Casas took his struggle on behalf of indigenous Americans to Europe, where, acting as perhaps "the first exponent of truly universal human rights," he tenaciously pushed his cause (Brysk, 2000, p. 193; Orique, 2009). His successes were fleeting and didn't stop the brutal anti-indigenous campaigns and systematic economic exploitation of the colonizers. It would be many centuries before a full-fledged transnational movement would begin to alter the behavior of repressive forces in the region. Transnational human rights networks (THRNs) have emerged in the past 50 years to empower Latin American activists pushing for justice from governments and other institutions. This process has been global in nature, but nowhere (with the possible exception of Europe) has it so fundamentally transformed the political life of a region.

This chapter provides a broad overview of THRNs as they emerged and responded to dictatorships and civil wars; took part in region-wide democratization and reconciliation; empowered indigenous activists; and used their growing presence to help create a culture of human rights throughout the region. It concludes with case studies of Guatemala and Argentina. The three-level analytical framework provides a means for understanding how human rights activism operates at local, national, and global levels (as depicted in Figure 6.1). The theoretical concern with networks and institutions, norms, and principles, and power and capacity is especially central to this chapter, as each is crucial to understanding how transnational activists have collaborated with local actors to make human rights politically meaningful to the people of Latin

America. More than any other transnational actor, human rights networks have worked to empower Latin American citizens, taking part in what Peter Evans describes as a "counter-hegemonic," bottom-up version of globalization (Evans, 2008, p. 272; Tarrow, 2005). At the same time, this analysis acknowledges the potential for tensions within the human rights network when questions of representation arise (Piewitt et al., 2010).

The Rise of Transnational Human Rights Networks in Latin America

The mid- and late 1940s was a promising moment for human rights in Latin America. Latin Americans were among the most significant supporters of, and contributors to, the process that led to the creation of the UN and the crafting of the Universal Declaration of Human Rights (Glendon, 2003). The global struggle against fascism and for democracy during World War II created genuine momentum for democratic change in Latin America. Aspiring democrats repeatedly referred to Franklin Roosevelt's Four Freedoms. Chile and Uruguay continued and deepened their democratic traditions. In nations such as Argentina and Brazil, members of middle class and labor organizations pushed for greater openness and electoral competition. National movements for democracy in Colombia, Guatemala, El Salvador, and Costa Rica pushed against repressive regimes with notable success. It seemed, momentarily, as if many Latin American regimes were moving in the direction of democracy and respect for human rights.

Instead, over the next four decades, national governments became singularly hostile to human rights, as the region became plagued by dictatorship, civil war, foreign intervention, widespread political repression, and genocide. In some cases, they swallowed up either enduring or fledgling democracies. In others, they bolstered and deepened undemocratic systems. Virtually everywhere in the region, governments either ignored or brutally repressed popular aspirations. Democracies fell in Colombia in 1948, Guatemala in 1954, Argentina in 1955, and Brazil in 1964. Mexico's one-party-dominant system calcified. Cuba's communist party monopolized national political life in the wake of Castro's revolution. Other leftist experiments largely failed in Bolivia in the 1950s and Peru in the 1960s, leading to undemocratic outcomes. Personalistic dictatorships entrenched themselves in nations such as Paraguay and (until 1979) Nicaragua. The 31-year rule of Rafael Trujillo in the Dominican Republic ended in 1961, but the nascent democracy was stamped out by a coup against the leftist Juan Bosch in 1963 and direct US military intervention in 1965. And two of Latin America's most enduring democracies, Chile and Uruguay, both fell to dictatorship in 1973. Guillermo O'Donnell's pioneering comparative work on Chile, Uruguay, Brazil, and Argentina pointed out that these "bureaucratic-authoritarian" nations failed as democracies not for random reasons, but because of the specific nature of their economic development and the militarization of their political systems (O'Donnell, 1978). While the US response to these events varied, a "national security" doctrine, emerging partly out of US training, served as a rationale for the military leaders of these nations as they systematically violated human rights (Weschler, 1998).

Furthermore, Central America was, in the 1970s and 1980s, swallowed by a wave of revolution, counter-revolution and repression that was even more extreme in its violence and murderousness than elsewhere in Latin America. A fraudulent election in 1972 set the stage for two decades of civil war and military repression in El Salvador, leading to the death or disappearance of close to 100,000 Salvadorans. Beginning in the late 1970s, the Guatemalan regime's brutal response to revolutionaries operating in indigenous areas reached genocidal levels. The successful revolution against the Somoza dictatorship in Nicaragua in 1979 led only to a decade of conflict between the Sandinista government and the US-supported "contras"—a group that was responsible for perpetrating violence that approached levels in El Salvador and Guatemala. In all three nations, this process was driven to a significant extent by US military and political support for the forces inflicting most death and repression.

Early on in the struggle against dictatorships and repression, the main protagonists were, first, mainstream opposition political parties. Then, as they were repressed and even destroyed, more radical insurgent organizations arose. These groups varied tremendously, but for the most part, human rights was a secondary goal, as they strove most immediately for replacing the existing regime and perhaps socioeconomic and political transformation. It was in this setting that transnational networks gradually emerged to defend human rights. Margaret Keck and Kathryn Sikkink describe the process through which local and global actors collaborated against repressive states as a "Boomerang Pattern," emerging repeatedly against undemocratic regimes throughout the region (Keck and Sikkink, 1998, p. 13). So comprehensive were the repressive forces at work that recourse to transnational solidarity and alliances became one of the few options available to threatened Latin Americans.

Information from the Transnational Social Movement Organization dataset (compiled by Jackie Smith and her collaborators) shows these trends, providing a decade-by-decade account beginning in 1953. Its concern with transnational organizations leads it to include groups with a presence in three or more countries. Around the globe, these groups increased in number 17-fold from 1953 to 2013. Their numbers grew from approximately 100 in 1953 to roughly 200 in 1963 (Smith et al., 2018, p. 382) and, as Table 6.1 shows, nearly doubled from 1973 to 1983, and then shot up in each successive decade after that. The percentage focusing explicitly on human rights ranged from 59.3% to 66.6% (in 2013). Many of these organizations had a presence in numerous regions: from 1973 to 2013, the percentage with a presence in Latin America fluctuated between 55.6% and 65.5% (Smith et al., 2018, p. 385). Extrapolating from

TABLE 6.1 Transnational Activist and Human Rights Organizations

	1973	*1983*	*1993*	*2003*	*2013*
Total Groups	255	489	844	1,434	1,767
% Human Rights	61.6%	59.3%	60.3%	63.9%	66.6%

Transnational activist organizations include those that have a presence in three or more nations. The human rights category includes groups focusing on human rights, and on gender, economic, social, and cultural rights. The % reflects the proportion of total transnational activist organizations involved in human rights activism.

Data are taken from the Transnational Social Movement Organization dataset, based on data from the Yearbook of International Organizations, published by the Union of International Associations. This table is based on Smith et al. 2018, pp. 382, 383, 385.

these data, hundreds of transnational human rights organizations have been at work in Latin America since the 1980s, and that number has risen to just short of 1,000 in recent years. Smith and her coauthors note that the intensity of these groups' engagement has increased with advances in communications and affordable transport, and make the crucial point that much of their work is "networked with national and local-level activists and organizations," acting as a kind of multiplier on their influence (Smith et al., 2018, p. 383).

In terms of this book's analytical framework, this process represents comprehensive collaboration between the local/societal and transnational levels, with varying degrees of cooperation or opposition at the national level. It is a story of organizations emerging in democratic nations, often from outside the region, and collaborating with local activists in Latin America looking outward for allies after being ignored or repressed by their own national governments. These transnational and local trends are of course related, as local actors collaborated with external ones even in the creation of groups, and it eventually became difficult to distinguish between what was local and what was external, precisely because these activists created and joined human rights networks. Collaboration among proliferating local and global groups took the form of transnational **networks** that were well situated to pressure recalcitrant Latin American governing institutions.

In theory, these network-based relationships are based on collaboration and empowerment of local activists and organizations. But, as noted, tensions are built into these transnational networks for a variety of reasons, as organizations with differential access to resources and distinctive goals work together. General accounts of networks in Latin America point to the genuine collaboration taking place. For example, this theme of bottom-up influence is central to Alison Brysk's account of transnational indigenous rights activism (Brysk, 2000). Jackie Smith and her collaborators make a similar point, noting that the data from their survey shows that transnational human rights organizations have become "more diverse, localized and less elite" in recent decades (Smith et al., 2018, p. 376). The extent to which transnational human rights activism avoided these tensions is addressed at the end of this chapter in light of the details provided in the analysis that follows.

As the above data show, the emergence of THRNs gained genuine momentum in the late 1970s and early 1980s. Yet there were also significant early examples of support and collaboration. Because of the established presence of the Catholic Church, and the radical tendencies nourished by the Vatican II and Medellín gatherings (as described in Chapter 3), the earliest independent human rights organizations often had explicit links to Catholicism. Cardinal Paulo Evaristo Arns was an early advocate for human rights, and beginning in the late 1960s, he made the Brazilian Conference of Bishops a hub for human rights activism (Weschler, 1998). Faith-based groups were among the first human rights organizations to emerge in Peru, Ecuador, and Colombia in the late 1970s (Bamat, 2009). On a more secular level, some of the earliest and most effective human rights organizations in South American dictatorships had close links to the Ford Foundation, including the Brazilian Center for Analysis and Planning, which provided effective sanctuary for a group of influential, endangered Brazilian academics (including future president Fernando Henrique Cardoso). This model, of local groups emerging from Ford Foundation protection and funding, was repeated in Chile and Uruguay in 1973 and in Argentina in 1976 (Keck and Sikkink, 1998, p. 101). These organizations became among the most prominent critics of their respective dictatorships.

Two transnational organizations that have become synonymous with human rights activism on a global scale played a crucial role in the struggles over human rights in Latin America during the 1970s and 1980s. Although originally founded in Britain in the early 1960s, the global human rights organization Amnesty International (AI) began to focus a disproportionate amount of its attention on human rights violations in Latin America in the 1970s. AI's reports provided crucial information about human rights abuses, and the group was often able to use its resources and reputation to unearth information on its own. Given its global reach as the world's largest human rights organizations, its efforts to sway governments and global organizations were extremely effective. For example, it was one of the first organizations to react to the coup in Chile, demanding that the Inter-American Court of Human Rights (IACHR) pressure the Chilean government to respect human rights and allow threatened individuals to leave the country (Hawkins, 2002, p. 53). Ropp and Sikkink note that the staff for Chile's Vicaria de la Solidaridad "was on the phone every day with Amnesty International in London throughout the early years of the dictatorship" (Ropp and Sikkink, 1999, p. 176). AI also provided threatened individuals sanctuary and positions from which to push for human rights in Latin America, which led to a flow of individuals from AI into national and local organizations. For example, the Chilean José Zalaguett had briefly worked for the Vicaría de la Solidaridad after the 1973 coup, then had been imprisoned and expelled by the Pinochet government. He became deputy executive director of AI in the mid-1980s, and then returned to Chile in 1986 to resume his local fight for human rights (Sikkink, 2011, p. 25). In another example, Mexican activist Mariclaire Acosta rotated from her staff position with AI to, in collaboration with several prominent Mexican activists, create the Mexican Academy for Human Rights in 1984 (Keck and Sikkink, 1998, p. 111).

Americas Watch was founded in 1981, and immediately prioritized the Central American conflicts in its work, reporting on human rights abuses and collaborating with local groups throughout Latin America. (Sister organizations for Africa, Middle East, and Asia emerged in following years, leading to the creation of Human Rights Watch in 1988.) The organization's primary mission is to provide information on human rights abuses in the form of annual reports and targeted visits to areas of conflict. Crucial moments related to human rights developments were almost invariably accompanied by influential and well-documented reports from Americas Watch. This was the case in the early 1980s in El Salvador and Guatemala, and throughout the South American dictatorships. Americas Watch also provided legal and political advice related to war crimes and human rights abuses, which became even more significant as international institutions such as the Inter-American Court of Human Rights and the International Criminal Court heard cases against human rights violators (Burgerman, 2001, p. 60; Sikkink, 2011, p. 107).

The work of these larger human rights organizations was accompanied by activism from groups focusing more explicitly on Latin America. The Washington Office on Latin America (WOLA) was created in 1974 with funding and office space (in the Methodist Building just northeast of the US Capital grounds) provided by the Methodist Church. In its own words, WOLA's mission was "to connect policy-makers in Washington to those with first-hand knowledge" of human rights abuses in Latin America, "not to 'represent' Latin Americans but to give them access in the United States to those making the policies that had such a profound impact on their lives" (taken from the WOLA website). A good example of its early influence was its central role in drafting the 1976 Harkin Amendment, which prohibited US military aid to governments that abuse human rights (Sikkink, 2011, p. 7). While WOLA worked primarily in Washington, the group Peace Brigades International (PBI) sent its members to the most dangerous parts of Latin America. It was formed in Canada in 1981, with the mission of sending citizens to accompany threatened individuals in conflict areas. Its first major operation began in Guatemala in 1983, and in the following years expanded its work to El Salvador, Chiapas, Honduras, and Colombia. There are hundreds of accounts of local activists claiming that they would have had very little chance of physical survival without this accompaniment, and that they owe PBI their lives (Mahony and Eguren, 1997). (This discussion does not include the Committee in Solidarity with the People of El Salvador and various Nicaraguan solidarity organizations, because of their alliance with the Salvadoran rebels and the Nicaraguan government, respectively (Perla, 2009).)

It is worth a brief account of several nations marked by human rights abuses in order to get a better sense of the local portions of the THRNs. (The Guatemalan and Argentinian cases at the end of the chapter also provide these local details.) The widespread human rights violations during and after the 1973 Pinochet coup forced Chileans to look outward for assistance. The World Council of Churches played a central role in getting Methodist, Lutheran, Catholic, Orthodox, and Jewish religious communities to support the formation of the first post-coup human rights organization, the Committee for Cooperation and Peace in Chile (COPACHI), which served as a lifeline to thousands of Chileans. COPACHI was closed by the dictatorship in late 1975, and out of it emerged the Vicaría de la Solidaridad, a group more explicitly linked to the Catholic Church, but equally dedicated to defending human rights (Bastias Saavedra, 2013, p. 98). It used its close work with Chilean human rights victims to collaborate with transnational groups, especially AI (Ropp and Sikkink, 1999, p. 176). As El Salvador descended into dictatorship and civil war in the 1970s, few organizations existed to protect human rights on the ground. The Salvadoran Catholic authorities created the human rights office Socorro Juridico in 1975, which was renamed and repurposed as Tutela Legal in 1982, to focus more explicitly on human rights documentation. In the face of extreme levels of government violence, it became the most prominent independent human rights group in the nation. Tutela Legal became an especially significant actor because its reports on human rights violations provided an alternative to the far more rosy (and arguably fraudulent) reports coming out of the US embassy (Valencia-Weber and Weber, 1986; Burgerman, 2001, p. 40). In this way, the work of Tutela Legal became closely linked to policy debates in the US. Other local human rights organizations were active in El Salvador, notably CoMadres, a "motherist" group emerging at roughly the same time as similar groups in Argentina (Bejarano, 2002). But the combination of extreme violence and politicization coming out of the massive US presence made the work of Tutela Legal especially important.

These local conditions in Chile and El Salvador can be contrasted to Uruguay, where the state was able to effectively cut off transnational access to Uruguayan society. In her comparative study, Mara Loveman argues that "society was thoroughly and deeply penetrated by the monitoring and repressive apparatus of the military state," and that "deep intervention by the military in all spheres of life closed off potential spaces for the emergence of HROs" (Loveman, 1998, p. 505; Weschler, 1998, pp. 123–159). An AI report at the time estimated that "one in every 500 inhabitants of Uruguay was in prison for political reasons and that one in every fifty citizens had been through a period of imprisonment, which for many included interrogation and torture" (quoted in Loveman, 1998, pp. 505–506). A crucial factor was the marginalization of the Catholic Church, which was simply unable to provide "protected places" in a nation where it was historically subordinate to the state. The Uruguayan dictatorship was equally effective at shutting out secular groups. The first human rights organization appeared only in 1981, an affiliate of the Argentinian group Servicio Paz y Justicia (SERPAJ), which, as a regionally based transnational actor, came to play a crucial role in reconciliation and the transition to democracy during the mid- and late 1980s (Loveman, 1998, p. 506; Roniger, 2011).

One of the key tactics of transnational activism is to work with powerful external national governments to support human rights. This was the case in the late 1970s with the Carter administration. Under Carter, the US Department of State was a stalwart ally of human rights activists at the highest levels with Secretary of State Cyrus Vance and especially Patricia Derian, the assistant secretary of state for the recently created human rights office. Keck and Sikkink maintain that Derian, in her government position, was "part of the human rights network in the sense that she shared many of their values, and she and her staff were in frequent communication with them" (Keck and Sikkink, 1998, p. 103). And at a key moment, the Carter administration provided generous funding for the Inter-American Commission on Human Rights, which enabled the Commission to increase staffing, establish a computerized documentation center, and engage in comprehensive on-site investigations in Latin American nations (Sikkink, 2011, p. 64).

Human rights suffered a setback when Ronald Reagan replaced Carter and the ultra-hawkish Elliott Abrams replaced Patricia Derian. The THRN often came to look at the new administration as an adversary. Yet a longer perspective shows that the growth of the network and the empowerment provided by the Carter administration's support gave it genuine leverage in Latin American and in Washington. Human rights advocates were also able to look elsewhere in the US government: the legislative branch became the central arena for activists pushing for a more human rights-oriented US policy in Latin America during the 1980s.

Democratization and the Transnational Human Rights Network in Latin America

THRNs may have reached the height of their influence as they confronted dictatorships and political violence in Latin America in the 1970s, 1980s, and early 1990s. And it makes sense to think of them as losing some centrality as political systems democratized and wars ended. Organizations looking for justice within their own boundaries were perhaps more likely to receive a fair hearing from their own national governments and not need the kind of international advocacy that this network provided. Yet the THRN continued to play an important role in more recent decades: in the peace processes of Central American nations, and in former South American dictatorships as they democratized and wrestled with questions of stability, justice, and accountability.

Actors linked to the transnational network continued to play a central role in influencing how the nations throughout the region would confront difficult questions of democratization and justice. The 1988 Chilean plebiscite that Pinochet believed would legitimate his rule instead led to a shocking repudiation of the dictatorship. The transnational network was a central actor in this outcome: Ropp and Sikkink note that "International groups provided extensive financial and technical support for intellectuals, NGOs, and political parties to carry out polling, voter registration drives, training for polling observers, and election monitoring" (Ropp and Sikkink, 1999, p. 187). In Uruguay at roughly the same time, SERPAJ and Americas Watch played a central role in ensuring the legitimacy of a referendum about transitional justice in Uruguay, and more generally pushing for post-dictatorial reconciliation (Weschler, 1998, pp. 173–236; Markarian, 2007; Roniger, 2011). In the wake of Alberto Fujimori's anti-democratic rule in Peru in the 1990s, AI and Americas Watch were crucial actors in the successful legal struggle to return him to Peru to face trial (Burt, 2014, p. 155), and transnational activists were able to assume almost state-like powers as they inserted themselves into Peru's post-Fujimori reconciliation process (Root, 2009).

That the fate of Augusto Pinochet was ultimately taken out of the hands of Spanish prosecutors in the late 1990s and left in the hands of a newly democratizing Chile represented anything but a failure, as it showed a reduced need for the kind of transnational advocacy of earlier decades. And it also demonstrated that Chile had returned to a genuine culture of democracy, which had been a strong part of its earlier history.

Transnational actors also played an important role in the peace processes in Central America. Both El Salvador and Guatemala's processes were marked by unprecedented levels of participation by international and transnational actors. In the case of El Salvador, the push for peace and stability was matched by a human rights imperative. Noting "the history of transnational activism in El Salvador throughout the 1980s," Susan Burgerman points to a central reason for this development:

> The involvement in the peace process of actors allied with the human rights network ensured that the UN verification operation that emerged from the negotiations would be centered on human rights promotion.
>
> *(Burgerman, 2001, p. 80)*

The dominance of the UN and of powerful national actors, who had a strong interest in the success of the peace agreements, sometimes created strains among the local, UN, and transnational actors (Burgerman, 2001, p. 90). Nevertheless, the THRN, as it had in earlier decades, worked to ensure that human rights were never far from the minds of officials crafting and implementing the Salvadoran peace accords.

Cuba under Fidel Castro and his successors is a case that departs in some ways from the more typical outcomes for transnational human rights activism. The most prominent transnational human rights organizations consistently criticized the regime for its monopolization of political power in Cuba and its persecution of dissidents, yet groups like AI and Americas Watch were far less central to anti-Castro struggles in Cuba. This difference can be attributed to a number of factors. First, Castro's hold on power was so tight that it was difficult for transnational organizations to form strong ties with local groups. This was based partly on his monopoly on political power and partly on a series of state-led initiatives that (for better or worse) penetrated and transformed Cuban society. Second, anti-Castro organizations became a powerful force in influencing US policy toward the regime. Well before AI became an influential human rights presence, the anti-Castro lobby was successful in working with successive US administrations to embargo and isolate Cuba (Haney and Vanderbush, 1999). The very closeness of anti-Castro activists to power in the US made the need for a transnational network less necessary. These factors are probably more significant than a third explanation: that human rights organizations had less ideological affinity with anti-Castro activists than with activists pushing human rights in nations ruled by right-wing dictatorships, although this explanation cannot be ignored.

While Latin America was the subject of intense human rights organizing in the 1970s and 1980s, the struggle for indigenous rights predates these efforts, and has grown in recent decades even as Latin America has democratized. In some nations with majority or near-majority indigenous populations, it is perhaps the central human rights concern. Due partly to the unresponsiveness and hostility of national governments and partly to the localized and subnational nature of many indigenous communities, concern about indigenous rights has inspired a powerful network of transnational activists who have come out of and collaborated with local organizations. Alison Brysk's comprehensive account of transnational activism for indigenous rights is worth quoting at length:

> Like David battling Goliath, tribal villages unexpectedly challenge the states, markets, and missions that seek to crush them. Even more unexpectedly, their scattered triumphs come from Goliath's own arsenal, from the United Nations to the World Wide Web. Indigenous movements derive much of their impact from an unlikely combination of identity politics and internationalization. In the spaces between power and hegemony, the tribal village builds relationships with the global village.
>
> *(Brysk, 2000, p. 2)*

A series of groups pushing for indigenous rights emerged throughout the region. The largest and most effective groups have arisen in Guatemala, Ecuador, Bolivia, and Peru, the nations with the greatest concentrations of indigenous populations. And Brysk describes how, by the 1980s, Mexico was marked by "hundreds of Indian organizations that ranged from single-community campaigns for land rights to associations of bilingual teachers across several regions to national peasant bodies" (Brysk, 2000, p. 82). In her comparative study, Deborah Yashar points to significant variations from nation to nation, and views the "changing and uneven role of the state" in individual nations as more consequential than global factors to indigenous rights movements. Yet she also points to "the weak reach…and presence of the state (in particular in the countryside)" throughout Latin America as a crucial factor to indigenous activism (Yashar, 2005, pp. 17, 307).

As they attempt to prod Latin American states into action, virtually all successful indigenous rights movements look up and outward to collaborate with regional or global organizations. This external strategy does not always bring complete success. Jose Lucero's account of Oxfam's work with indigenous groups in the Andean nations notes cultural and political tensions between local and transnational activists that ultimately stymied their efforts (Lucero, 2013). Yet it is also difficult to deny the successes of transnational collaboration in the area of indigenous rights. In response to protests and campaigns, even more substantive steps have been taken, with important legislation related to indigenous rights throughout the region, including specific provisions for either land reserves or autonomous zones in Brazil, Ecuador, Colombia, Panama, Venezuela, and Nicaragua. Bolivia, under indigenous leader Evo Morales, launched numerous comprehensive initiatives to bolster indigenous interests. These concrete steps have been accompanied by changing norms, closely linking human rights to the preservation and celebration of indigenous communities.

THRNs have from the start worked closely with global intergovernmental organizations. Very early on in the recent history of human rights activism, the UN began the process of giving formal observer status to groups of many kinds, including transnational human rights organizations (Willets, 1996). The EU has taken similar steps. This status does not confer direct political influence, but it does create the potential for it. The UN has at times fallen behind THRNs in applying its prestige and power to cases of human rights violations, and can be accused of responding to pressure rather than initiating it. Its role in Chile demonstrates both its strengths and weaknesses. In 1978, the UN appointed a special rapporteur for human rights in Chile, who was initially able to do almost nothing as local activists looked instead to groups such as AI. But the rapporteur was finally able to enter Chile as an independent actor in 1985, and by all accounts, played a crucial role in the 1988 referendum and more generally in the transition to democracy (Hawkins, 2002, p. 64). The UN's influence was greatest in the peace processes in Guatemala and El Salvador in the 1990s, as it engaged in unprecedented efforts to help these countries recover from civil war. To its credit, the UN formally incorporated transnational activists into its efforts on a massive scale.

The most notable human rights trend in recent decades is the dramatically increased role of the IACHR in trying and punishing human rights violators in Latin America. This multinational organization has become arguably the central actor in the Latin American human rights drama in the 21st century. Different nations chose to adopt dramatically different approaches as they reckoned with the legacy of dictatorship and widespread human rights abuses. But one thing that they virtually all ended up having in common was a national decision to agree to compulsory jurisdiction of the IACHR (Ropp and Sikkink, 1999, p. 191). With few exceptions, Latin American nations have agreed to hand over legal arbitration of high-profile human rights cases to a global intergovernmental entity, and many took the accompanying step of creating national offices dedicated to the protection of human rights. These offices, which in the 1970s or 1980s might have seemed like window dressing, have been empowered by a democratic setting, ties to transnational organizations, and the leverage provided by national commitments to the IACHR (Giannino, 2019; Zuloaga, 2020). To be sure, different nations have shown different levels of commitment, and in recent years, several nations have chafed at the strictures of the IACHR. Cuba has remained a holdout. Mexico's violent battle with drug cartels has led to widespread human rights violations that have not been adjudicated. For all its accomplishments, the IACHR has not penetrated the region's legal systems as deeply as its counterpart in Europe. Nevertheless, there is a great deal of truth to Kathryn Sikkink's and her collaborators' description of this trend as a "justice cascade" moving across Latin America (Sikkink, 2011).

As nations have become democratic, and human rights have become institutionalized in largely effective intergovernmental organizations like the IACHR, the transnational collaboration of the 1970s and 1980s has taken new forms. THRNs now routinely provide important legal advice in IACHR cases. They stand ready to resume pressure on nations which fail to live up to their human rights commitments. These groups are aware that democratization provides no guarantee that issues such as indigenous rights will be satisfactorily addressed. These campaigns have met with some of the same successes of the more general human rights movement, helping to elect pro-indigenous leaders in nations such as Bolivia and Ecuador, making great policy strides throughout the region, and successfully pushing the IACHR to take on indigenous rights cases. Since the 1970s, Latin America has seen, in Jackie Smith's words, "the growth of transnational organizing for a more democratic, equitable, and sustainable world-system" (Smith, 2018, p. 395), with collaboration at the local and transnational levels bringing on genuine policy results at national and global levels.

As an intergovernmental legal body, the IACHR has been unable to move expeditiously to hold leaders accountable in the current Venezuelan crisis. It's not inconceivable that the nation's internal political system can reconcile the deep divisions that run through Venezuelan society. But as the crisis drags on, it is increasingly likely that activists will be forced to engage in the kind of transnational, network-based activism that proved so necessary in the 1970s and 1980s. It's encouraging that these networks are already in place. Both AI and Human Rights Watch have provided accounts of the latest wave of repression in Venezuela (AI, 2020; HRW, 2020). Both organizations have established a presence in the nation, and are working with local human rights organizations. It is sobering to consider the implications of a relapse into the kind of rule that would allow no other option than transnational activism. Yet it is also encouraging that Bolivia and Chile have apparently been able to settle the deep crises that engulfed their nations in 2020 through peaceful, electoral means.

The prosecution of national officials implicated in Operation Condor, the multinational conspiracy among Latin American dictatorships to persecute and murder human rights activists in the late 1970s, is a particularly telling and significant way to finish this general account of transnational human rights activism in Latin America. Leaders from the Bolivian, Brazilian, Chilean, Paraguayan, Uruguayan, and Argentinian dictatorships (Dinges, 2004; McSherry, 2005) have been punished for "crimes transcending borders." This has been done by tribunals that, while based in Argentina, represent significant collaboration with the post-dictatorial authorities in all six nations, "effectively tackling the whole terror network in its geographical scope" (Lessa, 2015, p. 501). In 2016, the tribunal sentenced 15 high-level officials from multiple nations for over 100 human rights violations (Lessa, 2019).

The Politics of Transnational Human Rights Networks in Guatemala

Guatemala exhibited many of the typical features of an undemocratic, unequal, and dependent politico-economic system up until the early 1940s, with an added element of a large and fiercely persecuted indigenous population. A decade of reform and democracy ended in 1954, when the US worked with local elites and the United Fruit Company to overthrow Guatemala's democracy, and the nation was plunged into a 40-year period of repressive and largely undemocratic rule. A leftist insurgency emerged in response to this repression, but it was almost snuffed out with direct help from the US in the late 1960s. As a result of this defeat, and of a strategic reassessment, Guatemalan insurgents chose to relocate their struggle in rural indigenous communities in the early and mid-1970s. Given the remoteness of these communities, they were initially able to expand their presence and function as quasi-governments in many towns and villages (Manz, 2005). The insurgents' ability to entrench themselves in indigenous communities combined with a long history of state-sponsored racism to create an environment ripe for a violent response from the government.

These efforts began under the Lucas Garcia regime in 1979, and reached their peak during the rule of Ríos Montt from March 1982 to August 1983. The comprehensive UN report labels governmental policies during this period as "acts of genocide." Roughly, 150,000 civilians were killed, 440 villages were completely destroyed, and over 1,000,000 Guatemalans displaced. The UN attributes over 90% of the deaths to government forces and their allies, and indigenous Guatemalans (in a majority-indigenous nation) made up a disproportionately high number of the victims (CEH, 1999; REMHI, 1999). Most accounts of the genocidal behavior in Guatemala focus on this period. But government counterinsurgency efforts were sustained after Ríos Montt's removal, and lasted into the 1990s.

In the 1970s and prior to the most brutal periods of 1982 and 1983, Guatemalans did form groups to oppose government state-led violence. But the bulk of this mobilization was channeled through the growing guerrilla organizations and groups like the Committee for Peasant Unity, an indigenous-oriented peasant group with ties to the insurgency. Government violence going all the way back to 1954, but intensifying in the 1970s, effectively ruled out left-of-center political parties and union organizing. Elements of the Catholic Church opposed the regime in the late 1970s, but by the early 1980s progressive Catholics had been either killed or intimidated into silence. Religious offices that might have served as sanctuary or clearing houses for human rights information were shut down. European groups refused to maintain offices in Guatemala City because of fears for employees' safety (Ropp and Sikkink, 1999, p. 178). AI was able to craft reports on human rights conditions in Guatemala, and organizations like WOLA worked to pressure policymakers in Washington. But both organizations lacked local groups and individuals with which to collaborate. These transnational groups did little to immediately deter the Guatemalan military during the fierce repression of 1982 and early 1983. Indeed, for a brief period, the state succeeded in destroying or closing down all human rights organizations in the country, including the Guatemalan Commission for the Defense of Human Rights and the Committee for Justice and Peace (Ropp and Sikkink, 1999, p. 183).

In a classic case of the Boomerang Pattern, and of network-based collaboration more generally, transnational human rights groups played a central role in the reconstruction of Guatemalan civic society beginning in late 1983. The initial campaigns to hold the government accountable for the events of 1982 and 1983, and to prevent further violations, came about through close collaboration between threatened Guatemalans and the transnational group PBI. PBI's goal was to provide unarmed "bodyguards" from European and North American democracies to protect local Guatemalan activists. Their presence made it possible for Guatemalans to form the Mutual Support Group for Families of the Disappeared (GAM), which forced the government into important concessions beginning in October 1984. Pressure from PBI and GAM also prompted the embattled Guatemalan Catholic Church into action (Mahony and Eguren, 1997, pp. 17–29). In 1990, the Church opened the Archbishopric of Guatemala Office of Human Rights (ODHAG), and in 1993 the Myrna Mack Foundation, named in honor of a Guatemalan activist killed by the military, was founded by her sister. According to Ropp and Sikkink, these two organizations "formed the backbone of the revived domestic community that galvanized the transnational network." ODHAG benefitted from the ample resources of the Church, and the Mack Foundation received funding from the National Endowment for Democracy, the Fund for Global Human Rights, and the Rights and Democracy organization (Ropp and Sikkink, 1999, p. 189).

The THRN also influenced diplomatic and legal events. Americas Watch and the Lawyers' Committee for Human Rights filed an August 1983 advisory opinion with the IACHR, which led to the dissolution of Ríos Montt's special tribunals, which had condemned numerous activists to death sentences (Burgerman, 2001, pp. 61–62). Guatemala's most prominent individual activist, Rigoberta Menchú Tum, referred to a "Swedish-made bullet-proof vest" provided figuratively by her Nobel Peace Prize; international accompaniment repeatedly provided for her protection (Mahony and Eguren, 1997, pp. 102–110; Brysk, 2000, p. 111).

Several more general accounts demonstrate the THRN's ability to pressure and constrain the Guatemalan state in the mid- and late 1980s. Susan Burgerman describes how Guatemalan activists "universally attached great importance to their contacts with international NGOs, which gave them a modicum of security and brought outside scrutiny to the government and military" (Burgerman, 2001, p. 70). Stephen Ropp and Kathryn Sikkink point to a human rights "spiral," which led to the government's formal acceptance of the compulsory jurisdiction of the IACHR in 1987, one of the first in Latin America to do so. An empowered set of Guatemalan and transnational human rights activists then increasingly took advantage of this legal opening (Ropp and Sikink, 1999). In this way, Guatemalan victims of human rights abuses "reached beyond the state" to find justice through collaboration with transnational activists and the IACHR (Davis and Warner, 2007).

As the strength of the THRN grew in the 1980s, it faced a Guatemalan state which, for all its capacity to inflict genocidal violence, was fundamentally weak. Prior to the counterinsurgency campaigns of the early 1980s, it had virtually no presence in many rural areas. It was among the weakest-taxing states in the world, and it repeatedly failed to pass and implement tax reforms that would have forced Guatemalan business elites to contribute to efforts to control the countryside. Ambitious military schemes for rural civil defense patrols in the 1980s quickly lapsed into corruption and brutality. This weakness helps explain the long-run success of human rights activists. It also brings out larger theoretical points about different types of state capacity and the power of transnational actors (Shepherd, 2016).

Events in the 1990s further demonstrated the strength of the THRN in relation to the Guatemalan state. During the 1993 *autogolpe* staged by President Jorge Serrano, internal Guatemalan activists from across the political spectrum acted with increased confidence, staging protests, wresting concessions from potential nondemocratic forces, and working directly with Organization of American States' officials to push Serrano from power. The failure of Serrano's machinations provided the basis for comprehensive UN-led efforts to oversee and implement an accord for peace, democratization, and reconciliation. That these accords provided for a substantial UN presence in Guatemala—400 staff augmented by several thousand activists and supporters—was testimony to the influence of transnational activists. The Peace Accords further empowered local organizations by mandating and providing a central role for an Assembly of Civil Associations (many of which had been part of the THRN) in formulating and implementing the accords (McCleary, 1999, pp. 118–122, 132–137; Burgerman, 2001, pp. 73–74).

On a more general level, the Peace Accords set up comprehensive procedures for democratization and human rights. These procedures have institutionalized democracy as peaceful transfers of power have been the rule since 1996. And they have led to the creation of meaningful domestic human rights organizations linked to the government, including a national human rights ombudsman and an UN-backed International Commission Against Impunity in Guatemala (CIGIG). CIGIG was instrumental in the efforts to expose corruption and human rights abuses during the administration of Otto Pérez Molina, who was forced to resign in 2015 (Rutherford, 2017, p. 8). Yet these organizations have recently come under threat, as President Jimmy Morales began a campaign in 2018 to marginalize and shut down CIGIG by transferring its functions to other government ministries (Legal Monitor Worldwide, 2020). All these developments are also taking place against a backdrop of dramatic increases in criminal violence and the entrenchment of forces linked to gangs and transnational drug networks.

The 1996 Peace Accord also included ambitious provisions for protecting and empowering indigenous Guatemalan communities. Local indigenous rights organizations were among the most enthusiastic and effective participants in the Accord's Assembly of Civil Associations, and they were able to use this platform to accomplish a great deal, including a formal Agreement on the Identity and Rights of the Indigenous which established many specific rights for indigenous community and, more generally, a "pluricultural and plurilingual national project." The government agreed to set up an autonomous agency supported and funded by Fondo Indígena, a regional Latin American indigenous rights organization. Transnational collaboration was consistently a crucial element of successful efforts to push indigenous interests. Brysk notes that:

> International appeals were important in every phase and aspect of these
> developments, from Indian takeovers of the OAS site to protest civil

patrols to UN monitoring of land seizures and refugee repatriation to international insistence on the inclusion of indigenous organizations in the implementation commissions.

(Brysk, 2000, p. 271)

In 1996, the Guatemalan legislature approved formal incorporation of the International Labor Organization's strongly pro-indigenous standards in areas such as political autonomy and cultural preservation. It also created the position of Defender of Indigenous People's Rights in the Human Right Ombudsman's office. This step and others represented "important and unprecedented advances in the transformation of the Guatemalan state." Yet its record as an active enforcer of its mandate has been mixed (Brett, 2011). Indigenous activists have been most successful when they have continued to apply grassroots pressure, as was the case in successful efforts against mining companies in the La Puya and Sipacapa communities (Rutherford, 2017). The democratic opening and the continued collaboration between local and transnational organizations has pushed Guatemala closer to becoming genuinely representative of its sizeable indigenous population.

The domestic successes of the indigenous movement have had the unexpected result of making Guatemala a hub for transnational indigenous activism. Despite the current national crises related to drug organizations and criminal violence, Guatemala stands out in Latin America as a model for indigenous rights, as local and national actors have taken advantage of the peace accords and democratization to make significant political inroads. Rigoberta Menchú Tum's prominence as a Nobel Laureate and the work of the Rigoberta Menchú Tum Foundation has further raised Guatemala's profile. Menchú Tum led numerous continent-wide pan-Indian conferences and actions, and "spearheaded" protests over the commemorations of the 500th anniversary of 1492 (Brysk, 2000, p. 3). Since then, numerous regional indigenous rights gatherings have taken place in Guatemala (*Indigenous Policy Journal*, 2017).

Despite the accomplishments of the Peace Accords and the comprehensive move toward (imperfect) democracy, Guatemala was forced to continue to focus on human rights in the new century as it confronted the legacy of genocide. The effort to prosecute Ríos Montt first materialized in Spain, but activists, lawyers, families of victims, and select government officials ultimately chose to pursue justice in the Guatemalan court system. This decision initially bore fruit, as he was convicted of genocide in 2013. But his case was overturned on a technicality later that year, and the reprosecution of his case ended when he died in 2018. Transnational organizations played a central role in the prosecution of Ríos Montt, most notably the San Francisco-based Center for Justice and Accountability (CJA), led by the Spanish lawyer Almudena Indígena. Early on, the CJA worked closely with the Rigoberta Menchú Tum Foundation as it planned its legal strategy. With an explicitly legal focus, attorneys from

Guatemala, Spain, the US, and Europe collaborated with local and transnational human rights organizations and victim advocacy groups (McConahay, 2013; CJA, 2016).

The Politics of Transnational Human Rights Networks in Argentina

After World War II, Argentina seemed, like many of its large South American neighbors, to be moving decisively in the direction of democratization. The Perónist party, under the leadership of Juan Perón and his popular wife Eva, used its base among organized labor, leftist intellectuals, and the middle class to win the presidency in 1946 and re-election in 1952. The backlash against Perónism combined with the emergence of powerful military factions pushing a doctrine of "national security" to bring on a succession of military coups over the next few decades: first in 1955, leading to the direct removal of Perón; again in 1966, with the goal of repressing and controlling Perónists; and another intra-military coup in 1970. Argentina experienced a brief democratic opening with the Perónist's electoral victory, Juan Perón's return as President in 1973, and his wife Isabel's brief rule following his death in 1974. But the weakness of the government under Isabel Perón emboldened the military and shadowy right-wing militias. The military, led by General Jorge Rafael Videla, intervened decisively against democracy in March 1976. The coup led to the so-called "Dirty War," and by far the most comprehensive period of human right violations in the nation's history.

Under the leadership of General Videla, the regime murdered thousands of Argentinians; the numbers remain uncertain, with official government figures coming in at 8,960 and Argentinian human rights activists making strong arguments for 15,000–30,000 (Brysk, 1994). The regime became notorious for several particularly brutal practices: "death flights," in which drugged prisoners were dumped from airplanes flying at high levels; and the systematic kidnapping of children and infants of political prisoners born in captivity. Interrogation, torture, and ultimately murder took place at 340 detention centers throughout the nation. The broad outlines of government repression are most vividly reflected in the number of disappearances, which peaked in 1976 and 1977, and fell over the next four years. These rates reflect the fury of the government's initial crackdown on dissent, the easing of government policy following the March 1981 replacement of General Videla, and the more general delegitimization of the regime in the wake of the Falklands/Malvinas military defeat in April 1982 (CONADEP, 1986). Videla repeatedly asserted that repressive steps were necessary in the fight for Christianity and Western civilization against subversion and communism. As noted in Chapter 3, nowhere in Latin America was the Catholic hierarchy as explicitly supportive of dictatorship as in Argentina.

The Argentinian human rights movement during this period is generally grouped into three types of organizations; Alison Brysk describes it as "an informal—and at times unconscious—division of labor" (Brysk, 1993, p. 264). The Permanent Assembly for Human Rights, the Argentine League for the Rights of Man, and the Center for Legal and Social Studies (CELS) focused on legal work and documenting abuses. The Ecumenical Movement for Human Rights (MEDH), the Jewish Movement for Human Rights, and SERPAJ used their position within the (Jewish, Protestant, and Catholic, respectively) religious communities to push for human rights. And The Mothers of the Plaza de Mayo, The Grandmothers of the Plaza de Mayo, and the Relatives of the Disappeared and Detained for Political Reasons can loosely be grouped together as family-based groups (ibid).

Argentinian justice and human rights organizations have gained such global prominence that it is important to note that they began as local and embattled groups. The Relatives of the Disappeared first emerged in the city of Córdoba in response to the disappearance of 24 individuals in January 1976, and then broadened its activities to Buenos Aires later that year as the dictatorship entrenched itself. Rita Arditti describes the work of Azucena Villaflor de DeVincenti (whose son and daughter-in-law had been abducted) and a group of other mothers who were to become the Mothers of the Plaza de Mayo:

> They started meeting in her home to draft petitions, gather information, and plant the seeds of their future organization. It was Azucena's idea to go to the Plaza de Mayo and to ask for an audience with President Videla to find answers to their questions about the disappearances. On April 30, 1977, fourteen mothers gathered at the Plaza de Mayo, traditionally the heart of Argentine civic life. By meeting there, the Mothers placed themselves in the public eye in a desperate attempt to bring attention to their families' plight. Labeled Las Locas de Plaza de Mayo (the crazies of the Plaza de Mayo), they broke the conspiracy of silence that had permeated the country and found a way to channel their despair and frustration into action.
>
> *(Arditti, 1999, p. 35)*

As the kidnapping of women and children became widespread, The Grandmothers of the Plaza de Mayo emerged soon afterward. Azucena Villaflor was abducted, tortured, and murdered in December 1977, but by that time the mothers' and grandmothers' groups had grown substantially, staging weekly marches in which they held up signs with the pictures of their missing family members. Media outlets relayed these images to the nation and the world. But both these organizations emerged with little backing from established opposition groups, political parties, or the Catholic Church. Only later would they become part of a transnational network (Loveman, 1998, p. 512).

SERPAJ (and other religious organizations) differed from the Plaza de Mayo groups in the fact that they benefited from transnational links from the start. But early in the dictatorship, these external connections did little to guarantee activists' safety and effectiveness. Kathryn Sikkink notes that "[w]hen the Nobel Committee awarded the 1980s Peace Prize to the head of SERPAJ, Adolfo Pérez Esquivel, it brought great visibility to the organization; but in 1977…it was just one of various human rights organizations struggling during the dictatorship" (Sikkink, 2012, p. 67). As the Argentinian human rights movement grew, these groups became part of an increasingly effective transnational network. Isolated and with few allies to turn to in Argentina, local organizations came to rely on external funding as their international profiles grew. The Mothers received funds from Dutch churches and the Norwegian Parliament, and The Grandmothers was funded, at various times, by the Ford Foundation, the UN, Denmark, France, Switzerland, the World Council of Churches, and AI. The headquarters for The Families' office was purchased with externally provided funds. MEDH's work was subsidized by the World Council of Churches. CELS's archival work on disappearances and torture was funded by the Ford Foundation (Brysk, 1993, p. 273).

AI was the largest transnational human rights organization to fight the dictatorship. On an individual level, AI adopted Argentinians as "prisoners of conscience," including future Human Rights Watch leader Juan Mendez. Mendez noted in retrospect that his release was directly attributable to AI pressure: for the government, "I wasn't that important. It was easy enough to get Amnesty International out of my hair" (Sikkink, 2012, p. 8). The group's 1977 report, based on a formal visit in 1976, provided well-documented accounts, which alleged that as many as 10,000 people had been abducted by the government, and was instrumental in drawing global attention to human rights violations in Argentina. It was based on extensive collaboration with local human rights organizations. The AI report proved especially important as US policymakers relied on it, and not on US intelligence, to confront the regime about its abuses. Another AI report in 1980 revealed the existence of numerous secret government detention camps (Keck and Sikkink, 1998, p. 105).

It is also the case that AI was buoyed by the success of its work in Argentina. One of the explanations for the dictatorship's surprising decision to allow Amnesty a formal visit and to provide it with real access to Argentinian organizations is that the organization was at that time not regarded as a significant global actor. It had only recently opened its permanent office in Washington. As Alison Brysk notes:

> The trip backfired: Amnesty issued a highly critical report, the visit helped raise the consciousness of both foreign participants and domestic contacts, and the transnational NGO grew in stature.
>
> *(Brysk, 1993, p. 277)*

And there is little question that AI's work in Argentina was crucial to its winning the Nobel Peace Prize in December 1977.

As policy issues related to US policy in Argentina were debated, Washington-based groups, most notably WOLA, became deeply involved. Kathryn Sikkink describes her work there in the early 1980s:

> [P]art of my job was to receive human rights leaders and members of the opposition who arrived from Argentina or Uruguay, or from exile, and help them make contact with policy makers in Washington to explain their histories and their concerns. I set up interviews with congressional staff…, meetings in the State Department, interviews with the press, and receptions for civil society leaders. I accompanied our visitors to their meetings, translated for them, and sometimes put them up in my small apartment.
>
> *(Sikkink, 2011, p. 7)*

AI was also deeply involved in similar efforts, as it sponsored and organized numerous US and European trips for Argentinian groups and activists (Arditti, 1999, p. 2). The courage and compelling message of these organizations contributed to their global prominence; but the material and organizational assistance of transnational groups was also crucial to their ability to get their messages out.

The collaboration between human rights organizations and foreign governments, most notably the US, was so extensive that it not only transformed Argentinian government policy, it also deeply influenced transnational and global intergovernmental actors. Transnational activists were able to form remarkably strong relations with human rights-oriented officials in the legislative and executive branches. Assistant Secretary of State Patricia Derian made several visits to Argentina to bluntly inform regime leaders of US concerns over human rights policies—it was at these meetings that she used intelligence gathered by AI to pressure officials. She met repeatedly with local activists during her visits, and openly claimed that the Nobel Committee's award to Adolfo Pérez Esquivel was a "warning to all the nations that still practice repression" (Arditti, 1999, p. 40). The US Congress was also deeply involved, and formed strong ties with transnational activists. Its role was important because Congress had the power to cut aid to Argentina, which it did in late 1978. Robert Drinan, who had directly participated in AI's 1976 visit and met with Argentinian human rights activists, was a particularly effective and vocal Congressional advocate for human rights in Argentina (Brysk, 1993, p. 269).

The Carter administration funding for the Inter-American Commission on Human Rights enabled it to engage in comprehensive on-site investigations in Latin American nations. One of its first subsequent visits was to Argentina in 1979, where it met with numerous victims of human right violations.

The Commission worked closely with officials from both the Permanent Assembly for Human Rights and the Center for Legal and Social Studies. At the same time, beginning in 1979, members of the transnational Lawyers Committee for Human Rights met repeatedly with CELS and directly shaped its goals and legal tactics. It was in this larger, highly transnationalized setting that the Commission then produced a comprehensive report in 1980 that, for the first time, called for human rights prosecutions. This began a lengthy collaboration that was to have tremendous implications for the end of the dictatorship and post-conflict justice throughout Latin America (Sikkink, 2011, p. 67).

Analysts debate the significance of Argentina's misbegotten aggression against the Falklands/Malvinas and the subsequent ten-week war in the spring of 1982 to the dictatorship's downfall. To describe it as the determinative event in the move toward democracy is to ignore important events within civil society and the growing human rights movement. Yet there is little question that the regime's abject failure in this military conflict deepened and broadened opposition to the regime. It led many Argentinians to begin planning for the reintroduction of democracy. On a more theoretical level, it demonstrated that the despotic capacity of the brutal dictatorship did not translate into the kind of capacity needed to manage and mobilize resources for a conventional military conflict.

As the dictatorship began to topple, Argentinian groups forged strong ties with the American Association for the Advancement of Science (AAAS) for the very specific but crucial purpose of obtaining credible evidence about the regime's human rights victims, to bolster cases against the perpetrators and to find birth information about living infants and children who had been kidnapped by the regime. After several meetings with representatives of The Grandmothers in the US in 1983, the AAAS's Eric Stover (who himself had been briefly detained in Argentina in 1976) agreed to lead efforts to systematically analyze genetic material both from living children and from mass graves. As a result of this collaboration, victims and their advocates were armed with technically sound evidence of human rights violations. As Arditti notes:

> The Grandmothers had accomplished their goal…[T]heir investigative work could proceed on firmer footing. Empirical, objective evidence could now be used to convince previously skeptical judges. Faced with this new information, the government's Commission on Human Rights and the Department of Public Health of the city of Buenos Aires set up a technical commission to oversee the implementation of genetic testing.
> *(Arditti, 1999, p. 72)*

None of this could have happened without transnational cooperation.

Most human rights activists regard the government of Rául Alfonsín (1983–1989) with mixed feelings: moving far too slowly on human rights cases, not pushing hard enough to prosecute officials in the dictatorship, and passing laws that came close to providing amnesty and impunity for human rights violators; but also as a bulwark for democracy, creating important pro-human rights institutions, including the National Commission for the Disappeared and the Secretariat of Human Rights within the Foreign Ministry, and as committing Argentina to significant international treaties on human rights, effectively giving the IACHR jurisdiction over Argentinian human rights cases. The Alfonsín government also allowed and facilitated the initial trials of top officials in the dictatorships. These trials led to the prosecution of numerous top officials, including Videla, who was found guilty of numerous crimes, including murder, torture, and kidnapping, and sentenced to life imprisonment in 1985.

Transnational collaboration remained an important feature of human rights activism in Argentina even as it democratized. This was the case partly because the IACHR remained such an important arena for human rights decisions. But a crucial factor in continuing transnational collaboration was the passage of the Due Obedience Law in the last years of the Alfonsín administration, which blocked future human rights trials, and the election of Carlos Menem in 1989, who moved quickly to pardon high-level Argentinian military officers. These actions brought on a tactical shift among human rights activists, throwing virtually all the struggle into a courtroom setting. And given the unresponsiveness of the new Menem administration, activists' focus once again shifted outward: "When Argentine groups were blocked by amnesty laws from pursuing trials in their domestic courts, they did a judicial version of the boomerang: they sought out judicial allies to pressure their government at home" (Sikkink, 2012, p. 77). Previous human rights work and the concessions of the newly democratic government ensured that there were multiple potential legal arenas. CELS brought cases to the IACHR, which in 1992 had the leverage to come down with a binding verdict that found that amnesty laws and Menem's pardons contradicted Argentinian commitments to the American Convention on Human Rights. CELS also worked with allies in Spain to open human rights cases in their national courts. Spurred partly by this implicit external pressure, courts in Argentina began to assert themselves on the issue of amnesty and impunity.

Argentinian human rights activists and organizations became less dependent on outside support from the THRN in the last several decades, in a setting of democratization and (more or less) responsive domestic political institutions. This trend did not, however, imply an Argentinian withdrawal from the THRN. Rather, local activists expanded their efforts by becoming important actors in this network well beyond Argentinian boundaries, channeling their energies and wisdom outward. Kathryn Sikkink describes how Argentina has "exported" its examples and models of human rights activism, and "has gone on to become an important international protagonist in the human rights realm, involved in actively modifying the international structure of human rights activism" (Sikkink, 2008, p. 23). This "exporting" began as early as the

1970s, as SERPAJ, led by Nobel Prize winner Adolf Pérez Esquivel, helped to create extremely effective sister organizations in Ecuador, Uruguay, and Mexico (Weschler, 1998, pp. 154–156). But it mushroomed after the dictatorship fell. On the individual level, Sikkink points to figures such as Juan Mendez, who has filled numerous top positions in multinational and transnational human rights organizations, and Luis Moreno Ocampo, the founding Prosecutor for the International Criminal Court. There are now dozens of groups around the world based on the original Mothers and Grandmothers groups in Argentina, including in China and New York. Forensic practices pioneered in Argentina have been replicated in many post-conflict settings. And Argentinian legal and activist figures (including Moreno Ocampo) have been important actors in the creation of the International Criminal Court and other global justice organizations (Sikkink, 2008).

To be sure, some of these organizations and individuals owe much of their early successes (and even survival) to support by external actors. But these distinct forms of Argentinian participation in the THRN are a sign of the network's versatility and enduring importance to Latin America and to the world.

Theoretical Conclusions

This concluding section begins by describing precisely how THRNs fit into the three-level framework of analysis used throughout the book. It then uses this framework to more deeply understand and analyze transnational human rights activism in reference to institutions and (especially) networks, capacity, and power, and principles and norms.

In the most general terms, THRNs can be understood as residing at global and local/societal levels, and attempting to influence and, in some cases, bypass states at the national level. In other words, as depicted in Figure 6.1, first and third levels collaborate in order to empower themselves at the second level of national government policy; Keck and Sikkink's Boomerang Pattern and Brysk's phrase "from tribal village to global village" present this scenario succinctly. And these three-level relationships have been, to some extent, formalized with the emergence of the IACHR as an effective global intergovernmental legal arena for Latin America. At the same time, the very success of the transnational human rights movement has helped to make Latin American states more democratic and responsive to local human rights concerns. The following more specific discussion of networks and institutions, norms, and capacity and power examines the complexities of these larger relationships.

The collaboration between transnational and local human rights activists described in this chapter comes very close to meeting the ideal of democratic, "counter-hegemonic" globalization (Evans, 2008). The details from this chapter demonstrate the transnational human rights movement in Latin America's status as a genuine **network**. In this regard, much of what has been described

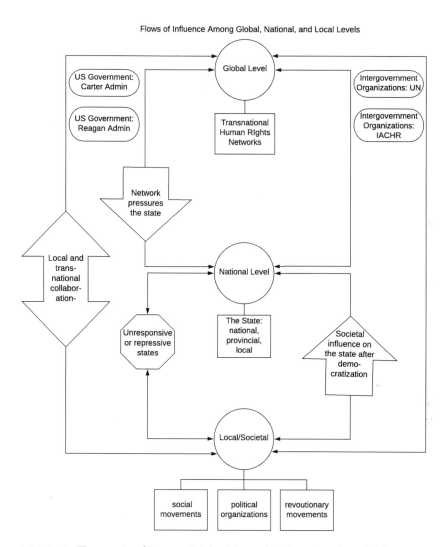

Flows of Influence Among Global, National, and Local Levels

FIGURE 6.1   Transnational Human Rights Networks Three-Level Model for Transnational Influence.

in this chapter involves transnational human rights organizations working directly with imperiled local groups in nations plagued by human rights violations: Argentinian groups such as SERPAJ and The Mothers working directly with AI and the WOLA; Guatemalan groups such as GAM working with PBI; and many more such collaborative relationships across Latin America. Local groups reach up and out and transnational groups reach downward to form networks against repressive national states and their allies. This partly reflects the dangerous conditions in which they operated, and the need to be nimble and flexible in response to state-inflicted violence.

But the network form also reflects intentional decisions by global actors to empower local ones. And most of the details show that, despite some tensions, this relationship was based on the ultimate goal of local empowerment. Smith and her collaborators' general comments about bottom-up tendencies in the hundreds of groups they examined demonstrate this point, as do most details from the cases examined in this chapter. The narrative of this chapter is very much about the growth and proliferation of this collaboration throughout Latin America. The numbers show that transnational networks have grown dramatically in size and scope over the past 70 years.

The networks were, from the start, even more complex and diverse than is suggested by simply focusing on transnational and local groups. They incorporated allies in foreign governments—often in powerful democracies or neighboring countries—and intergovernmental organizations. Particularly notable is the UN's practice of formal observer status and the kind of opportunities this allows for collaboration within networks. A measure of the networks' success can be seen at the national and global levels: national states have become more democratic throughout Latin America; and much decision-making power related to human rights has moved from national governments in Latin America to formal intergovernmental organizations, most notably the IACHR. The threat of widespread human rights abuses is never far away. And several nations have taken backward steps in recent years. Yet the entrenched and increasingly formalized THRN stands as a bulwark against the kind of human rights violations that occurred before and during the rise of transnational human rights activism in Latin America.

A central theme in this book has been the weakness of Latin American states in relation to local and transnational actors; it is this weakness that makes the **capacity and power** of THRNs in relation to Latin American states an interesting and complex issue. And it becomes even more so with a nuanced approach to the power and capacity of states and transnational actors. Analyzing Latin American states in the context of weakness may seem counterintuitive, given the widespread human rights violations that were inflicted from the 1960s through the 1980s. Yet the distinction between despotic and infrastructural capacity can clarify this analysis and lead to important conclusions about the power of states and human rights networks. A key initial point is that, if one takes a broad view of the kind of activities that are included in the category of state infrastructural capacity, human rights networks' work in the area of protecting citizens and providing safety represented a state-like activity that national governments were simply unable or unwilling to perform. Figure 6.1 provides an image of the national-level political vacuum.

There is a more important general theoretical argument to be made about repressive regimes, human rights, and state capacity. Even as Latin American governments exercised significant despotic state capacity, the infrastructural weakness of Latin American nation-states created a political vacuum which, in the long run, empowered the THRN as it penetrated national political systems. For all the despotic strength being demonstrated by states that were able to dominate all that was narrowly political, most Latin American states remained infrastructurally weak during this period. Even as the Guatemalan regime was implementing its genocidal policies in the early 1980s, it was not able to convince the Guatemalan business elite to fund the effort with increased taxes. The competing religious and political power center of the Catholic Church was able to provide "protected places" to Chileans in the early months and years of the Pinochet dictatorship. And in an interesting application of the "bellicist" approach, the Argentinian dictatorship was unable to mount the most rudimentary conventional military operation in the Falklands/Malvinas conflict even as it was pursuing a "national security" campaign against vulnerable internal "enemies." All of these examples point to a profound long-term weakness in these states, which provided a vacuum for THRNs.

This argument becomes even clearer in reference to the Cuban and Uruguayan counter-examples. Uruguay had, well into the 1960s, been widely regarded as the most advanced political system in Latin America, with ambitious welfare provisions, a strong educational system, a functioning physical infrastructure, and a secular tradition that had wrested power from the Catholic Church. Soon after his rise to power, Castro launched ambitious health care and educational reforms, and set up a comprehensive system for political and social control of the island. To an extent unmatched in the rest of Latin America, the Cuban and Uruguayan authorities were able to employ this relatively high level of infrastructural capacity to deeply penetrate national society as Castro ruled a one-party communist system and ten years later, the Uruguayan government transformed into a military dictatorship. It is no coincidence that, as transnational human rights groups reached out to Uruguay and Cuba, they could find no local organizations with which to collaborate. Contemporary accounts described Uruguay as more closely resembling an Orwellian totalitarian system than any other Latin American nation, and even those who saw some redeeming features in the Cuban system were forced to acknowledge how closed off it was to outside human rights groups. In both cases, the state's sinister combination of despotic and infrastructural capacity provided no political vacuum for a local branch of the THRN until the political systems started to open up: in Uruguay in the 1980s and in Cuba only recently. The absence of such infrastructural capacity in much of the rest of Latin America is an important factor in understanding the long-term successes of the THRN.

In formulating the Universal Declaration of Human Rights in 1948, the UN presented a potential norm for the consideration of the global community. What has occurred since then is a classic example of an abstract principle gradually transforming into a norm, with meaningful political implications and genuine consequences for perpetrators and victims of human rights violations. Rigorous studies have also shown that **human rights norms** also deeply influence, and can serve as a deterrent to, the behavior of powerful actors in the global setting (Sikkink, 2011). Most significantly, these norms often serve as the basis for the daily operations of legal institutions that transcend national boundaries—Latin America is close behind Europe in creating and empowering a regional human rights court system to which national governments have pledged allegiance. This general outcome is significant, but it is also important to understand how this occurred and the complexities that might make this victory for human rights norms something less than total.

There is little question that for several decades after 1948, conditions got worse for human rights in Latin America. Early actions by the Catholic Church and largely apolitical groups like the Ford Foundation represented important first steps in the face of widespread human rights violations. In the most general terms, the transnational network came of age just as an international ally—the US under the Carter administration—played a crucial role in supporting human rights norms in Latin America (as indicated in Figure 6.1). The human rights network became adept at framing human rights goals in a way that made them both compelling and realistic. The "motherist" groups in Argentina (and elsewhere) provided a vivid and relatable face for human rights violations. Sophisticated use of ever-evolving communications media technology was an important part of these campaigns. And the human rights network was often able to focus on specific goals, such as the issue of international aid to human rights violators such as Argentina in the late 1970s and El Salvador in the early 1980s. These specific campaigns provided momentum for other more general human rights efforts.

The progress from initial formulation of human rights norms in 1948 to the institutionalization of a generally effective IACHR represents a significant set of steps in the "life cycle" of norms as they become more politically meaningful (Khagram et al., 2002, p. 15). Elsewhere, Sikkink has called this phenomenon, both in Latin America and on a global level, a "justice cascade" (Sikkink, 2011). Some of this process can be explained by the nature of the institutions supporting or opposing it, or by pure power considerations. But the increasing viability of the human rights norm, and the growing advocacy for it by transnational human right networks, is a central part of this development. That groups from Argentina and Guatemala currently act as "exporters" of human rights to other parts of the world demonstrates the centrality of Latin America to this universal struggle.

References

AI (Amnesty International), 2020. *Venezuela: Announcement of Pardon of More Than One Hundred People Is Only the First Step to Reversing Policy of Repression.* New York: Amnesty International, August 31, 2020.

Arditti, Rita, 1999. *Searching for Life: The Grandmothers of the Plaza de Mayo and the Disappeared Children of Argentina.* Berkeley: University of California Press.

Bamat, Thomas, 2009. "The Rights of the Poor: Christian Theology and Human Rights Practices in Latin America's Andean Region," in Frederick M. Shepherd, editor, *Christianity and Human Rights: Christians and the Struggle for Global Human Rights.* New York: Lexington Books, pp. 179–194.

Bastias Saavedra, Manuel, 2013. "The Unintended Legacy of September 11, 1973: Transnational Activism and the Human Rights Movement in Latin America," *Iberoamericana* 13/51 (September), pp. 87–103.

Bejarano, Cynthia, 2002. "Las Supermadres de Latino America: Transforming Motherhood by Challenging Violence in Mexico, Argentina and El Salvador," *Frontiers* 23/1, pp. 126–150.

Brett, Roddy, 2011. "Confronting Racism from within the Guatemalan State: The Challenges Faced by thee Defender of Indigenous Rights of Guatemala's Human Rights Ombudsman's Office," *Oxford Development Studies* 39/2 (June), pp. 215–228.

Brysk, Alison, 1993. "From Above and Below: Social Movements, the International System, and Human Rights in Argentina," *Comparative Political Studies* 26/3 (October), pp. 259–285.

Brysk, Alison, 1994. "The Politics of Measurement: The Contested Count of the Disappeared in Argentina," *Human Rights Quarterly* 16/4 (November), pp. 676–692.

Brysk, Alison, 2000. *From Tribal Village to Global Village: Indian Rights and International Relations in Latin America.* Stanford, CA: Stanford University Press.

Burgerman, Susan, 2001. *Moral Victories: How Activists Provoke Multilateral Action.* Ithaca, NY: Cornell University Press.

Burt, Jo-Marie, 2014. "The Paradoxes of Accountability: Transnational Justice in Peru," in Steven Stern and Scott Straus, editors, *The Human Rights Paradox: Universality and Its Discontents.* Madison: University of Wisconsin Press, pp. 148–176.

CEH (Historical Clarification Commission), 1999. *Guatemala: Memory of Silence.* Guatemala City: CEH.

CJA (Center for Justice and Accountability), 2016. *Genocide of Mayan Ixil Community: Guatemala Genocide Case.* San Francisco: CJA.

CONADEP (Nacional Commission of the Disappeared), 1986. *Nunca Mas: The Report of the Argentine National Commission of the Disappeared.* New York: Farrar, Straus, and Giroux.

Davis, Jeffrey and Edward Warner, 2007. "Reaching Beyond the State: Judicial Independence, the Inter-American Court of Human Rights, and Accountability in Guatemala," *Journal of Human Rights* 6, pp. 233–255.

Dinges, John, 2004. *The Condor Years: How Pinochet and His Allies Brought Terrorism to Three Continents.* New York: The New Press.

Evans, Peter, 2000. "Fighting Marginalization with Transnational Networks: Counter-Hegemonic Globalization," *Contemporary Sociology* 29/1 (January), pp. 230–241.

Evans, Peter, 2008. "Is an Alternative Globalization Possible?" *Politics and Society* 36/2 (June), pp. 271–305.

Giannino, Domenico, 2019. "Are We Looking Up or Are We Looking Out? The Transnational Constitutionalism of the Inter-American Court of Human Rights: Conventionality Control and the Fight against Impunity," *Transnational Legal Theory* 10/1, pp. 6–29.

Glendon, Mary Ann, 2003. "The Forgotten Crucible: The Latin American Influence on the Universal Human Rights Idea," *The Harvard Human Rights Journal* 16, pp. 27–54.

Haney, Patrick and Walt Vanderbush, 1999. "The Role of Ethnic Interest Groups in U.S. Foreign Policy: The Case of the Cuban American National Foundation," *International Studies Quarterly* 43/2, pp. 341–361.

Hawkins, Darren, 2002. "Human Rights Norms and Networks in Authoritarian Chile," in Sanjeev Khagram et al., editors, *Restructuring World Politics: Transnational Social Movements, Networks, and Norms*. Minneapolis: University of Minnesota Press, pp. 47–70.

HRW (Human Rights Watch), 2020. *Venezuela: A Police State Lashes Out Amid Covid-19*. New York: Human Rights Watch, August 28, 2020.

Indigenous Policy Journal, 2017. "The Declaration of Tecpan: 3rd International Peoples Corn Conference," *Indigenous Policy Journal* 28/1 (Summer), pp. 276–281.

Keck, Margaret and Kathryn Sikkink, 1998. *Activists beyond Borders: Advocacy Networks in International Politics*. Ithaca, NY: Cornell University Press.

Khagram, Sanjeev, James Riker and Kathryn Sikkink, 2002. "From Santiago to Seattle: Transnational Advocacy Groups Restructuring World Politics," in Sanjeev Khagram et al., editors, *Restructuring World Politics: Transnational Social Movements, Networks, and Norms*. Minneapolis: University of Minnesota Press, pp. 3–23.

Legal Monitor Worldwide, 2020. "Guatemala Pol Wants Probe of UN Anti-Corruption Commission," *Legal Monitor Worldwide*, January 14, 2020.

Lessa, Francesca, 2015. "Justice beyond Borders: The Operation Condor Trial and Accountability for Transnational Crimes in South America," *International Journal of Transitional Justice* 9, pp. 494–506.

Lessa, Francesca, 2019. "Operation Condor on Trial: Justice for Transnational Human Rights Crimes in South America," *Journal of Latin American Studies* 51/2, pp. 409–439.

Loveman, Mara, 1998. "High-Risk Collective Action: Defending Human Rights in Chile, Uruguay, and Argentina," *Journal of Sociology* 104/2 (September), pp. 477–525.

Lucero, José Antonio, 2013. "Seeing Like and International NGO: Encountering Development and Indigenous Politics in the Andes," in Eduardo Silva, editor, *Transnational Activism and National Movements in Latin America: Bridging the Divide*. New York: Routledge, pp. 80–105.

Mahony, Liam and Luis Eguren, 1997. *Unarmed Bodyguards: International Accompaniment for the Protection of Human Rights*. West Hartford, CT: Kumarian Press.

Manz, Beatriz, 2005. *Paradise in Ashes: A Guatemalan Journey of Courage, Terror, and Hope*. Berkeley: University of California Press.

Markarian, Vania, 2007. "Uruguayan Exiles and Human Rights: From Transnational Activism to Transitional Politics, 1981–1984," *Anuario de Estudios Americanos* 64/1 (enero-junio), pp. 111–140.

McCleary, Rachel, 1999. *Dictating Democracy: Guatemala and the End of Violent Revolution*. Gainesville: University Press of Florida.

McConahay, Mary Jo, 2013. "Prosecutor without Borders," *California Lawyer* 33/9 (September), pp. 24–32.

McSherry, J. Patrice, 2005. *Predatory States: Operation Condor and Covert War in Latin America*. Lanham, MD: Rowman & Littlefield.

O'Donnell, Guillermo, 1978. "Reflections on the Patterns of Change in the Bureaucratic-Authoritarian State," *Latin American Research Review* 13/1, pp. 3–38.

Orique, David, 2009. "Journey to the Headwaters: Bartolomé de las Casas in a Comparative Context," *Catholic Historical Review* 95/1, pp. 1–24.

Perla, Hector, 2009. "Heirs of Sandino: The Nicaraguan Revolution and the US-Nicaragua Solidarity Movement," *Latin American Perspectives* 36/6 (November), pp. 80–100.

Piewitt, M., et al., 2010. "Civil Society in World Politics: How Accountable are Transnational CSOs?," *Journal of Civil Society* 6/3, pp. 237–258.

REMHI (Recovery of Historical Memory Project), 1999. *Guatemala: Never Again!* Maryknoll, NY: Orbis Books.

Roniger, Luis, 2011. "Transitional Justice and Protracted Accountability in Redemocratised Uruguay, 1985–2011," *Journal of Latin American Studies* 43/4 (November), pp. 693–724.

Root, Rebecca, 2009. "Through the Window of Opportunity: The Transitional Justice Network in Peru," *Human Rights Quarterly* 31/2 (May), pp. 452–473.

Ropp, Stephen and Kathryn Sikkink, 1999. "International Norms and Domestic Politics in Chile and Guatemala," in Thomas Risse et al., editors, *The Power of Human Rights: International Norms and Domestic Change.* Cambridge: Cambridge University Press, pp. 172–204.

Rutherford, Amanda, 2017. "How Non-violent Resistance Effects Positive Change Toward Protecting Indigenous Rights and Environmental Integrity in Guatemala," *Arizona Journal of Environmental Law and Policy* 8/1, pp. 1–28.

Shepherd, Frederick, 2016. "State Strength, Non-State Actors and the Guatemalan Genocide: Comparative Lessons," *Genocide Studies International* 10/1, pp. 65–83.

Sikkink, Kathryn, 2008. "From Pariah State to Global Protagonist: Argentina and the Struggle for International Human Rights," *Latin American Politics and Society* 50/1 (Spring), pp. 1–29.

Sikkink, Kathryn, 2011. *The Justice Cascade: How Human Rights Prosecutions are Changing World Politics.* New York: W.W. Norton.

Smith, Jackie et al., 2018. "Transnational Social Movement Organizations and Counter-Hegemonic Struggles Today," *Journal of World-Systems Research* 24/2, pp. 372–402.

Stern, Steven and Scott Straus, editors, 2014. *The Human Rights Paradox: Universality and Its Discontents.* Madison: University of Wisconsin Press.

Tarrow, Sidney, 2005. *The New Transnational Activism.* Cambridge: Cambridge University Press.

Valencia-Weber, Gloria and Robert Weber, 1986. "El Salvador: Methods Used to Document Human Rights Violations," *Human Rights Quarterly* 8/4 (November), pp. 731–770.

Weschler, Lawrence, 1998. *A Miracle, A Universe: Settling Accounts with Torturers.* Chicago, IL: University of Chicago Press.

Willets, Peter, 1996. *"The Conscience of the World": The Influence of Non-Governmental Organizations in the UN System.* Washington, DC: The Brookings Institution.

Yashar, Deborah, 2005. *Contesting Citizenship in Latin America: The Rise of Indigenous Movements and the Postliberal Challenge.* Cambridge: Cambridge University Press.

Zuloaga, Patricio, 2020. "Judging Inter-American Human Rights: The Riddle of Compliance with the Inter-American Court of Human Rights," *Human Rights Quarterly* 42/2 (May), pp. 392–433.

7

TRANSNATIONAL INFLUENCE IN LATIN AMERICA

Conclusions

Accounts in previous chapters provide the details and the drama of the transnational presence in Latin America. The focus on four markedly different actors is meant partly to demonstrate the great extent and variety of the region's penetration by external forces. There are very few portions of Latin American political, cultural, economic, and religious life that have been unaffected by at least one of these transnational actors. But this focus on diverse actors is also meant to serve as a basis for meaningful comparisons about how they exert influence and the different responses to this influence from the region. Furthermore, these comparisons can lead to larger theoretical conclusions about transnational actors, states, and society in Latin America. The goal is greater understanding of how transnational actors function in Latin America and, ultimately, how the people and the institutions of the region can come to terms with the legacy of external domination.

This concluding chapter begins with an overview of the impact of institutions and norms on transnational actors in Latin America. It makes broad comparisons concerning how important these factors were in explaining the behavior of the Catholic Church, transnational corporations (TNCs), transnational drug networks (TDNs), and transnational human rights networks (THRNs). The second part of the chapter focuses on relations among transnational actors, states, and society in the context of power and capacity, and will be divided into two sections: the first explores instances of unconstrained and direct transnational influence; the second addresses instances of local, national, and global challenges to transnational actors. Each section of this second part presents both contrasts and similarities in the ways that transnational actors have influenced Latin America from afar. The third part of the chapter provides a brief account of how the findings of the book both bolster and undercut several broader theories of global politics. This chapter, and the book, concludes with a call for theoretical perspectives and policy prescriptions that prioritize local and national conditions in a setting of overwhelming transnational influence.

The Impact of Institutional Form and Norms: An Overview

Tables 7.1 and 7.2 provide an overview of this book's findings regarding institutions and norms. Discussion of institutional forms has been based on a distinction between formal organizations and networks. As indicated in Table 7.1, TDNs and THRNs take the form of networks, while the Catholic Church and TNCs are relatively hierarchical and coherent organizations. This distinction is far from absolute, and masks important variations. Yet it does provide genuine insight into the workings of these transnational actors. The network form that TDNs take has been forced on them by the illegal nature of their operations: by their ruthless competitors and by national states in collaboration with the US government. A similar dynamic is at work with THRNs, especially during eras of fierce repression of human rights by Latin American states. Yet it is also the case that THRNs use the network structure because of a mostly unwavering commitment to empowerment at the global level.

The Catholic Church and TNCs more closely resemble hierarchical organizations. And these institutions fit well with an early history of direct dominance of Latin American societies and states, applied transnationally in a largely seamless way by highly structured organizations. More recently, challenges to this dominance have led to changes within their structures. Greater external control over TNCs has been the result of processes taking place at the local level, with social revolutions and worker-based protests; at the national level with

TABLE 7.1 Institutions and Networks

	Catholic Church	Transnational Corporations	Transnational Drug Networks	Transnational Human Rights Networks
Level of hierarchy	Hierarchical	Hierarchical	Network, under siege	Network
Flow of influence	Flowing both ways, but more down	Flowing down, corporate model	Flowing down	Flowing both ways, with collaboration
Tensions, collaborators, and threats	Regional, national, and local influence; Protestant threat	Regulation and expropriation from national and local levels	National and global collaboration for eradication	National repression, genuine collaboration?

TABLE 7.2 Norms: Impact and Sources

	Catholic Church	Transnational Corporations	Transnational Drug Networks	Transnational Human Rights Networks
Overall impact of norms	High: norm-driven organization	Moderate: external impact on behavior	Low: illicit, mostly immune to pressure	High: central to mission and existence
Specific norm, source	Neo-Christendom: internal, from hierarchy	Resource nationalism: external, from national, local	Eradication: external, from global, national	Human rights: internal, from global, local
Specific norm, source	Vatican II: internal, from hierarchy and grassroots	Corporate social responsibility: external, from global, local	Indigenous rights: external, from local	
Specific norm, source	Modern social issues: external, from societies			

expropriation, regulation, and more equitable negotiation over concessions to TNCs; and at the global level, with increasingly rigorous systems for corporate social responsibility (CSR). Challenges to the Catholic Church coming from Latin America have taken a different form. Vatican II placed far greater power in the hands of local grassroots actors. But the model of a completely top-down organization had already largely disappeared with Catholicism's deep cultural and religious penetration of the region centuries earlier, beginning a long history of bottom-up, distinctly "Latin American" influence over the Church. This influence was deepened with Vatican II, the regional group Conference of Latin American Bishops, more or less powerful national Catholic communities, and grassroots Catholics pushing for radical change.

The influence of norms has varied widely among the four transnational actors, as demonstrated in Table 7.2. A single norm—that of universal human rights—has been central to the very existence of THRNs. It has been applied internally, and is equally salient at the global and local levels of the network. The Catholic Church has been a largely norm-driven institution, although its domination of the region has led to significant struggles within the Church over competing norms. The norms of "neo-Christendom" and the "preferential option for the poor" (and others coming out of Vatican II) are different enough so that the stakes for this struggle have been quite high. Critics of neo-Christendom would argue that it justified such a cozy relationship with political power in the region that it really wasn't a norm at all.

TNCs operated free of norms for much of their early history in the region. But their economic dominance provoked two norms that were ultimately introduced from outside and, to varying degrees, imposed on them: resource nationalism and CSR. Groups from societal, national, and global levels took part in efforts to use these norms to constrain TNCs in Latin America. TDNs have been far less constrained by norms. Their formally illicit status is important in this regard, as norms-driven groups struggle to exert any leverage over organizations which operate based primarily on violence and meeting the demand for a lucrative product.

Norms have had an influence in the region far greater than would have been anticipated when they emerged. They "outperformed" predictions based solely on questions of power and leverage, and have been a crucial factor in either constraining or empowering transnational actors in Latin America. The genuine influence of these principles in the face of overwhelming political and economic power demonstrates the influence of norms both within nations and in the larger global system. They have had an impact within transnational groups, influencing the highest levels of the Catholic Church in the wake of Vatican II and representing the heart of the work of THRNs. And they have been central to efforts by states and societal groups to exert greater national control over TNCs. They have transformed relations among transnational actors, states, and societies in Latin America. This has happened both in opposition to and in alliance with transnational actors. For the most part, their presence has empowered marginalized groups in Latin America, and has been central to grassroots and democratic globalization in the region. Their general absence in the case of TDNs only makes their impact on the Catholic Church, THRNs, and TNCs that much clearer.

This broad comparative overview of institutional forms and norms leads to four general classifications. The Catholic Church is a relatively hierarchical organization which is norms-driven, even as its penetration of Latin America has led to a significant and lasting presence in societies and alongside states. TNCs are also relatively hierarchical organizations, but are influenced by norms primarily when they are imposed on them by outside forces. TDNs are decentralized and are virtually immune to pressure from norms. Finally, THRNs are decentralized and highly norms-based in their actions. In themselves, these distinctions provide insight into these transnational actors' presence in Latin America, and are more fully explored in reference to questions of power and capacity.

Power and Capacity: Direct and Unconstrained Transnational Influence

Preceding chapters demonstrate how transnational actors have directly influenced conditions in Latin America, bypassing or controlling local and national organizations, and transcending national boundaries (as presented in the top row

TABLE 7.3 Infrastructural and Despotic Capacity for States, Transnational Actors, and Society

	Catholic Church	Transnational Corporations	Transnational Drug Networks	Transnational Human Rights Networks
Direct application of infrastructural capacity by transnational actor	State-like functions, providing political legitimacy	Enclave: total economic and political control	State-like functions: "security," taxing, social spending	Providing safety and legal arena for justice
Levels of infrastructural and despotic capacity applied by state	Low infrastructural capacity, with occasional despotic capacity	Low infrastructural capacity, with occasional exceptions	Low infrastructural capacity, with high despotic capacity	Low infrastructural capacity, with high despotic capacity
State inroads into transnational capacity	Gradually reducing some Catholic state-like functions	Expropriation and attempts to manage state-run companies, with increased regulation	With help from US, destruction of individual networks, but not drug trade as a whole	Temporary destruction of THRNs in repressive eras, but not permanent

of Table 7.3). The Catholic Church was an early practitioner of transnational domination in Latin America. It worked in concert with the colonial authorities to establish its presence well before nations and states existed in Latin America, and sustained this presence as new nations emerged with independence. With rare exceptions, such as Uruguay in the early 20th century and Cuba under Castro, the leaders of most nations left the Catholic cultural presence mostly in place, to such an extent that most Latin American national cultures can be loosely viewed as "Catholic." At a political level, Catholic power was such that many new states either supported the Church authorities or simply handed over basic state functions to Catholic authorities, allowing them to directly exercise their own version of infrastructural capacity within national boundaries. The Church, in turn, provided legitimacy and support for states, many of which were highly undemocratic. This arrangement was supported at the local level by entrenched Catholic culture, at the national level by religious establishments closely linked to the state, and at the global level by the powerful Catholic hierarchy. These relations allowed for an almost seamless exercise of transnational power.

TNCs also enjoyed lengthy periods of largely unconstrained dominance in many parts of Latin America. These companies were less entrenched culturally at the local level than the Catholic Church, but in most cases possessed economic resources far out of proportion to local economic actors. Enclaves, in which TNCs directly controlled political and economic life and exercised their own narrow version of infrastructural capacity, emerged throughout Latin America. Their outsized influence often enabled them to effectively control political institutions in the nations in which they operated, either through economic pressure or direct political threats. And, especially early in the 20th century but also as recently as 1973 in Chile, they could often rely on the US government to support them and aid in overthrowing governments that did not favor their narrow interests. On a more general level, global economic forces empowered these technologically advanced and physically mobile transnational organizations as they prevailed over local and national economic interests in Latin America. This was especially the case in eras marked by market-oriented economic trends, such as the early 20th century and the 1990s.

TDNs represent a more recent version of unconstrained transnational influence. They have used their control of the lucrative and illegal drug trade to directly control parts of Latin American nations. They perform state-like functions in these areas, exercise a kind of private infrastructural capacity, and often gain the loyalty of local communities. Extreme levels of violence and plentiful proceeds from the drug trade have enabled them to control national and local political institutions, at various times and to varying degrees, in Colombia, Mexico, Bolivia, Honduras, Guatemala, and El Salvador. The very illegality of the drug trade allows TDNs to be largely immune from the political and norms-based pressure that has influenced TNCs. Yet, like corporations, TDNs benefit from market-based resources which dwarf those available to the infrastructurally weak Latin American states. For this reason, national governments have had to look outward, primarily to the US government, for assistance in efforts to control and stamp out the drug trade.

A different dynamic has driven the rise of THRNs. While working closely and directly with local organizations, these networks have bypassed national governments to provide a kind of alternative justice and legal arena for victims of human rights abuses throughout Latin America. This collaboration between transnational organizations and local groups has more than occasionally met defeat at the hands of repressive Latin American governments in the short term. Yet in the medium and long term, these networks have dramatically reduced the ability of Latin American governments to violate human rights with impunity. THRNs have collaborated extensively with intergovernmental organizations, most notably the UN and the Inter-American Court of Human Rights. The US government has also been a significant supporter—most notably during the key period of the late 1970s under the Carter administration and ever since by at least parts of the divided US democratic structures. In turn, the growing strength of THRNs has transformed the states they initially tried to influence, playing a significant role in the democratization process. Furthermore, the network has helped to empower the regional and global intergovernmental organizations which have increasingly taken formal responsibility for human rights in Latin America.

These specific variations are related to a more general contrast among the four types of actors. These transnational actors represented different versions of globalization as they exerted unconstrained influence on Latin America. The actions of TNCs and TDNs have been, for the most part, driven by external factors, imposed on Latin American nations. They fit the model of top-down globalization, and are viewed by many in Latin America as a sign of the region's powerlessness. The Catholic Church's European-centered hierarchy presents a similar model. Early in the history of colonialism, this closeness to the political authorities led the Church to collaborate in exploitation, cultural destruction, and even genocide. More recently, the Church's entrenched presence at the local level in Latin American societies has made the issue more complex, as individuals and organizations inspired by Catholicism have challenged structures of power, especially in the wake of reforms that placed power in the hands of Latin American laypeople. Of the four transnational actors studied in this book, human rights networks come closest to representing a bottom-up version of globalization. The cases explored in this book show that they, for the most part, collaborate with and empower grassroots organizations in Latin America.

All four types of transnational actors have exercised direct power in a larger setting of weak nation-states: a weak sense of nationalism among the people living within the boundaries of Latin American nations; and weak state institutions ruling these nations. Furthermore, the superficial despotic capacity demonstrated by repressive regimes was generally accompanied by a more profound infrastructural weakness (as demonstrated in row 2 of Table 7.3). This was the case immediately after Latin American independence, and for a variety of reasons, it has continued to be the case since then. Infrastructurally weak Latin American nation-states have thus provided immense opportunities for transnational influence in Latin America. In many cases, these organizations have simply prevailed over weak and ineffectual national political institutions. And citizens, with few ties to these states and a weak sense of national belonging, have found it easy to either tolerate or actively celebrate the political, economic, cultural, and religious influence of transnational actors. In this regard, then, these transnational organizations have been able to, for better or worse, deeply penetrate the national systems of Latin America and raise profound questions of national sovereignty.

Power and Capacity: Global, National, and Local Challenges

These brief descriptions of direct transnational influence are important. But they only tell a part—and the least complicated part—of the story of transnational influence in Latin America. The more complex reality of this influence comes through clearly in the following analysis of key moments of conflict and tension, in which transnational power and capacity was transformed by challenges coming from local, national, and global levels (the subject of row 3 of Table 7.3). But close analysis also demonstrates the enduring power of each of the four transnational actors as they faced these challenges. This section begins with the local challenges, moves to the global level, and then concludes with analysis of the struggle between states and transnational actors.

Given the extent to which transnational influence has been applied in a direct and unconstrained way to many Latin American nations, it makes sense to begin with **local societal challenges** to this influence. The Mexican revolution was, among other things, a response to excessive external domination of a nation. High-profile parts of the 1917 constitution called explicitly for limiting outside control of Mexico's natural resources, for constraining the power of the Catholic Church, and for setting the stage for future actions against transnational actors. Lázaro Cárdenas's moves against the oil companies in the late 1930s were pushed and supported by the oil worker unions. A similar, much more accelerated, series of events took place during the Cuban revolution, as mobilization coming out of the revolution and the mass organizations which emerged were a key factor in pushing policies that threatened the Catholic Church and TNCs. During the 1952 Bolivian revolution, pressure from the radicalized tin unions was central to the swiftness of the state's nationalization policies. Half a century later, a loosely structured social movement led by indigenous and environmental activists waged "war" on foreign ownership of Bolivian water and oil. These struggles brought about the removal of a neoliberal government and the rise of a new regime, led by Evo Morales, committed to assert control over TNCs. Centrist and leftist political parties throughout the region successfully pushed nationalization policies in the 1970s and again in the early 2000s.

Local grassroots organizations have successfully challenged the power of TDNs on a variety of occasions. The peasants and leftists leading the Revolutionary Armed Forces of Colombia (FARC) effectively took over key steps in the drug trade during from the early 1990s to the early 2000s, enriching their movement and significantly weakening Colombian-based transnational drug organizations. During the Morales era, Coca farmers worked closely with the Bolivian government—led by a President with roots in coca farmer organizing—to bolster production of legal coca and loosen the grip of the drug organizations over their livelihoods. With the rise of the drug trade in Mexico, certain indigenous communities resisted pressures to collaborate with transnational drug organizations, grounding their opposition on their indigenous identity and a history of local and regional organizing (while also receiving assistance from Catholic activists and transnational social justice organizations).

Local pressure from Latin America and elsewhere was crucial to the dramatic theological and political reassessment that emerged from within the

Catholic Church during Vatican II. The grassroots precedent of Catholic Action was significant, and Dom Hélder—the Brazilian who had worked closely with grassroots activists and created and ran several key Latin American organizations—deeply influenced Vatican II. Inroads from protestant, syncretistic, and secular traditions in the Latin American countryside were a spur to action. The provisions of Vatican II empowered lower-level Catholics and the laity, which meant that much of its implementation would occur at the grassroots level. And it was animated by norms which were oriented toward grassroots activism and more marginalized elements of Latin American society.

Global challenges to transnational actors have been initiated by a variety of global actors. As the world's largest intergovernmental organization, the UN has played a central role in the global movement for CSR. In collaborating with transnational organizations and, in some cases, representatives of corporations, the UN has provided leverage to a CSR campaign which has changed the way that many companies behave. It may ultimately empower local communities, states, and intergovernmental organizations in their dealings with TNCs. In contrast, the UN decision to bow to US pressure and adopt an eradicationist approach to the global drug trade ultimately empowered illegal drug networks, and weakened global intergovernmental efforts to constrain the drug trade. Regional and global anti-drug organizations have been almost entirely ineffectual, opening the door to other global actors, most notably the US government.

The US has met significant success in collaborating with Latin American states to oppose, constrain, and, in some cases, destroy transnational drug organizations: removing the main elements of a narco-state in Bolivia in the 1980s, destroying the Medellín and Cali drug networks in the 1990s, and forcing fragmentation among Mexican networks in the 2000s. These campaigns failed to bring about a significant reduction in the flow of drugs into the US, and the extent to which these campaigns represented genuine collaboration with Latin American states is addressed in the following section. It is also worth noting that US commitment to the anti-drug effort wavered when it clashed with larger geopolitical goals in Central America during the 1980s. Yet in no other area has the US government had such a sustained commitment to constraining the power of a transnational organization in Latin America.

Certain US administrations have been broadly supportive of transnational human rights activists. But there have also been notable instances of US administrations opposing and constraining THRNs. This was particularly the case in the 1980s, as the Reagan administration was often at loggerheads with human rights organizations, while openly supporting regimes which systematically violated human rights. But the divided structures of the US political system allowed for key parts of the government to continue significant collaboration with human rights activists. The opposite occurred in 2009, when factions of the US Congress and the Defense and State Departments supported the coup in Honduras, which was widely condemned by the human rights community.

Probably the most significant global challenge to the Catholic Church came from within itself during Vatican II, as the Church at the very highest levels presented and, to a certain extent, supported radically new ideas about theology, politics, and social justice. But it was also the case that Vatican II came partly out of the Church's perception that it was being challenged by rival Christian and non-Christian traditions. Some of these challenges were entirely local. But others came out of global traditions administered by transnational religious organizations, most notably various Protestant denominations—never more dramatically so than when Rios Montt and his Protestant followers, linked to a California-based sect, persecuted Catholic activists during the Guatemalan genocide. These intra-Catholic and intra-Christian developments represent genuine global challenges to Catholicism, changing the Church's position in a region it once dominated.

A final area of global-based challenges to the power of transnational organizations is notable largely for its absence. Many other regions of the world are marked by a history of traditional military rivalries, which prompted states to strengthen themselves in relation to actors that challenged national sovereignty and interests. As Centeno notes for the 19th century, and as a quick survey of the 20th century and 21st century history shows, Latin America has been largely free of conventional international military conflicts. These types of conflicts have strengthened states and encouraged nationalism in regions around the globe. An alternative, hypothetical narrative for a study of transnational power in Latin America would be of states and societies asserting themselves in relation to transnational forces as they are drawn into international conflicts. And Bolivia's nationalization of its small transnational oil sector in the wake of the Chaco War in 1937 fits this narrative, as does Cuba's general clamping down on transnational actors in response to a very real threat of US invasion. These examples are discussed more fully in the section on state-led challenges. Yet their rareness speaks to the absence of a dynamic that could have empowered or emboldened states and societies against transnational actors. Instead, transnational actors have only rarely been challenged by Latin American states coping with international military conflict.

At the national level, **state-led challenges** to transnational influence in Latin America often rely on nationalist rationales, never more so than in the case of TNCs. Leftist Bolivian and Mexican leaders in the 1930s enjoyed widespread popular support as they seized foreign-owned oil facilities. Regimes further to the left pursued widespread and initially popular expropriation of TNCs in the early 1960s in Cuba and the early 1970s in Chile. But nationalization of TNCs was also pursued by less radical regimes in Peru in the 1960s and Venezuela in the 1970s. Brazil's rightist dictatorship intentionally excluded transnational companies from key technology sectors; and the Pinochet dictatorship favored local business over TNCs in the first ten years of its rule, and refused to completely denationalize the key copper sector. During the pink revolution, leaders in Venezuela, Argentina, Ecuador, and Bolivia reacted to the excesses of neoliberalism by nationalizing key sectors.

Yet these policies inspired by resource nationalism have been the subject of almost perennial political and economic contention once they have been initiated. They were launched in a setting of traditionally weak states and powerful global market forces bearing down on Latin America. Sustaining these policies implied states effectively managing the sectors that they had expropriated. This would prove to be a test of state strength generally, but especially of state infrastructural capacity, of the state's ability to "reach down and centrally coordinate" people and institutions in the society which it formally rules. With some notable exceptions, Latin American states have struggled to provide the resources and management needed for viable state-run enterprises, even as antagonistic governments and global market forces have applied external pressure. The result has been numerous privatizations and denationalizations over the decades. And it led some of the leftist regimes that rose to power during the pink revolution of the early 2000s to eschew nationalization and encourage increased foreign investment. Evo Morales, one of the more leftist of the group, chose to pursue a mixed, "negotiated" approach to TNCs even as he publicly emphasized nationalization.

Anti-TNC nationalism reflects a legitimate and often popular frustration with external leverage over key economic resources. But from a broad historical and theoretical perspective, the nationalist step of expropriating a key industry, although politically sensitive, is far more straightforward than mobilizing the resources, management skill, and political will to run the enterprise. This form of nationalism represents political calculations that are divorced from the levels of infrastructural capacity that states may need to effectively implement them. This infrastructural weakness is both a symptom and a cause of deep external economic penetration.

State-led challenges to the THRN would, at first glance, seem to have little in common with economic policies based on resource nationalism. Yet these state-led campaigns against human rights resemble other national efforts in what they reveal about the weakness of states and the strength of transnational actors. This analysis becomes especially convincing with reference to different types of state capacity. There is little question that the highly repressive Latin American states of the 1960s, 1970s, and 1980s were able to prevail against many human rights activists in the short run, exercising unaccountable power and dominating all that was narrowly political. This rule represented almost a textbook case of despotic capacity across much of the region. But even as they exercised despotic capacity, most of these regimes possessed little of the capacity to influence society in a more lasting, constructive way. For the most part, they lacked infrastructural capacity. The Guatemalan state, for example, had among the lowest capacities to tax its citizens in the world, and was unable to get the local business elite to agree to tax increases as it pushed its genocidal policies in the countryside. The Argentinian state, while able to crack down on dissent and kidnap the children of activists, could not muster an effective military campaign against British troops on the Malvinas islands just off the Argentinian coast. It is also no coincidence that both nations had a history of US support, which provided them short-term political benefits but also allowed them to avoid reforms that would have increased their infrastructural capacity. Their inability to exercise infrastructural capacity created a societal vacuum, which THRNs filled with great courage. And the leverage provided by transnational networks eventually gave these human rights activists unusual influence over states that were ultimately strong only in their despotism.

The Uruguayan and Cuban cases depart from this model, but in doing so demonstrate a similar point about state capacity and the THRN. Both the Uruguayan and Cuban states possessed unusually high levels of infrastructural capacity by regional standards. The combination of despotic and infrastructural capacity during the two nations' dictatorships provided a more comprehensive challenge to THRNs. They were far less able to establish links with local organizations, and ultimately exercised less influence in Cuba and Uruguay than in other Latin American dictatorships. This was especially the case with relations between the Cuban and Uruguayan authorities and the Catholic Church, a crucial factor in the two states' ability to control human rights activists.

Catholicism had such a dominant position within Latin American societies at independence that state-led challenges to the Church have been common throughout the region. Only a few of these challenges have led to sustained changes, and even in most of these cases the Catholic Church has outlasted the national initiatives that threatened it. This was certainly the case with Liberal attempts to circumscribe Catholic influence: for roughly a century after independence, Liberals generally prevailed over the more pro-Catholic Conservatives, but there was so much compromise and so many short-term setbacks that it is simply inaccurate to see some kind of region-wide anti-Catholic trend. The most significant and telling state-led challenges came more recently. The Mexican and Cuban revolutions represented genuine challenges to Catholic influence, and both revolutionary systems took strong steps against the Church. But despite the anti-Catholic provisions of the 1917 Constitution, the Mexican authorities often compromised with Catholic interests; and the 1992 Constitutional reforms represented an unambiguous victory for the Catholic Church. The growth of religiosity in Cuba and the well-attended papal visits show, in Cuba as well, the Catholic Church's long-term ability to survive state-led challenges. The Nicaraguan revolution was more deeply influenced by Christianity than either the Cuban or Mexican revolution. And Catholicism's triumph over a leftist state-led challenge was far quicker in Nicaragua. This was clear as early as 1983, when the Church defied the Sandinista National Liberation Front (FSLN) military conscription policy. But it was also evident in successful Catholic opposition to the FSLN in the 1990 presidential campaign, and Ortega's eventual decision over coming decades to align himself with key figures from the Catholic hierarchy. As noted above, the more serious challenges to Catholicism may come from within Latin American society, as non-Catholic Christian traditions gain followers and secularism grows.

It is worth briefly noting the case of Uruguay, the one nation that seems to have irreversibly marginalized the Catholic Church as an institution. This marginalization has its roots in a historically weak Catholic presence in the nation. The policies of President Batlle in the early 20th century not only further weakened the Church, but also strengthened the state as an actor in Uruguayan society. These developments help to explain the state's success in deeply penetrating Uruguayan society during the dictatorship and sidelining the Catholic Church as a human rights defender. They are also partially responsible for Uruguay's recent passage of pro-choice and pro-lesbian, gay, bisexual, and transgender (LGBT) legislation in the face of Catholic opposition. And they show that a Latin American state can mount a comprehensive and lasting challenge to the Catholic Church. But the conditions—a historically weak national Catholic presence and an infrastructurally strong state—are so unique that the Uruguayan case can also help to explain the continued strength of the Catholic Church in the rest of Latin America.

Efforts by Latin American states to challenge the power of TDNs have led to the destruction and fragmentation of specific networks, but have done little to reduce the global drug trade. The nature and extent of state capacity is a crucial factor in understanding the successes and limitations of challenges to TDNs in Latin America. The use of the phrase "war on drugs" makes this focus especially relevant, given the extent to which conventional wars in other regions and eras have strengthened state infrastructural capacity and empowered states in relation to transnational actors. The "wars" against this trade are, in theory, collaborations between the US government and various Latin American states. But the reality is that the US is the dominant partner in the project. At the same time, due to a combination of historical weakness and recent neoliberal reforms, the Latin American states involved in the drug wars lack the capacity to challenge the TDNs on their own. And a heavy reliance on the US government has likely made this weakness more pronounced.

US-led efforts succeeded in ousting key officials in the Bolivian "narco-state" of the 1980s, but did nothing to strengthen the state's reach into the drug trade; externally dictated "structural adjustment programs" made the Bolivian state even weaker in the following decade, as did similar neoliberal programs in Colombia and Mexico. Colombia and the US collaborated to smash the Medellín and Cali networks, but the state's inability to even access large areas of Colombian territory left smaller "cartelitos" in place, and allowed the FARC to control key parts of the drug trade. Mexican authorities worked with the US to craft comprehensive military-like campaigns, which succeeded in capturing and killing top figures in the drug trade. Yet the trade only grew and new networks emerged. In all cases, TDNs emerged as powerful actors within society, performing government-like functions and gaining the loyalty of citizens. All these developments fit the model of states, with a powerful outside benefactor, exercising significant despotic capacity in violent crackdowns against drug organizations, but doing nothing to increase their infrastructural capacity. It is a genuine infrastructural capacity that would most likely serve as a counter to powerful transnational networks. Eliminating US largesse would force states to improve tax collection, increase government funding for salaries, and make drug-related bribes and corruption less likely. In another key government function, getting rid of extradition to the US would force Latin American states to create legal institutions strong enough to prosecute drug operatives. Under current conditions, it is not uncommon for drug networks to substitute their own infrastructural capacity for that of the state, funding social welfare initiatives, providing running water, building athletic fields, or providing a skewed version of public safety. Infrastructurally weak states are no match for the global drug trade.

Two cases separated by almost 50 years provide interesting examples of sustained state-led efforts to counter TDNs. The Castro government took drastic and immediate steps against drug interests in the immediate wake of the revolution. The Cuban state was able to associate the drug trade with the US, capitalism, and corruption, and its initial popular support and deep penetration of society was a central part of its ability to take these dramatic steps against organizations linked to that trade. While the drug trade was not nearly as institutionalized in the late 1950s as it would be in following decades, it had deeply penetrated Cuban society and had strong global ties. It is hard to imagine an infrastructurally weaker state having the capacity to move against such a powerful outside actor. From the outset of his administration, Evo Morales explicitly chose not to work with the US in its efforts to challenge drug interests in Bolivia. Rather, it encouraged legal cultivation of coca—with strict limits—and collaborated with *cocaleros* to increase governmental monitoring. The Morales government also mounted one of the first serious campaigns to change UN drug policy, which resulted in a substantive UN shift on coca legality in 2013. These multi-level efforts, led by the Bolivian state, did not seriously affect the larger global drug trade. But they did benefit coca growers and constrain drug networks operating in Bolivia, making the nation safer and more prosperous in the process.

Global Implications

This book focuses more on politics within the Latin American region than on the global system as a whole. In this regard, its central concern is how transnational actors apply their influence within particular Latin American nations and how actors at local, national, and global levels respond. Yet analysis of transnational power in Latin America does provide insight into certain global dynamics, and can contribute to theories of global politics.

Powerful global actors transcending national boundaries, and acting primarily in the interest of elites or consumers in wealthy nations, would fit well into a theoretical narrative which emphasizes global class divisions and economic processes. In this regard, Marxism generally and the globally oriented "world-systems" approach in particular apply well to parts of this analysis (Wallerstein, 1991; Chase-Dunn, 2005). Economic developments during and since colonialism, which are crucial to understanding much of the region, are the inspiration for the closely related "dependency" approach to economic and political inequality in the world (Frank, 1967; Cardoso, 1979). And William Robinson's similar treatment of the highly penetrated Central American political systems provides genuine insight as it focuses almost entirely on economic and class-based factors (Robinson, 2003). These Marxist global approaches can also explain the growing power of THRNs, emerging out of local grievances against externally supported regimes, and representing a "counter-hegemonic bloc" and a "post-capitalist alternative." Indeed, some of the best work on quantifying the depth and scope of the transnational movement for social justice is being done by scholars linked to the world-systems approach (Smith, 2018). These Marxist theories contribute a great deal to understanding the politics and economics of a region that, 500 years since the imposition of colonialism and 200 years since formal political independence, is still wrestling with economic dependency. But, as is the case with many theories of a global system, it is less able to explain granular events within particular nations. Marxist-based theories, for all their insight, struggle to explain particular processes that depart from class-based outcomes and the emergence of ideas and norms that cannot be reduced to larger economic relationships.

The approach to global politics known as "social constructivism" offers less of a comprehensive and systematic explanation for the forces that drive world politics. But its focus on the forces bringing about changes in the global system, the complex relationships among national and global politics, and especially the importance of ideas and norms to a global system enables it to provide insight to questions raised in this book (Wendt, 1999). Indeed, some of the authors most frequently quoted in this book, such as Kathryn Sikkink, Alison Brysk, and Emanuel Adler, are explicitly identified with social constructivism. And the emergence of the study of norms as a consequential factor in global politics is directly attributable to this theoretical approach (Finnemore and Sikkink, 2001; Adler et al., 2011). Transnational actors pushing ideas such as human rights and a preferential for the poor, and transforming global politics in the process, are developments which do not fit easily into traditional approaches to global politics. Nor can the rise of resource nationalism in the face of transnational corporate power, or the use of indigenous solidarity to head off the power of TDNs, be understood without privileging the role of ideas and norms. Social constructivism does just this, and many of the central points of this book correspond closely to its larger approach.

Yet what happens within Latin American nations, even as they are being buffeted by global forces, is best understood by theories that devote special attention to local and national conditions and their complex interactions with transnational actors. This book endeavors to provide insight into the actions of transnational organizations by scrutinizing not only the power that they often directly apply to Latin American societies, but also the local and national forces that, to the surprise of many observers, constrain them. A central theoretical point of this book is to endorse an approach that both blends and transcends the distinction between national and global politics. It also endorses the more focused theoretical undertaking of globalizing the concept of infrastructural capacity to include not only states, but also transnational actors as they function within national boundaries and in the larger global system. This measure of an organization's capacity to influence the world around it can provide insight when applied to a nation, and when applied to larger global settings.

At a superficial level, this emphasis on state power and capacity resembles the most entrenched and traditional of all theories of global politics, "Realism." A concern with the power and capacity of states, as they represent nations in the global system, is a central feature of the Realist approach. But even more nuanced recent "neo-Realist" incarnations of this approach, for example, in the work of Kenneth Waltz and Robert Gilpin (Waltz, 1979; Gilpin, 2008; as well as Keohane, 1986), remain focused on global political dynamics and are largely reductionist in their treatment of the relationship between national and international politics. Their concern with the state is largely limited to its status as a representative of the nation in the global arena, and they have little to say about its place within the society that it formally rules. Scholars with ties to Realism such as Steven Krasner have attempted to turn their approach inward to understand politics within nations (Krasner, 2020), but these efforts have been rare. Rival global theories' emphasis on factors such as economic dependency, transnational influence, and norms comes out of a reaction against Realism and neo-Realism. A cursory understanding of Latin American history shows that conventional military conflict, the central concern for Realism, has been largely absent in the region since independence. Centeno's deep analysis of the implications of this absence appropriately addresses the impact on Latin America's nation-states. And it then makes the crucial point that these internal conditions set the parameters for transnational actors' deep penetration of Latin America's political systems. This book has adopted similarly nuanced treatment of the relationship between internal politics and the global system; it has a central theoretical goal of extending theories of local and national politics outward.

Institutions and Networks, Capacity, and Norms in a Transnational Setting

Preceding sections on unconstrained transnational power, and the three levels of challenges to it, present the tremendous variety of outcomes associated with transnational actors in Latin America. The first general point to emphasize is that these four actors do indeed transcend national boundaries and often act beyond the control of Latin American states. They deeply penetrate Latin American national units and exert influence from a distance, raising profound issues of sovereignty and accountability. At the same time, the nature of the particular transnational actor leads to notable variety in how they exercise this influence. Transnational corporations and the Catholic Church operate as relatively seamless, hierarchical organizations. THRNs are far more loosely organized. Out of necessity, TDNs have also become fragmented and decentralized, as they compete with one another and attempt to survive in a setting of illegality. Both the Catholic Church and the THRN have been deeply influenced by local actors, a result of the Church's deep penetration of Latin American societies and human rights activists' commitment to empowering their local collaborators. These factors, in turn, influence how these transnational actors respond to challenges to their unconstrained power.

A second key point is that these organizations are, according to the "state in society" approach, best viewed as one of many actors trying to influence Latin American societies. They are empowered by the ability to call on resources from outside of the region. Yet they each are still vying for influence with local, national, and global forces. At times, given their history of directly influencing Latin American societies, their struggles or collaboration take place with local societal groupings; at other times, transnational organizations capture, oppose, fall victim to, or collaborate with state institutions in Latin America; or they compete with other global actors that also have a presence in Latin America. At each of these levels, powerful actors either undercut or bolster transnational groups. This three-level framework applies well to Latin American political systems, and should be emphasized precisely because it is less prevalent in other regions with more established and sovereign political systems.

A third important point is that questions of power and capacity are a crucial factor in assessing how these political struggles, at all three levels, play out. A particular element of this focus is based on understandings of state infrastructural and despotic capacity. Considerations related to state capacity, and especially to the distinction between these two types of capacity, are central to analysis of the four transnational actors' influence on Latin America at key moments. For example, the distinction between infrastructural and despotic capacity helps explain the limited success but larger failures of the US-led "drug-wars." It provides insight into the ability of THRNs to ultimately prevail over repressive governments. It helps to bring greater understanding to the complexities associated with efforts to nationalize and manage key economic sectors formerly controlled by TNCs. And it comes to terms with the entrenched nature of Catholic culture in a region marked by weak nationalism. In a broader sense, it helps to explain the ability of transnational actors to exert state-like powers in societies even as they are formally ruled by despotic states. It is the infrastructural weakness of most Latin American states that provides much of the backdrop for transnational power. And it is often rare cases of genuine infrastructural capacity that explain successful state efforts to constrain the power of transnational organizations.

This book's repeated use of the concept of infrastructural capacity, as it explores the influence of transnational actors, leads to a more specific theoretical point: infrastructural capacity should be broadened as a concept to apply to the global level. It should be used to assess the power and capacity of states as they interact with the global arena, and to assess the power and capacity of transnational actors as they act within nations. A more externally oriented approach to infrastructural capacity is a logical outcome of a study that analyzes the power of transnational actors in a deeply penetrated region. This expansion of Michael Mann's original concept to the global level provides genuine theoretical insight in several ways. First, it allows for analysis of a state's capacity to not only reach down and influence society, but also effectively interact with external actors and other forces as they bear down on nations and the states that rule them. This is a fruitful way to formally incorporate analysis of state power and capacity in relation to each of the four transnational actors studied in this book, and it could apply to other external actors as well. Second, it encourages analyzing the ability of external actors to exert infrastructural capacity within the ostensibly sovereign boundaries of a nation-state. The previous five chapters demonstrate that this kind of external penetration is more the rule than the exception in Latin American history, and an externally oriented approach to infrastructural capacity is a particularly effective way to understand these conditions.

A final point is that the use of principles and norms can transform political relations among societies, states, and transnational actors. Norms, and people and groups inspired by them, have deeply influenced the actions of the Catholic Church, TNCs, and THRNs. At times, these norms have come from within these organizations and have been used by them to advance the cause of citizens in Latin America. On other occasions, activists have used them to constrain transnational actors. TDNs are distinctive in this regard, in that their illegal actions are largely immune to norm-based behavior. But even in this case, activists inspired by indigenous rights norms have successfully constrained these illicit transnational organizations. The conclusions of this book confirm the work of scholars who put norms in the center of their analysis of national and global politics.

The central goal of this book is to bring clarity to a vast topic. That there is no single theoretical explanation for the power of transnational actors in Latin

America should come as no surprise to anyone who has closely analyzed their actions. Yet it is also the case that certain theoretical tools can bring greater understanding of their behavior and the behavior of institutions and individuals affected by them.

★★★

This book focuses on the influence of transnational actors in Latin America. But a central theme emerging throughout the book is the shortcomings of Latin American states. This concluding chapter has raised the theoretical implications of state infrastructural weakness for transnational actors as well as for the people of Latin America, and it recommends applying the concept of infrastructural capacity to local, national, and global developments in the region. But these discussions also raise significant moral and policy-related questions. A central theme of this book is the thwarting of Latin American aspirations at the local and national level. Discussions of this theme are often accompanied by discussions of state infrastructural capacity and, in Centeno's words, the state's ability "to perform even a limited set of tasks" (Centeno, 2002, p. 3). This point leads to a second, more policy-oriented recommendation coming out of this study of transnational actors: that local, national, and global actors collaborate to increase state infrastructural capacity in Latin American nations. Such a development would benefit states and societies, as it would lead to more equitable interactions between government institutions and grassroots organizations. It would increase the capacity of the state to address key issues on a genuinely national scope, and in this way attack social, racial, and gender-based inequity. And in a less tangible way, it would heighten the sense among Latin Americans that they belong to functioning national units, and can exert greater leverage over transnational actors. In the long run, an infrastructurally strong state in a Latin American setting would increase the chance of genuine and mutually beneficial collaboration with transnational organizations and networks.

Whether advocacy for greater infrastructural capacity can eventually take the form of a meaningful norm is a question for both activists and theorists. There is certainly an abundance of worthy—and more elegantly expressed— norms being pushed by local, national, and global actors. But the principle of increasing state infrastructural capacity in Latin America does have an urgency to it. The absence of infrastructural capacity leaves Latin American states unable to address a series of pressing issues. Several nations in the region are engaging in interesting experiments involving a deeper, more effective, and democratic state presence in society, even if the term "infrastructural" rarely appears. If successful, efforts to increase the constructive presence of the state could transform Latin American societies and change the way they interact with transnational groups. Ultimately, states with strong infrastructural capacity would be in a far better position to work collaboratively with the transnational actors that have coerced and exploited them in the past. This is a realistic goal for Latin American nation-states. It has been accomplished to some degree and in differing ways in nations like Uruguay, Chile, and Bolivia. And in other regions, far poorer nations such as South Korea and Taiwan, have crafted systems that have over many decades attained prosperity, democracy, and infrastructural capacity (Amsden, 1992; Chang, 2008). The ultimate goal might resemble the social democracies of Western Europe, which operate from a position of genuine leverage in their interactions with transnational actors. And, in the age of COVID-19, it represents the kind of societal mobilization needed to effectively combat a pandemic.

The analysis in this book attempts to present the actions of transnational actors in a neutral and theoretically rigorous way, and to use theoretical tools to more deeply understand these actions. Yet it is impossible to be completely detached when describing and comparing, for example, a THRN and a TDN. It is indisputably the case that one collaborates with threatened populations to advance the cause of human rights, and the other lays waste to communities and profits from addiction. While it's theoretically meaningful to note the difference between pre- and post-Vatican II Catholicism, the shift in Church teachings had dramatic and inspiring consequences on the ground, empowering many marginalized Latin Americans (and representing a threat to others). And shifting power dynamics for transnational corporations should not distract from the powerlessness that many Latin Americans feel at their hands or, more recently, their hope at the prospect of large companies practicing genuine CSR. These same moral and political concerns also animate what might seem to be academic discussions of infrastructural capacity and transnational actors.

In this way, the study of transnational actors in Latin America proves to be a rich source for theorizing about the drama of conditions in a region marked by a history of extreme external penetration. The lack of accountability that accompanies such conditions has frustrated and radicalized Latin Americans for generations. The tensions and conflicts emerging from these grievances has been an important part of recent Latin American history. Local, national, and global efforts have constrained some transnational actors. Other transnational actors have played a central role in these same efforts. Yet those seeking to constrain or democratize transnational power have by no means completely succeeded. Each of the four transnational actors studied in this book has shown tremendous staying power in the face of a wide variety of challenges. Yet the struggle for accountability has irreversibly changed political conditions in Latin America, and given Latin Americans a far better chance to influence the behavior of these far-flung groups.

References

Adler, Emanuel and Vincent Pouliot, editors, 2011. *International Practices.* Cambridge: Cambridge University Press.

Amsden, Alice, 1992. *Asia's Next Giant: South Korea and Late Industrialization.* Oxford: Oxford University Press.

Cardoso, Fernando Henrique, 1979. *Dependency and Development in Latin America.* Berkeley: University of California Press.

Centeno, Miguel Angel, 2002. *Blood and Debt: War and the Nation-State in Latin America.* University Park: Penn State University Press.

Chang, Ha-Joon, 2008. *Bad Samaritans: The Myth of Free Trade and the Secret History of Capitalism.* New York: Bloomsbury Press.

Chase-Dunn, Christopher, 2005. "Social Evolution and the Future of World Society," *Journal of World Systems Research* 11/2, pp. 171–192.

Finnemore, Martha and Kathryn Sikkink, 2001. "Taking Stock: The Constructivist Research Program in International Relations and Comparative Politics," *Annual Review of Political Science* 4, pp. 391–416.

Frank, Andre Gunder, 1967. *Capitalism and Underdevelopment in Latin America.* New York: Monthly Review Press.

Gilpin, Robert, 2008. *War and Change in World Politics.* Cambridge: Cambridge University Press.

Keohane, Robert, 1986. *Neorealism and Its Critics.* New York: Columbia University Press.

Krasner, Stephen, 2020. *Defending the National Interest: Raw Materials Investments and US Foreign Policy.* Princeton, NJ: Princeton University Press.

Robinson, William, 2003. *Transnational Conflicts: Central America, Social Change, and Globalization.* New York: Verso.

Smith, Jackie et al., 2018. "Transnational Social Movement Organizations and Counter-Hegemonic Struggles Today," *Journal of World-Systems Research* 24/2, pp. 372–402.

Wallerstein, Immanuel, 1991. *Geopolitics and Geoculture: Essays on the Changing World-System.* New York: Cambridge University Press.

Waltz, Kenneth, 1979. *Theory of International Politics.* Longlake, IL: Waveland Press.

Wendt, Alexander, 1999. *Social Theory of International Politics.* Cambridge: Cambridge University Press.

INDEX

Abrams, Elliott 134
Acosta, Mariclaire 132
Adler, Emanuel 70, 172
Alemán, Arnaldo 48
Allende, Salvador 36, 83, 84, 91
Alfonsín, Raúl 148–149
American Association for the
    Advancement of Science (AAAS) 148
Americas Watch 132, 135, 136, 141
Amnesty International 75, 131–133,
    135–137, 139, 140, 146, 147, 149,
    152, 155
Anaconda Copper 65, 81, 83, 84
Andean Pact 71, 78, 84, 92
Anderson, Charles 11
Áñez, Jeanine 43
Aramayo company 76
Arbenz, Jacobo 37, 69, 91
Arce, Luis 81
Archbishopric of Guatemala Office of
    Human Rights (ODHAG) 141
Arditti, Rita 145, 148
Arellano Félix Organization 115
Arévalo, Juan José 69
Argentina 21, 42, 77; Catholic Church in
    35, 36, 39, 40, 41, 146; democracy in
    24–25, 26, 128, 144; "Dirty War" in 39,
    42, 144–145; Falklands/Malvinas war
    144, 148; Protestantism in 145; resource
    nationalism in 73, 168; transnational
    corporations in 65, 67, 71, 72, 73;
    transnational human rights networks

in 5, 11, 131, 139, 144–150; US policy
    toward 147–148
Argentine League for the Rights of
    Man 145
Arns, Cardinal Paulo Evaristo 52, 53, 131
Assembly of Civil Associations
    (Guatemala) 142
Aylwin, Patricio 85

Bachelet, Michelle 73, 85, 87
Baer, Madeline 86
Báez, Auxiliary Bishop Silvio José 49
Bagley, Bruce 100, 105, 110
Bailey, John 114
Banzer, Hugo 103
Barco, Virgilio 108
Battle y Ordóñez, José 24, 35, 170
Bechtel company 78, 79
Benedict XVI 40, 53, 56, 57
Boff, Clodovis 52
Boff, Leonardo 52, 53
Bolivia 5, 15, 20; 1952 revolution 76, 128,
    165; 2019 coup 43–44, 81, 89; 2020
    elections in 89, 139; Catholic Church in
    44; coca farming in 105–107, 110, 123,
    165, 171; enclave economy in 76–77;
    indigenous activism 136–138, 165;
    resource nationalism in 77–80; state
    weakness in 76–77, 119, 121, 122, 163,
    170, 177; transnational corporations
    in 66, 67, 71, 74, 75, 76–81, 165, 168;
    transnational drug networks in 26,

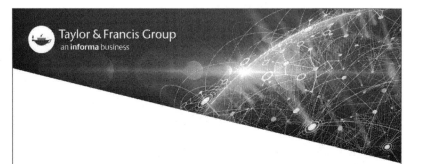